Anti-Blanchard Macroeconomics

Anti-Blanchard Macroeconomics

A Comparative Approach

SECOND EDITION

Emiliano Brancaccio

Professor of Economic Policy, University of Sannio, Italy

With

Andrea Califano

Visiting Professor, Federal University of Bahia (UFBA), Brazil and Researcher, University of Milan, Italy

Edward Elgar
PUBLISHING

Cheltenham, UK • Northampton, MA, USA

Back cover image: Emiliano Brancaccio and Olivier Blanchard in the debate 'Thinking of an Alternative' (Feltrinelli Foundation, Milan, Italy, 19 December 2018)

A revised and updated version of the fifth Italian edition: Brancaccio, Emiliano (2021), Anti-Blanchard. Un approccio comparato allo studio della macroeconomia (quinta edizione), Milano, Italia: Franco Angeli. ISBN: 978-88-351-1088-0.

Translation by Andrea Califano

Published by
Edward Elgar Publishing Limited
The Lypiatts
15 Lansdown Road
Cheltenham
Glos GL50 2JA
UK

Edward Elgar Publishing, Inc.
William Pratt House
9 Dewey Court
Northampton
Massachusetts 01060
USA

A catalogue record for this book
is available from the British Library

Library of Congress Control Number: 2022931059

This book is available electronically in the **Elgar**online
Economics subject collection
http://dx.doi.org/10.4337/9781802200768

Printed on elemental chlorine free (ECF)
recycled paper containing 30% Post-Consumer Waste

ISBN 978 1 80220 075 1 (cased)
ISBN 978 1 80220 076 8 (eBook)

Typeset by Cheshire Typesetting Ltd, Cuddington, Cheshire
Printed and bound in the USA

Contents

Presentation to the first edition   viii
Mauro Gallegati

Preface to the first edition   xi
Robert Skidelsky

Acknowledgements   xiv

1   Introduction   1

2   Blanchard's AS–AD model   7
    2.1   Structure of the traditional AS–AD model   7
    2.2   From the IS–LM model to the aggregate demand   7
    2.3   Monetary wage and real wage demanded by workers   12
    2.4   Price level and the real wage offered by firms   14
    2.5   "Natural" equilibrium in the AS–AD mainstream model   18
    2.6   Only the "natural" equilibrium can guarantee price and
          wage stability   19
    2.7   From the labour market to the aggregate supply   21
    2.8   AS–AD model   25
    2.9   Expansionary policy is not essential in order to overcome
          a crisis   26
    2.10 "Natural" equilibrium and the limits to expansionary policy   29
    2.11 Neutrality of money, contractionary policy, crowding out
          and austerity   31
    2.12 Conflicts over wage are useless and harmful   32
    2.13 Virtues of wage moderation   34
    2.14 Oil, anti-trust, technological unemployment   36
    2.15 Conclusions reached by the AS–AD model   39

3   The alternative model   41
    3.1   A different view on the economic system   41
    3.2   Blanchard's downward sloping AD curve: a critique   41
    3.3   Critique of the exogenous nature of μ and z 44
    3.4   Complete alternative model   46

3.5   Market forces alone cannot put an end to the crisis   47
3.6   Expansionary policy can have a permanent effect on the
       equilibrium   49
3.7   Conflict versus wage moderation   51
3.8   The case of the horizontal AS   54
3.9   The case of the upward sloping AD: debt deflation   57
3.10   The alternative model: other examples   59
3.11   Mainstream replicas – and critical economists' rejoinder   60
3.12   Actual limits of the alternative model and perspectives for
       further research   64

4 Blanchard's "new approach": the IS–LM–PC model   66
   4.1   From the AS–AD model to the IS–LM–PC model   66
   4.2   Horizontal LM, real interest rate and risk premium   66
   4.3   The "extended" IS–LM model   70
   4.4   The labour market and the Phillips curve are added to
         the model   72
   4.5   The complete IS–LM–PC model   75
   4.6   The economic crisis according to the IS–LM–PC model   77
   4.7   From the AS–AD model to the IS–LM–PC model:
         continuity or break-up?   80
   4.8   Critiques of the IS–LM–PC model from the perspective
         of the alternative approach   82

5 The competing approaches: theory and policy   85
   5.1   Comparing the two models: an algebraic representation   85
   5.2   Two competing interpretations of the economic crisis   90
   5.3   Alternative monetary policy rules   102
   5.4   Sustainability of public debt   108
   5.5   Hysteresis of unemployment   116
   5.6   Wage competition between countries in the framework of
         an open economy   121
   5.7   Financial globalization, Tobin tax and capital controls   123
   5.8   The dispute over the crisis of the European Economic and
         Monetary Union   128
   5.9   Speculators against central banks   133
   5.10 Labour flexibility, employment and unemployment   137
   5.11 A few notes on immigration, unemployment and wages   140
   5.12 Alternative theories of growth and income distribution   144
   5.13 A comparative approach to the stock market   152
   5.14 Growth and climate change   158

5.15 The economic consequences of Covid-19   161
5.16 Market versus planning: the Covid-19 pandemic   165

Appendix 1   Labour flexibility and unemployment   172
Domenico Suppa
    A1.1   Introduction   172
    A1.2   Correlation index and simple regression in brief   173
    A1.3   The relationship between EPL and unemployment rate   179

Appendix 2   Contractionary fiscal policy and fiscal multipliers 184
Andrea Califano and Fabiana De Cristofaro
    A2.1   Introduction   184
    A2.2   Austerity and fiscal multipliers   184
    A2.3   Blanchard and Leigh's test   186
    A2.4   Debate around the test   189
    A2.5   Blanchard and Leigh's test and macroeconomic theory   190

Appendix 3   On the pandemic trade-off between health and
              production   192
Emiliano Brancaccio and Raffaele Giammetti
    A3.1   Is there a trade-off between health and production?   192
    A3.2   More victims from the economic crisis than from the
            virus?   192
    A3.3   Is lockdown good for economic recovery? The IMF
            thesis   193
    A3.4   Overcoming the pandemic trade-off   196

Crisis and revolution in economic theory and policy: a debate   199
Olivier Blanchard and Emiliano Brancaccio

Further reading   221
Index   225

Presentation

Mauro Gallegati

Olivier Blanchard, among the most prominent representatives of main-stream economics and saltwater economists, has shown – most notably in recent years – increasing awareness of the limits of the dominant theoretical approach. His advocacy for rethinking macroeconomics contributed to setting up a growing debate on the founding assumptions of the dominant paradigm, also leading to the opening of a new window of discussion with the alternative theoretical approaches.[1] Blanchard, referring to the great recession, also recognized that: "Turning from policy to research, the message should be to let a hundred flowers bloom. Now that we are aware of nonlinearities and the dangers they pose, we should explore them further theoretically and empirically – and in all sorts of models. This is happening already, and judging from the flow of working papers since the beginning of the crisis, it is happening on a large scale".[2] Furthermore, in an interview released at the end of his mandate at the International Monetary Fund (IMF), Blanchard went as far as declaring that the earthquake of ideas generated by the so-called great international recession has brought about a significant mutation in economists' intellectual milieu: in his view, within mainstream literature there is much more scope nowadays for the study of theses that belong to the critical schools of thought and until recently were considered "anathemas" by orthodox economists.[3]

These words seem to suggest that bridging dominant economic theory and heterodox streams of research might now be possible, after years of "watertight compartments" and absolute lack of communication. Among the other custodians of the orthodoxy, reopening a debate that would unavoidably dwell on the epistemological and theoretical shortcomings of the mainstream might not be a warmly welcomed novelty. But Blanchard's view seems to be different. His warning about research drying up due to

---

[1]   O. Blanchard (2018), "On the future of macroeconomic models", *Oxford Review of Economic Policy 34(1–2)*, 43–54.

[2]   O. Blanchard (2014), "Where danger lurks", *Finance & Development 51(3)*, 28–31.

[3]   Interview with Olivier Blanchard, *Looking Forward, Looking Back*, IMF Survey, 31 August 2015.

an excess of conformism between scholars dates long back in time, like his "openness of mind": I remember his copy of Hyman Minsky's *Can "It" Happen Again*,[4] lying full of annotations on his office table at MIT: it was 1989. This is why there is reason to think that he might see a renewed dialogue with critical schools of thought as a fruitful occasion to bring lifeblood to mainstream literature itself.

This is the viewpoint – I believe – from which to look at Blanchard's endorsement of *Anti-Blanchard Macroeconomics*. The Italian version of this book, authored by Emiliano Brancaccio, has got to the third edition; now, it is also available in English, in the present edition co-authored with Andrea Califano. This little and smart textbook deeply analyzes and criticizes Blanchard's theoretical evolution, and raises strong points supporting a view that is alternative to the dominant one. The major contribution of the volume consists in the use of a very effective comparative method, which helps to show that few but crucial changes to mainstream macroeconomic models are enough to radically alter the theoretical perspective and the related evaluation on the efficacy of mainstream economic policy prescriptions. From the issue of public debt sustainability to policies to fight unemployment, this book challenges a number of commonplaces whose validity is generally taken for granted in the realm of public debate. In critically dealing with these issues, Brancaccio and Califano draw inspiration from a noble stream of research, which dates back to the contributions of classical economists and Marx, and is developed around the unconventional interpretations of Keynes's thought. However, as is clear from the authors' proposals for further reading, their book is open to more recent alternative theoretical insights, such as behavioural and evolutionary approaches to the study of economics. In this regard, even if designed for students, the textbook offers food for thought also to researchers interested in the reopening of a debate on the foundations of contemporary macroeconomics.

Anti-Blanchard Macroeconomics is provocative in its title, but rigorous in its contents. The fact that the former Chief Economist of the IMF has acknowledged the importance of this alternative textbook can be considered a hint signalling that the time of the self-referentiality of the dominant approach is finally coming to an end. And the fact that we have to change the DSGE mainstream models on which economics is currently built is now acknowledged. But do we have to change the paradigm or continue with the strategy of adding epicycles onto epicycles, as the Ptolemaic astronomers

---

[4]   H.P. Minsky (1982), *Can "It" Happen Again? Essays on Instability and Finance*, New York, USA: ME Sharpe.

did with astral anomalies? The easiest part of the answer is that DSGE models should be extended to the financial system and be enriched with heterogeneities. And this has been done. There are now several models of this kind that include banks and admit heterogeneity. The crisis has thus helped to produce richer, and therefore more realistic, DSGE models. In the already mentioned 2014 article, Blanchard himself asked whether these models should also be able to describe how the economy behaves in crisis, and the answer he gave was both disarming and ingenious: when things go well we can still use the DSGE, but another class of economic models, designed to measure systemic risk, can be used to give warning signals when we are getting too close to a crisis and evaluate policies to reduce risk. Trying to create a model that integrates both normal and crisis times – and thus is suitable for all seasons – is beyond the conceptual and technical capacity of the mainstream, at least at this stage.

After the crisis, the prevailing approach to macroeconomics seems to be going through a deadlock, characterized by only partial solutions to problems of a general nature. If economic science is to avoid drying up, the way ahead is to open up more and more to the comparison between paradigms, and it would be desirable for this to happen both at the most advanced frontier of research and in the realm of didactics, which is by no means less crucial. The brilliant comparative technique applied in this book represents a fruitful methodology that goes in the right direction.

Preface

Robert Skidelsky

Contrary to the suggestion of its title, *Anti-Blanchard Macroeconomics* is more textbook than polemic. Its novel feature is the juxtaposition of two sparse alternative macroeconomic models, the first labelled "imperfectionist", or more familiarly, New Keynesian, the second, labelled "critical", being a mixture of old Keynesianism and Marxism.

Professor Brancaccio, the author of the three Italian editions of *Anti-Blanchard Macroeconomics*, much prefers the second to the first, but his critique of Olivier Blanchard's "imperfectionist" textbook *Macroeconomics* (sixth and seventh editions) is so respectful that Blanchard himself is able to endorse its spirit, if not its substance. The fact that one of the cardinals of pre-crash macroeconomic orthodoxy is willing to commend this heterodox text, now revised and translated for the first time into English by Andrea Califano, is evidence of the mess in which orthodox macroeconomics finds itself after the collapse of 2007–2009. As Blanchard acknowledges, "questions such as whether we can expect the economy to return to health by itself, whether recessions have permanent bad effects, whether the interest rate channel of monetary authority works" are essentially open.

In the macroeconomic model presented in the first six editions of Blanchard's textbook (1997–2012) "the economy" is simply the summation of the standard inverse relationship to be found in all markets between demand and supply. In the labour market, the lower the price of labour, the more labour will be bought. This leads to the conclusion that flexible wages will always maintain full employment. In actual labour markets, monopolistic competition leading to sticky prices can delay, but not prevent, the recovery of full employment following a shock to demand or supply. How much intervention is needed to "speed up" recovery is essentially a matter of political choice, but because of the strength of its belief in the automatic nature of recovery forces, "with few limited exceptions, the model reaches conclusions essentially against public intervention into the economy ...". Rather, governments should undertake anti-trust reforms to increase price and wage flexibility.

In 2016, Blanchard, published a seventh edition of his textbook, which tried to take into account the failure of the world economy to bounce back rapidly after the "shock" of 2008. The new model – reverting to a standard IS–LM framework – pushed the dynamics of adjustment away from a rapid return to optimal equilibrium. Its central feature is the inverse relationship between real interest rates and investment. The argument now is that, following a shock to investment, a fall in the rate of inflation increases the real debt burden; the increased risk of default on debts causes real interest rates to rise, which pushes investment lower and unemployment higher. Once the economy has left its unique point of equilibrium, debt deflation will cause it to roll further and further away to a very inferior equilibrium. Government intervention is needed to restore a satisfactory equilibrium, but it does not equate to Keynesian stimulus. Blanchard believes that the 2008–2009 crisis was overcome by central banks "anchoring" inflationary expectations, thus enabling banks to avoid having to charge default premiums on their loans. This policy sustained investment. His earlier theoretical work also justified "expansionary fiscal contraction" on the ground that it would be useful in keeping down interest rates – a view that justified the austerity policies recommended by the IMF when he was its chief economist. As the authors of this book rightly point out, Blanchard's new approach only represents minor theoretical manoeuvrings within the New Keynesian universe, aiming to achieve a minimum contact between theory and reality.

What Brancaccio and Califano call the "critical" alternative to Blanchard I and II rests on a mixture of Keynes's original insights and on the "conflictual" nature of social relations under capitalism diagnosed by Karl Marx.

The "critical" approach follows Keynes's liquidity preference theory of the rate of interest in denying that a fall in the price level and a rise in the value of money necessarily lead to a fall in interest rates. Neither would flexible interest rates lead to a full employment level of investment if the expected profit rate had fallen below the zero lower bound.

The "critical" approach follows Marx in rejecting the idea of a "fixed mark-up" of profit over cost. This assumption underpins the argument that flexible wages will suffice to restore full employment. But there is no warrant for a downward sloping aggregate demand curve: the slope of the curve depends entirely on the state of the class struggle. Therefore no stable full employment equilibrium is available: the economy oscillates between inflation and depression. The Marxist model gives a political economy explanation for "sticky" wages that eluded Keynesians: the stickiness of wages depends on the strength of the trade unions and the legislation protecting workers.

The two models lead to two different interpretations of the economic crisis of 2007–2009 and two different sets of prescriptions for preventing its recurrence. In Blanchard I and II the crisis starts with an unexplained shock to the financial sector, which it then transmits to the real sector through the freezing of credit. In the "critical" perspective, one of the other possible roots of the crisis can be found in the under-consumption of the real sector that is transmitted to the financial sector through the build-up of unsustainable debt. The two explanations do not exclude each other. It is a matter of levels of analysis. For the mainstream macroeconomist, the "deeper" level is a distraction. The student, writes the mainstream professor, does not need to know about "critical" research topics such as under-consumption or surplus value to answer a question about bank rate.[1] But the under-consumptionist perspective is useful in explaining both the fragility of aggregate demand before 2008 and the failure of quantitative easing to drive up the inflation rate since the start of the slump.

The two models yield two different sets of policy prescriptions. The first is to secure the banking system from the danger of over-lending; the second is to improve the employment equilibrium by strengthening trade unions and legal protection of workers, capital controls against capital flight and public investment. To this second set of policies redistributive taxation could be added as well.

The technical level of *Anti-Blanchard Macroeconomics* is suitable for second – or third – year students of macroeconomics, but the volume can be recommended for more advanced courses. As Brancaccio and Califano write, the book provides "a useful tool for trying to overcome the current contradiction between the opportunity to offer students a preliminary mainstream education and the need to nurture rather than crush their critical spirit".

I am pleased that, in their appendix on the multiplier, Califano and De Cristofaro attack Blanchard and Co for the "mutability" of their use of the terms "short run" and "long run". This language serves the ideological purpose of minimizing the impact of economic disruption, the short run being the time it takes for an economy to regain its "natural" or "long run" equilibrium position. In the first edition of *Macroeconomics* this was one year. By 2017 it had become "a few years". On this mutability of language, Keynes, it seems to me, had the last word, when he wrote in 1923: "Economists set themselves too easy, too useless a task if in tempestuous seasons they can only tell us that when the storm is long past the ocean is flat again."[2]

---

[1]   See Martin Weale, Letter to the *Financial Times*, 18 January 2018.
[2]   J.M. Keynes (1971), "A tract on monetary reform", p. 65 in *Collected Writings*, vol. 4, London, UK: Macmillan.

Acknowledgements

In May 2011 the publisher Il Mulino, in collaboration with Alessia Amighini and Francesco Giavazzi, organized an event at Milan's Bocconi University entitled: "Teaching macroeconomics after the great recession". Those invited to take part in the discussion included Andrea Boitani, Efrem Castelnuovo, Carlo Favero, Giuseppe Ferraguto, Donato Masciandaro, Luigi Spaventa and Emiliano Brancaccio. The latter's report, dedicated "to the Anti Blanchard teaching method", was the subject of a lively and constructive discussion. The merits of an academic narrative designed to present macroeconomics as an area for comparing alternative theoretical paradigms were recognized from several quarters. In particular, broad consensus was expressed regarding the idea that this teaching method, by developing the critical spirit of students, is able to stimulate their interest in the methodological and theoretical foundations of the subject. We would like to thank those who took part in the Milan event, whose contributions have been used extensively even in this *Anti-Blanchard* edition. Our thanks are also extended to Pietro Alessandrini, Riccardo Bellofiore, Sergio Beraldo, Mario Biagioli, Roberto Cellini, Sergio Cesaratto, Roberto Ciccone, Enrico Colombatto, Lilia Costabile, Angelo Cuzzola, Salvatore D'Acunto, Domenico Delli Gatti, Giovanni Dosi, Giuseppe Fontana, Guglielmo Forges Davanzati, Antonio Maria Fusco, Mauro Gallegati, Nadia Garbellini, Raffaele Giammetti, Heinz Kurz, Giorgio Lunghini, Daniela Marconi, Alessio Moneta, Gary Mongiovi, Juan Carlos Moreno-Brid, Marco Musella, Torsten Niechoj, Guido Ortona, Ugo Pagano, Paolo Pini, Riccardo Realfonzo, Francesco Saraceno, Roberto Scazzieri, Robert Skidelsky, Anna Soci, Antonella Stirati, Mario Tiberi, Guido Tortorella Esposito, Carmen Vita, Gennaro Zezza and Luigi Zingales, for reading and commenting on previous versions of this text. Special thanks go to Olivier Blanchard and his co-authors Alessia Amighini and Francesco Giavazzi for having accepted the intellectual challenge launched by this small book. All responsibility for the contents of this text and any errors or omissions obviously lies solely with the authors.

30 April 2021
E.B. and A.C.

1. Introduction

Olivier Blanchard is one of the world's most renowned, cited and influential economists. Emeritus Professor at Boston MIT and former director of the International Monetary Fund's (IMF) research department, Blanchard has published a huge number of pioneering contributions in the field of contemporary economic research and is also the author of *Macroeconomics*, one of the most widely circulated textbooks in universities throughout the world.

In our view, Blanchard's textbook[1] represents the most complete, accurate and advanced teaching narrative of the so-called "mainstream" macroeconomics, an analytical method that stems from those developments in neoclassical theory that are sometimes incorrectly labelled as "New Keynesian", which in fact should more accurately be called "imperfectionist". This approach is proposed to describe the operation of an economy marked by various types of imperfections, asymmetries and concentrations of power. These phenomena share a common feature: they generate market failures that distance the economic system from a hypothetical optimal equilibrium, where labour and other production resources are employed in the most efficient way. The exponents of this line of research, which is prevalent nowadays, claim that its goal is to try to make the traditional neoclassical analysis less abstract and more pertinent to the complex functioning of contemporary capitalism.

In the first six editions of his textbook, Blanchard provided a teaching version of this approach based on a specification of the so-called aggregate supply and aggregate demand (AS–AD) mainstream model. The distinctive features of Blanchard's model focused on the prominent role assigned to the large oligopolistic enterprises and the workers' trade unions, on a price formation mechanism based on production costs and on a profit margin dependent on the degree of competition in the goods markct. For years Blanchard's AS–AD model represented a cutting-edge contribution to the teaching of macroeconomics. With this model, the French economist managed to combine the need for clarity of presentation with the aim of providing a teaching tool in step with the

---

[1]   O. Blanchard (2021), *Macroeconomics* (8th edn), Boston, USA: Pearson.

developments in prevalent economic research. However, this model also retained a feature typical of the mainstream approach that has always been the subject of keen debate: this is the argument whereby, at least in principle, an economic crisis could be overcome simply by relying on the spontaneous play of market forces, and particularly on the wage and price flexibility caused by unemployment.

After the great global recession that exploded in 2008, critiques of the idea that deflation alone can resolve recessions intensified. The fact that Blanchard's AS–AD model may contemplate this idea meant that his model also was called into question by important sectors of the scientific community. However, Blanchard did not remain insensitive to the blast of criticism. Indeed, the seventh edition of his textbook contains an important novelty. Both in the European version written in collaboration with Alessia Amighini and Francesco Giavazzi, and in the American version of the book, the former IMF Chief Economist claims that the traditional AS–AD model "gave too optimistic a view of the return of output to potential", describing a situation of so-called "natural" equilibrium of the economic system. In order to overcome this limitation, Blanchard removed the AS–AD model from the seventh edition of the volume and replaced it with an analysis that goes under the name of IS–LM–PC. For the sake of simplicity, we will sometimes call this model a "new approach" even though it actually combines two well-known macroeconomic tools from the last century: the Hicks macroeconomic model and the Phillips curve. The basic change in the new analytical method concerns a different concept of the effects of wage and price dynamics: whilst the AS–AD model suggested that movements in such variables might contribute to the convergence of output and employment towards the respective equilibrium levels, the new IS–LM–PC analysis focuses on the risk of wage or price inflation or deflation having destabilizing effects, distancing the economic system from its "natural" equilibrium.

The inability to analyze the potential destabilizing effects of deflation was one of the main limitations of Blanchard's previous model. The seventh edition of his volume filled this major gap, at least in part, by tackling significant problems of instability that had been ignored previously. Thus, Blanchard once again placed his manual at the frontier of mainstream macroeconomics teaching, proposing a model that attempts to address the rising critiques on the actual capacity of the prevailing approach to interpret the great recession and provide effective remedies to overcome it.

However, on closer inspection, the changes in Blanchard's new approach, as repeated in the recent eighth edition, are more limited than they might appear at first sight. If not for anything else, one will notice that also in the new model the author persists in considering the profit margin to be immune to wage bargaining, and re-affirms the idea that an inverse relationship exists between interest rates and investment. Yet, he himself, years ago, had cast relevant doubts on the empirical reliability of this argument. In this way Blanchard chooses instead to preserve a crucial feature of the old AS–AD model: namely, the existence of a level of "natural" equilibrium for employment deemed to be independent from effective demand, and a level of "natural" equilibrium for real wages considered to be independent from the distributive conflict between social classes. More generally, it can be stated that the new IS–LM–PC model reaches the same conclusions as the old AS–AD model regarding the existence and unique nature of the natural equilibrium, which is also grounded on the same theoretical tenets. Between the lines, one can clearly get the implication that these tenets are still of a neoclassical nature, even in the newer editions of Blanchard's textbook: net of market imperfections and asymmetries, a fundamental supposition holds, namely that the equilibrium is ultimately caused by "optimal" behaviours of economic agents driven by the so-called "fundamentals" of preferences, technology and, above all, the capital and labour resources available. Blanchard's use of the neoclassical growth model as a point of reference for "long run" analysis represents clear evidence of this way of reasoning.

Among the consequences of this theoretical continuity, is the fact that both Blanchard's old and new approach reach broadly similar economic policy conclusions. To quote an example from the many mentioned in this volume, the new IS–LM–PC model reiterates an argument typical of the old AS–AD model, whereby a policy of wage moderation may help to increase the level of employment's natural equilibrium without affecting real wages. The only difference is that in the most recent model, wage moderation does not lead automatically to the new equilibrium, but the contribution of an expansionary monetary policy is required.

Overall, if it is true that Blanchard has decided to abandon the form of the old AS–AD model, the same cannot be said for the theoretical and political substantial features of that model, which are confirmed in more than one respect. Thus, as far as pioneering contribution is concerned, his latest approach to macroeconomics teaching also seems to replicate existing well-known models. This difficulty in distancing himself from the old interpretation should not ultimately come as a surprise. Although the latest Blanchard has the honesty to express strong reservations on the capacity of mainstream macroeconomics to interpret contemporary capitalism and its crises, he eventually chooses to remain within the theoretical scope of the prevailing approach and does not breach its bounds.[2] Even the eighth edition of his manual, published after the world crisis unleashed by Covid-19, albeit amended in various respects, remains in general firmly anchored to the prevailing approach.

However, there is another way of trying to respond to the questions raised by the international great recession. Both in the old and new version of his teaching model, Blanchard's approach can be debated in the light of an alternative paradigm inspired by the contributions of the exponents of the so-called schools of critical economic thought. Although characterized by epistemological and theoretical variety, the alternative schools of thought share a view of capitalism as a monetary reproduction economy marked by irreducible class divisions. This alternative view denies any relevance to the traditional idea of a "natural" equilibrium caused by "optimal" behaviours of agents driven by the so-called neoclassical "fundamentals", and disputes the mainstream interpretation that reduces conflicts between the different social groups to the rank of mere market "imperfections".

The debate between the prevailing approach and the alternative schools has always been a tricky topic to present to students. This is due both to the intrinsic difficulty of the terms of the debate and to the fact that the mainstream analysis and the lines of critical thought feature their own diverse variants and connotations. For these reasons, critical economics textbooks usually tend to present the various theoretical paradigms in a purely narrative form, and only rarely manage to go through their analytical differences. The authors of mainstream textbooks, on the other hand, resolve the problem by actually choosing to expunge any criticism of the prevailing approach from their works. *Anti-Blanchard Macroeconomics* was conceived precisely to overcome these typical limitations of contemporary textbooks. By retrieving and updating a comparative process that was greatly in vogue in the second half of the twentieth century, this volume offers an extremely succinct comparison between Blanchard's mainstream model and the alternative approaches to macroeconomics. In particular, the Anti-Blanchard approach shows that making simple changes to the initial hypotheses of the dominant macroeconomic model can lead to an alternative model, a model that essentially "overturns" the logical relationships between the involved variables and the related implications for economic policy. While the limitation of this method is to reduce to a bare minimum the intricate tangle of issues running through the debates

---

[2]   For further insights, see the debate between Blanchard and Brancaccio at the end of the present volume.

between the schools of economic thought, the merit of this method is to suggest a new, more detailed and subtle way of interpreting Blanchard's celebrated textbook. Based on a long experience using the Italian edition of the volume in the academic field, we think that the Anti-Blanchard approach represents a useful tool for trying to overcome the current contradiction between the opportunity to offer students a preliminary mainstream education and the need to nurture rather than crush their critical spirit. As a matter of fact, albeit in very elementary terms, the volume helps students to understand that, just like and perhaps even more than any other area of scientific knowledge, economics is not a discipline that changes in a smooth, linear manner but, on the contrary, represents a field of research that develops through intense theoretical debates, continual empirical testing and resultant disputes about economic policy.

This text is the second English edition of a book by Emiliano Brancaccio (at its fifth Italian edition): it has already generated a number of interesting discussions and has been translated in Spanish as well (first edition). The translation from Italian to English has been edited by Andrea Califano, who has also helped with the revision and general updating of the text. This edition includes several unpublished paragraphs and updates with respect to the first English edition; within the new paragraphs, several pages are dedicated to the economic analysis and implications of the Covid-19 pandemic. This is also the object of an inedited appendix by Emiliano Brancaccio and Raffaele Giammetti, focussed more specifically on the trade-off between health and production. Two other statistical appendices are part of this volume: one by Domenico Suppa, which reproduces a well-known Organisation for Economic Co-operation and Development (OECD) test on the empirical relationships between statutory employment protection and unemployment, and another by Andrea Califano and Fabiana De Cristofaro, which reproduces a test performed by Blanchard and Leigh on the gross domestic product (GDP) forecasting errors made by major international institutions after the onset of the global crisis. The purpose of these appendices is to provide students with practical examples of the ways in which economists try to verify whether and to what extent their theories are supported or denied by empirical assessments. This edition also includes the transcript of a debate between Olivier Blanchard and Emiliano Brancaccio held in December 2018 at the Feltrinelli Foundation. The volume is concluded by some reading suggestions for further, more detailed treatment of the topic and some opinions on *Anti-Blanchard Macroeconomics* expressed by scholars belonging to different schools of thought.

Anti-Blanchard Macroeconomics is extremely versatile and is well suited to various types of teaching uses and to courses of different length.

Although it has been designed to counterbalance Blanchard's book, the volume offers the opportunity to examine any mainstream macroeconomics textbook that, at least in part, is dedicated to the AS–AD model or the IS–LM model with the Phillips curve. But this volume, above all, makes for a completely autonomous approach and can also be adopted as the main textbook for a comparative macroeconomics course. In addition, the volume as a whole, or parts of it, can be included in academic programmes so as to be used to different degrees of detail as part of undergraduate or graduate courses. It gives hints for critical reflection for courses in macroeconomics or political economy and it can even be used as a supplement to courses on economic policy, monetary economics or labour economics.

2. Blanchard's AS–AD model

2.1 STRUCTURE OF THE TRADITIONAL AS–AD MODEL

The subject of this chapter is the AS–AD (aggregate supply and aggregate demand) model. Blanchard used this model for many years as a basis for the didactic exposition of his textbook. However, since the seventh edition of his book, Blanchard chose to leave the AS–AD out and to provide a "new approach" to macroeconomics. We will show in Chapter 4 that this new approach nonetheless shares many features with the traditional AS–AD model. Moreover, the latter still represents a landmark for many macroeconomics textbooks adopting the "mainstream" point of view, thus it is still a key topic to deal with.

The AS–AD model determines the aggregate demand for goods (AD) moving from the IS–LM analysis, while it relies on the analysis of the labour market to determine the aggregate supply of goods (AS). Once the aggregate demand and the aggregate supply have been determined, the AS–AD model is completed (Figure 2.1).

2.2 FROM THE IS–LM MODEL TO THE AGGREGATE DEMAND

First, we would like to describe the logical steps leading from the IS–LM model to the aggregate demand function AD. The IS–LM macroeconomic model defines all the combinations of the interest rate i and production Y that bring the aggregate supply and demand of goods into equilibrium. The relation IS expresses the couples of i and Y able to guarantee

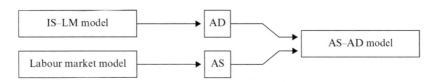

Figure 2.1   How Blanchard's mainstream model is derived

the equilibrium between the aggregate supply and demand of goods. According to Blanchard, this is an inverse relationship in accordance with the teaching model typical of mainstream literature: *ceteris paribus*, a reduction in the interest rate *i* stimulates firms to increase their demand for investment goods *I*, thus boosting aggregate demand. Production (realized and supplied) *Y* will increase accordingly. On the other hand, the LM relationship traces the *i* and *Y* couples that ensure the equilibrium between the supply and demand of money in real terms. Again, Blanchard follows the mainstream approach in considering this relationship to be of a direct type: *ceteris paribus*, when production *Y* increases, there is an equal increase of income and transactions. As a consequence, the agents involved need more real money in order to perform a higher number of transactions. The thirst for additional money is quenched by an increase of the supply of assets in the market, which causes a fall in the price of assets and an upswing of the interest rate *i*.[1] The IS–LM model can thus be described by the following equations, of which the IS gives the equilibrium between production and aggregate demand, and the LM the equilibrium between money supply and demand (in real terms):

$$\text{IS)} \quad Y = C(Y - T) + I(Y, i) + G$$

$$\text{LM)} \quad \frac{M}{P} = YL(i) \tag{2.1}$$

Figure 2.2 represents the two relationships: the shape of the curves corresponds to generic functions; a representation of specific (e.g. linear) functions could have been chosen as well. For example, by defining with c_0 and I_0 the autonomous components of consumption and investment; with c_1 the population's propensity to consume; with d_1 and d_2 investment sensitivity respectively to the trend of the interest rate and to production; with f_0 a fixed parameter; and with f_1 the sensitivity of the interest

---

[1] Why does a variation in the asset price P_T bring about an opposite variation in the interest rate *i*? To make things clearer, let us suppose that the assets are "fixed-income securities", which last for one year. A typical case is the treasury bonds issued by governments to get money lent by private agents. An asset is of the fixed-income type when the issuer is obliged to make a payment of a fixed amount to the holder when the asset expires (e.g. 100 euro). The interest rate on the asset will thus be given by the difference between the 100 euro obtained by the owner at the expiry date and the price P_T that he/she paid to buy the asset, divided by the price P_T: $i = (100 - P_T)/P_T = 100/P_T - 1$. For instance, if one buys an asset for 95 euro knowing that it will yield a fixed amount after one year (100 euro), one will profit from an interest rate equal to $i = 100/95 - 1 = 0.05255.2$ per cent. If the asset would be issued at the price of 90 euro, it would yield a higher interest rate: $i = 100/90 - 1 = 0.111 = 11.1$ per cent. Things would be opposite if the asset had been bought at a higher price (i.e. the interest rate would be lower). This explains the inverse relationship between asset prices and the interest rate.

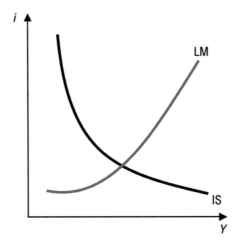

Figure 2.2   IS–LM model

rate to the quantity of money expressed in real terms, and assuming for simplicity that production does not affect labour demand, it is possible to represent the IS and the LM in the following way:

$$IS) \ Y = c_0 + c_1(Y - T) + I_0 - d_1 i + d_2 Y + G$$
$$LM) \ M/P = (f_0/f_1) - (1/f_1)i$$
(2.1b)

And therefore, rearranging the terms:

$$IS) \ Y = \frac{1}{1 - c_1 - d_2}(c_0 + I_0 + G - c_1 T - d_1 f_0 + d_1 f_1 \frac{M}{P})$$
$$LM) \ i = f_0 - f_1(M/P)$$
(2.1c)

In which the term $(c_0 + I_0 + G - c_1 T)$ represents the so-called autonomous expenditure, the term $[1/(1 - c_1 - d_2)]$ represents the so-called autonomous expenditure multiplier, sometimes referred to as the fiscal policy multiplier, and the term $[d_1 f_1/(1 - c_1 - d_2)]$ is the monetary policy multiplier. In the linear framework just described there is no need to make the relations explicit. However, in section 5.1 we will further develop these equations to examine the different models also from the algebraic point of view.

Going back to the generic function and the representation of it, it is obvious that any variations of variables that are not included in the graph will cause changes in the two relationships, hence movements of the equilibrium. For example, if public spending G increases, the IS will shift to the right, hence the interest rate i will increase and equilibrium production Y

as well; instead, an increase in the quantity of money M will cause the LM to shift to the right, with a corresponding reduction in i and an increase of the Y level of equilibrium, and so on.

In line with the mainstream tradition, Blanchard's IS–LM model gets to a fundamental macroeconomic relationship by linking the level of the prices of goods with the level of the aggregate demand for goods, hence with production. The relationship is the following: variations in the price level of goods cause the real value of the quantity of money to change, thus causing the interest rate to move, hence investment, aggregate demand and eventually production. For instance, if – for whatever the reason – the prices of goods P increase, the actual purchasing power of the money M/P present in the system declines. This decrease in the real value of the money held will lead many agents to look for more money by selling assets. This will determine an excess supply of assets in the market, therefore leading to a fall in the price of assets P_T. However, a falling asset price entails an increase of the interest rate i related to those same assets. Such a rise in the interest rate of the involved assets will bring a general increase in the interest rates linked to any contract. Debtors will thus need to offer higher rates in order to persuade creditors to lend. At that point, even the interest rates attached to bonds issued by firms and to the funding provided by banks to firms in order to invest will increase. As a consequence, firms will find it more expensive to borrow money and will tend to decrease their demand for loans that are usually taken out to buy investment goods I (machinery, plants, equipment ...). The demand for investment goods I will thus fall, bringing about a general contraction of the aggregate demand Z, with production Y and employment N decreasing and unemployment u rising. It can be expressed as follows:

$$P \uparrow \Rightarrow \frac{M}{P} \downarrow \Rightarrow \text{supply of assets} \uparrow \Rightarrow$$

$$\Rightarrow P_T \downarrow \Rightarrow i \uparrow \Rightarrow I \downarrow \Rightarrow Z \downarrow \Rightarrow Y \downarrow \Rightarrow N \downarrow \Rightarrow u \uparrow \qquad (2.2)$$

Indeed, if the price level decreases, an exactly opposite sequence stems out: the real value of monetary stocks increases, money holders are induced to use the exceeding stocks to buy assets, leading to an excess demand for assets in the market; the price of assets increases while the interest rate falls, stimulating firms' investment and thus the aggregate demand for goods, production and employment.

Thus, according to the mainstream analysis, there is an inverse relationship between the price level on the one hand and demand and production on the other. In the IS–LM model, this corresponds to a shift of the LM: lower prices entail a shift of the LM to the right and a new equilibrium characterized by a higher level of production. Another equation can be used to describe the same relationship:

$$\text{AD)} \quad Y = f(G, T, M/P) \tag{2.3}$$

The equation implies that aggregate demand – and the accordant level of production – is dependent on a set of elements. Among them, the level of the price of goods P clearly stands out, as it affects the real supply of money M/P, hence the actual purchasing power of the liquid stocks in the hand of the economic agents. The quantity of money M issued by the central bank matters as well, together with the level of public expenditure G and the level of taxation decided by the government. The equation can be represented on a chart that has the price level on the vertical axis and production on the horizontal axis, and which describes the function for the aggregate demand of goods AD (for clarity's sake drawn in Figure 2.3 as a straight line).

For the above mentioned reasons, the AD is downward sloping (from the left to the right): a movement along the function points to an increase in demand and production following a fall in prices. Instead, the function shifts when there are changes in those variables that are not present on the axes. For instance, if public spending increases or the central bank increases the quantity of money, we will have a rise in aggregate demand and in production Y, with P constant; this will reflect in a shift of the AD towards the right. On the contrary, if taxation is increased, aggregate demand and production Y will reduce, with P constant, thus implying a shift of the AD

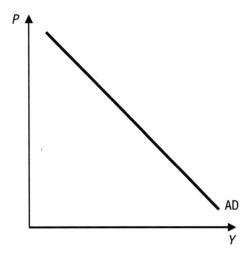

Figure 2.3   Aggregate demand AD

towards the left. The same result (a leftward shift) will stem from a wave of pessimism experienced by firms, inducing them to suddenly reduce the purchase of investment goods, hence bringing the aggregate demand down.

2.3 MONETARY WAGE AND REAL WAGE DEMANDED BY WORKERS

Let us move now to the analysis of the labour market, from which we will derive the aggregate supply of goods. Blanchard obtains the monetary wage from the following equation:

$$W = P^e F(u, z) \qquad (2.4)$$

where W is the monetary wage, P^e the expected price level, u the unemployment rate. The parameter z gathers various elements able to affect the wage demanded by workers: from the entity of unemployment benefits, to the legal framework concerning the protection of labour and to the degree of unionization of workers; the parameter z reflects the level of workers' bargaining power, that is, their higher or lower capability of claiming a higher wage. The relationship between u and W is assumed to be inverse: when unemployment lowers, monetary wage goes up. On the contrary, the hypothesis is that z and W are linked by a direct relationship: if z is enhanced – due, for instance, to more protective norms in the labour market (making it harder to fire workers) or to an upsurge in the number of the members of very confrontational unions – W will increase as well. F is a function resuming the relationship between these variables. Lastly, if workers are expecting higher prices in the future (P^e), they will ask for higher wages in order to avoid losing purchasing power.

In the short run, it is possible that workers make forecasting errors, i.e. actual equilibrium prices P are different from the prices expected by workers P^e. Nonetheless, it is reasonable to suppose that such errors tend to smooth out progressively as workers adjust their expectations, taking into account the actual trend. It is thus safe to assume that in the medium to long run $P^e = P$, so that the monetary wage set through bargaining between workers and firms is given by:

$$W = PF(u, z) \qquad (2.5)$$

from which one can derive the negotiated real wage, that is, the actual purchasing power of monetary wages: this is the value workers have the major interest into.

$$\frac{W}{P} = F(u, z) \qquad (2.6)$$

The equation points to an inverse relationship between unemployment and the negotiated real wage: the higher u, the lower will be the demanded W/P. This is intuitive when considering that the bargaining power of trade unions is reduced by a high unemployment rate. In effect, when unemployment is high, it is harder to find a new job, so the threat of being fired induces workers to moderate their claims and to accept lower real wages. On the contrary, when unemployment is low, workers think it would be easier to get a new job in case they are fired: the threat is less effective and they will claim a higher real wage. Moreover, the equation points to a positive relationship between the parameter z and the real wage. The parameter z is a synthetic indicator of the political and institutional situation in which the bargaining process takes place: a "catchall variable", as Blanchard calls it, to express workers' bargaining power. The more favourable the political and institutional framework is to workers, the higher the parameter. For instance, if there are high unemployment benefits, strong legal protection against unfair dismissal and a high unionization rate, then z tends to reach higher levels. Such an environment will increase workers' strength; they will perceive a higher bargaining power and thus adopt a more claimant stance. On the basis of these remarks, we can say that Equation 2.6 is the equation of real wage matching a given level of monetary wage, and able to express the real wage demanded by workers.

Figure 2.4 provides a graphical representation of Equation 2.6: it shows two charts with the unemployment rate u on the horizontal axis and the real wage W/P on the vertical axis. Equation 2.6 is represented by a downward sloping curve to show how an increase in the unemployment rate implies a lower wage demanded by workers, due to the less favourable situation they face. The opposite will happen when there is a reduction in unemployment. For a change in the value of a variable that is in one of the axes, such as u, we will witness movements along the curve; if there is a change in a variable not present in the axes, such as z, the curve itself will move.

In the left chart, we can see the effects of a variation in the unemployment rate u, so that a movement on the curve takes place, for instance, a decline in u emboldens workers' claims, and the real wage W/P requested is higher. The left chart describes instead the effects of a variation of workers' bargaining power z, which entails a movement of the curve: if z sets to a higher level, the curve $F(u,z)$, representing the demanded real wage, shifts upwards. This means that workers feel stronger in their bargaining power, so that – with the same level of unemployment, fixed by hypothesis – they demand a higher real wage.

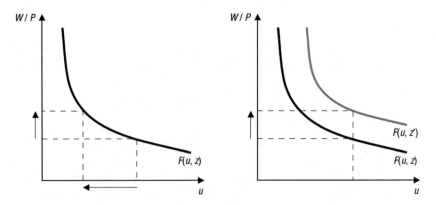

Notes: The left chart shows a movement on the curve of the real wage demanded by workers: a reduction in unemployment lifts the demanded real wage up. The right chart shows a movement of the curve: workers' bargaining power rises, so does the demanded real wage.

Figure 2.4   Real wage demanded by workers

Therefore, mutations in the political and institutional situation, as they bring changes in workers' bargaining power z, might affect the slope of the curve of the real wage demanded by workers. As a matter of fact, if workers are loosely protected by the law, have precarious contracts and are not unionized, it is likely that they will oppose a feeble reaction to a reduction in unemployment, increasing by a small amount the real wage demanded. In such a scenario, the demanded wage curve should be traced almost flat. If the political and legal environment is instead favourable to workers, a decreasing unemployment might be followed by claimant requests on the real wage. The curve will thus be very steep.

2.4   PRICE LEVEL AND THE REAL WAGE OFFERED BY FIRMS

Let us focus on the way in which firms set the prices. First, we will describe the peculiar shape of the production function chosen by Blanchard:

$$Y = AN \qquad (2.7)$$

This function implies that the production of goods Y depends on the number of workers N, multiplied by the productivity A of each single worker, that is, the quantity of goods produced by a worker in a given time span (a working day, or a working year, for instance). In the mainstream model, A is determined by the available technology. It is thus to be considered as a given, not subject to variations, unless there are specific technical innovations that make working more productive.

In his book, for the sake of simplicity, Blanchard considers $A = 1$, meaning that each worker produces one unit of good. In this way, the term A is not included in Blanchard's analysis. We do not share this simplification here. In our treatment, productivity can assume different values, and the term A will be always present: both in the production function and, as we will see, in the equation for the offered wage.

Once the term A is set according to the available technology, it is then possible to compute the cost of any produced good. We assume as an example that the wage of a worker is $W = 10$ euro per hour, and his/her productivity is $A = 5$ units per hour. The cost of labour for a single unit of good is then given by W/A, which is equal to 2 euro per unit of good.

$$W/A = 10 \text{ euro per hour} / 5 \text{ units per hour} = 2 \text{ euro per unit} \quad (2.8)$$

Let us assume that firms set the selling price of goods by summing up a profit margin (or mark-up) to the cost of labour W/A for a unit of good. The profit margin does not correspond to the entrepreneurs' remuneration only; it also covers costs other than labour, such as raw materials (oil, and so on). In our equation, the profit margin, or mark-up, is μ:

$$P = (1 + \mu)\frac{W}{A} \quad (2.9)$$

The mark-up multiplies the cost of labour. The result gives the actual monetary profit, which is the difference between the price and the cost of labour for each unit of good. In our example, the cost of labour is W/A52 euro per unit; if we assume that firms aim for a profit margin of 25 per cent over each unit, the selling price will be given by: $P = (1 + 0.25)(W/A) = (1 + 0.25)2 = 2.5$ euro per unit. The monetary profit will be 50 cents, equal to the difference between the selling price 2.5 and the cost of each unit (2). If firms manage to increase the mark-up to 50 per cent, we will have $P = (1 + 0.5)(W/A) = (1 + 0.5)2 = 3$ euro per unit. The monetary profit will thus rise to 1 euro.

At this point, if we rearrange Equation 2.9 we get to:

$$\frac{W}{P} = \frac{A}{(1 + \mu)} \quad (2.10)$$

This is the equation for the real wage W/P determined by firms' mechanism of price setting. We can say that the equation simply points to the real wage that firms are willing to offer. The offered real wage depends exclusively on the productivity of labour A and on the mark-up μ.

According to the mainstream model, both these variables are to be considered exogenous, as their values come from "outside" the model. More specifically, the productivity of labour is considered a function of the technological progress, hence of the improvement of the plants and of the machinery available to workers. In reality, labour productivity is also the result of the productive effort requested from workers and, as such, is a variable object of harsh negotiations between firms and unions. With respect to the mark-up, Blanchard claims it to be determined by the current structure of the market: if the market is characterized by a high degree of competition between firms, these are forced to keep the selling price low, so the mark-up they can gain is little as well. If competition is instead limited and perhaps there are just a few big firms, they will enjoy some degree of monopolistic power and they will have the possibility to set soaring prices and keep the margin high. Blanchard argues that the market structure is essentially the outcome of the anti-trust legislation in force. A loose anti-trust regime will favour bigger and more powerful firms, allowing them to get higher margins. On the contrary, a strict anti-trust law will foster competition, forcing firms to curtail their mark-up.

Is the mark-up influenced, beyond anti-trust legislation, by the bargaining between workers and firms? Blanchard's answer is negative. In the mainstream model, once the anti-trust regime, hence firms' market power, is known, the profit margin μ is determined. Firms will then manage prices so as to get that level of μ exactly – nothing more and nothing less than that. Accordingly, in line with the objective of keeping their margin untouched, firms will react to an increase in monetary wage with a corresponding increase in prices. Any increase in the monetary wage obtained by workers will always be offset by an equal increase of P, thus neutralizing it and leaving μ unchanged. In the framework of the mainstream model, the possibility that the real wage offered by firms could be modified by workers' claims on their monetary wage is ruled out. Provided that firms can always pass increases in W to the selling price P, it is obvious that the offered real wage turns out to be an autonomous decision of firms. Workers can decide whether to work for that wage or not, but cannot affect the level of the real wage that is offered by firms.

Let us move to the case of an increment in labour productivity and assume that the number of goods that a worker can produce in one year (A) increases following a technological improvement or a more intensive effort required from workers. From Equation 2.10 it is evident that an increase in A causes the real wage offered by firms to rise. In effect, given the monetary wage W, a growth in A implies a reduction in the cost of labour for each unit of good W/A, hence a reduction in the price level

$P = (1 + \mu)(W/A)$, and then an increase in the real wage $W/P = A/(1 + \mu)$ offered by firms. Thus, according to the mainstream model, although in absolute terms both wage and profit will grow, any increase in labour productivity will benefit real wage only, with no effect whatsoever on the profit margin. This conclusion relies on the assumption that the mark-up is exogenous: following an increase in A, firms are supposed to leave μ untouched and not to raise it. If they adjusted it instead, prices P might remain unchanged (not show any reduction), hence the real wage W/P would not increase. The assumption just mentioned seems in fact controversial and we will get back to it later.

The chart on the left in Figure 2.5 shows the equation of the real wage offered by firms (Equation 2.10) as a horizontal straight line. This is due to the fact that the wage supplied by firms depends on the level of productivity A and on the mark-up μ only, while it is not influenced by unemployment. Whatever the level of u, the offered real wage is not affected.

The graph on the right describes the effects of a change in the mark-up on the offered wage. If we suppose, as an example, that a stricter anti-trust law brings the mark-up level down to $\mu' < \mu$, we will see that the price level $P = (1 + \mu)W/A$ reduces as well: the real wage $W/P = A/(1 + \mu)$ will thus rise and the line representing it will move upwards (we will have a similar shift in the case of an increase in productivity).

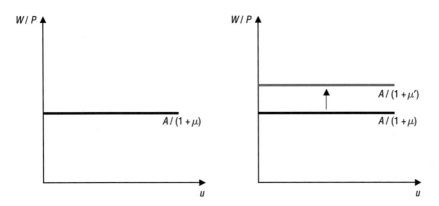

Note: The line is horizontal, as the offered wage is not influenced by unemployment. Within the mainstream model, variations in the offered wage are produced only when productivity or the mark-up change.

Figure 2.5   Line representing the wage supplied by firms

2.5 "NATURAL" EQUILIBRIUM IN THE AS–AD MAINSTREAM MODEL

Equations 2.6 and 2.10 can be drawn in a simple chart describing the equilibrium in the labour market according to Blanchard (see Figure 2.6).

The graph shows that there is just one level of unemployment where the wage demanded by workers matches the wage offered by firms.

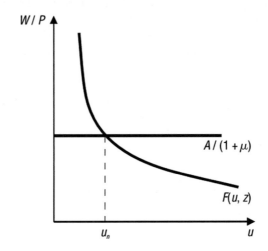

Figure 2.6   "Natural" equilibrium in the labour market

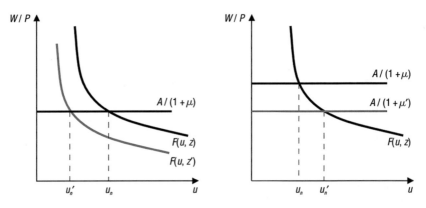

Notes: In the left chart, the effects of a reduction in workers' protection against unfair dismissal (implying a new $z' < z$) are represented.
In the right chart, the effects of loosening the anti-trust legislation (implying a new $\mu' > \mu$) are represented.

Figure 2.7   Variations in the natural rate of employment

This equilibrium level is defined as "natural unemployment rate" by Blanchard: it is the term u_n in the graph. Please notice that any other unemployment level corresponds to a gap (mismatch) between the demanded wage and the offered wage.

As made clear by Figure 2.6, the level of the natural unemployment rate depends on the parameters that determine the position of the wage requested by workers and of the wage offered by firms: z, μ, A. Variations in the parameters shift the curve, bringing a change in the natural rate of unemployment u_n.

Figure 2.7 is meaningful on the matter. In the right chart a loosening of the anti-trust legislation is considered. Competition is thus reduced, the mark-up μ increases, so do prices set by firms $P = (1 + \mu)W/A$; consequently, the offered real wage $W/P = A(1 + \mu)$ declines, bringing the horizontal line downwards. It can be seen that the natural unemployment rate u_n rises as a consequence. As a matter of fact, only a higher level of unemployment makes workers weaker, to the point of accepting a lower level of wage offered by firms.

A reduction in the legal protection against the unfair dismissal of workers is represented in the left chart. Clearly, such a policy makes workers weaker and therefore reduces the value of workers' bargaining power z. The wage that workers can demand will be lower, hence the attached line moves downwards. There is therefore a reduction in the natural rate of unemployment. As workers are now more worried about losing their job – which is now more likely – they will be available to accept the wage offered by firms, even with a lower level of unemployment.

We have just described how variations in the parameters of the model affect the natural rate of unemployment u_n, which in turn makes workers demand a wage that is equivalent to the wage offered by firms. However, this is a static description, as it is not helpful in explaining how the economic system tends exactly towards the rate of unemployment that makes the demanded wage equal to the offered wage. We shall investigate how we get from a given level of unemployment to another one, following mutations in A, μ, z. The next paragraphs will deal with this topic also.

2.6 ONLY THE "NATURAL" EQUILIBRIUM CAN GUARANTEE PRICE AND WAGE STABILITY

In the framework of the mainstream model, the natural rate of unemployment is the only rate that makes workers' claims on wage match the wage offered by firms. In addition, it is the only rate that is compatible with a situation of wage and price stability. The system will thus tend towards the natural rate, even though Blanchard's textbook does not go into the detail of the mechanism of convergence towards the natural equilibrium. We will now bring to the surface what is tacit in Blanchard's pages on the subject.

Looking at Figure 2.8, one may wonder what happens when the unemployment rate differs from the natural rate. When $u_0 < u_n$, unemployment is low and workers' bargaining power is high. The demanded wage (point A) will therefore exceed the real wage offered by firms (point B). The gap between what is offered and what is demanded, represented by the AB segment, will cause an upward spiral involving monetary wage W and prices P, as workers will request increases in monetary wage again and again, aiming for the desired real wage. Firms will in turn react with corresponding increases in prices, so as to maintain their profit margin μ unchanged. Thus, if firms succeed in keeping the mark-up untouched, the real salary too will not change, being given by $W/P = A/(1 + \mu)$.

An unemployment rate $u_0 < u_n$ will therefore set a mutual reinforcing upward trend of W and P, hence inflation. On the other hand, a rate $u_1 > u_n$ makes workers weaker. Their claims over the wage level will be lower than the offered wage (CD segment). In this case, the tendency will be one of reduction of W, hence of the costs W/A faced by firms. If they decide to leave the profit margin untouched – as we assumed in the previous case – the costs reduction will bring a proportional fall in prices P, that is, a deflation.

Therefore, levels of unemployment different from the "natural" level bring monetary instability. Only at the natural rate of unemployment

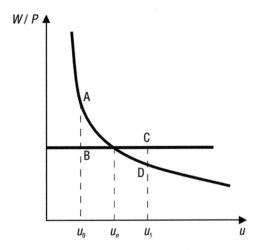

Figure 2.8   Deviations from the natural rate of unemployment cause either inflation or deflation

workers demand exactly what firms are willing to offer, and the upward (or downward) price–wage spiral stops.

2.7 FROM THE LABOUR MARKET TO THE AGGREGATE SUPPLY

It is now possible to move from the labour market to the analysis of the aggregate supply of goods. Let us start by recalling the equations of wage and price:

$$W = P^e F(u, z) \tag{2.11}$$

$$P = (1 + \mu) \frac{W}{A} \tag{2.12}$$

Prices appear in Equation 2.11 with their expected value, P^e. It means that in the short run actual prices may temporarily deviate from the prices expected by workers. Substituting Equation 2.11 into Equation 2.12, we get to the following price equation:

$$P = \frac{(1 + \mu)}{A} P^e F(u, z) \tag{2.13}$$

By definition, the unemployment rate u is given by the ratio between the total number of unemployed people U and the total labour force L, that is, $u = U/L$; the labour force is given by the sum of the unemployed people U and the actual workers N, that is, $L = U + N$. It is then obvious that the total number of unemployed people is given by the difference between the labour force and the employed workers, or $U = L - N$. Overall:

$$u = \frac{U}{L} = \frac{L - N}{L} = 1 - \frac{N}{L} \tag{2.14}$$

Furthermore, we know that production is given by the productivity of each worker multiplied by the number of workers: $Y = AN$; hence the number of employed people may be seen as $N = Y/A$. We can thus write that:

$$u = 1 - \frac{Y}{AL} \tag{2.15}$$

By substituting this latter expression in the previous price equation, we get that:

$$\text{AS)} \quad P = \frac{(1 + \mu)}{A} P^e F\left(1 - \frac{Y}{AL}, z\right) \tag{2.16}$$

This equation represents firms' aggregate supply (AS). It describes the relationship between the level of production and the price level: for any given level of Y, the equation gives us the attached level of P set by firms. It is a direct relationship. This is due to the fact that an increase in production Y, implies a surge in the level of employment N necessary to realize the new level of production, thus unemployment u drops. Workers' bargaining power is enhanced as a consequence, hence the monetary wage W they demand. However, firms will increase the price level P in proportion to wage in order to maintain the mark-up unchanged:

$$\text{if } Y \uparrow \Rightarrow N \uparrow \Rightarrow u \downarrow \Rightarrow$$
$$\Rightarrow \text{Workers' claims} \uparrow \Rightarrow W \uparrow \Rightarrow P \uparrow$$

(2.17)

If we draw a chart with production Y on the horizontal axis and the price level P on the vertical axis, we obtain an upward sloping aggregate supply (for the sake of simplicity, drawn as a straight line in Figure 2.9: it may well be a curve).

So far, we have described the movement on the AS caused by variations in Y. Upward or downward shifts of the AS are instead due to changes in the variables included in Equation 2.16 but not on the axes. For instance, if the parameter for workers' bargaining power z increases, then W increases as well, so does P – with constant Y – and thus the AS shifts upwards. If it is μ to rise with equal Y, again there is an increase in P and an upward shift of the AS. The opposite occurs if the parameters mentioned decrease: the AS will shift downwards.

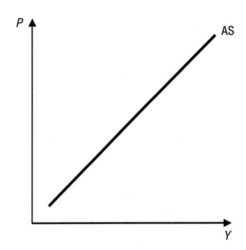

Figure 2.9   Aggregate supply AS

Another possible reason for the AS to shift upwards is the spiral involving wages and prices. In a situation where the level of unemployment does not correspond to the "natural" rate and there is no agreement on the real wage between workers and firms, we will have a race to the top of monetary wage and prices, as we have already seen. For instance, if the actual unemployment rate is $u_0 < u_n$, workers have a strong bargaining power and the spiral will drive wages and prices higher and higher. It is an environment where actual prices will always be higher than the prices expected by workers ($P > P^e$). Consequently, workers will continuously adapt their expectations on prices. Workers will demand compensation for this increase in expected prices through a rise in the monetary wage W (see Equation 2.11). Firms in turn want to keep their mark-up untouched, so the rise in monetary wage will lead to a further increase of prices (Equation 2.12), and so on. The wage–price spiral can be described as follows:

$$W \uparrow \Rightarrow P \uparrow \Rightarrow P^e \uparrow \Rightarrow W \uparrow \Rightarrow P \uparrow \dots \tag{2.18}$$

How is the AS affected by this race to the top? In order to answer this question, let us move to Figure 2.10, where we drew the aggregate supply chart just below that of the labour market. It is to be noted that the labour market chart has been here overturned with respect to previous representations. The origin of the axes is now on the right, that is, the more we move right, the less unemployment we have. We propose a representation that is not present in Blanchard's textbook; this has been done only for teaching purposes, to make more evident the link between the two charts, and does not have any significant theoretical implication whatsoever. Most notably, capsizing the labour market graph makes clearer that production Y and unemployment u move always in opposite directions. For instance, a rise in production (rightward movement on the horizontal axis of the lower chart) is always matched by a reduction in unemployment (a rightward movement too, on the horizontal axis of the upper graph). Intuitively, in order to produce more, more workers need to be employed (unemployment decreases), and the opposite if production falls.

The "natural" level of unemployment u_n is matched by the "natural" level of production Y_n. These two natural rates correspond to the unique situation in which the wage demanded by workers is equal to the wage supplied by firms (the point N in Figure 2.10).

However, if we stick to a hypothesis of disequilibrium with $u_0 < u_n$ (therefore $Y_0 > Y_n$) and with workers relatively strong in their bargaining power, the demanded wage will exceed the wage offered by firms (the difference is traced by the AB segment). An inflationary spiral is set, involving monetary wage, prices, expected prices, monetary wage, prices, and so on.

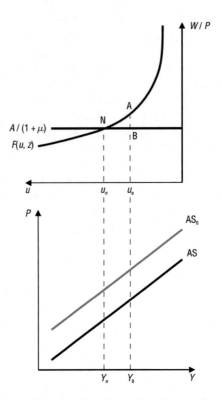

Note: With a level of unemployment that is lower than the natural rate ($u_0 < u_n$), workers are strong in their bargaining power, claim higher real wages and a gap emerges between the demanded wage and the offered one (AB segment). The wage–price spiral makes the AS shift upwards.

Figure 2.10   Aggregate supply chart and the labour market

With production held constant at Y_0, there is an increase in prices P (as it is clear from the equation of the AS). From a graphical point of view the aggregate supply AS shifts upwards. This upward shift does not stop until the "natural" rate of unemployment is somehow reached (and the accordant "natural" level of production), which, as we know, is the only point where the wage demanded by workers is equal to the wage offered by firms, and where the race to the top stops. It goes without saying that, if we had moved from an unemployment rate higher than the "natural" rate, we would have witnessed a race to the bottom, a wage–price downward spiral and eventually a downward shift of the AS.

2.8   AS–AD MODEL

We can now analyze the two curves together: aggregate demand and aggregate supply. Figure 2.11 shows once again the labour market in the upper panel and both the AS and the AD in the lower one. The intersection between the AS and the AD corresponds to the natural level of production, which in turn is linked to the natural rate of unemployment identified by the equilibrium in the labour market.

As we will see, the complete AS–AD mainstream model brings theoretical support to a set of traditional free market economy claims. First of all, the thesis that the market – if freed from constraints – will spontaneously rebalance towards its equilibrium (that is, to the "natural" levels of real wage, unemployment and production). This is to say that the "spontaneous

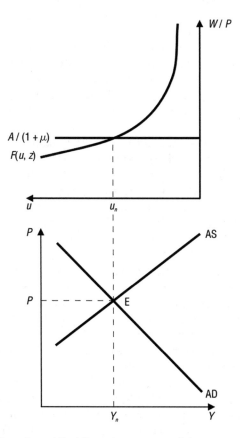

Figure 2.11   Complete AS–AD mainstream model

forces" of the market are by themselves able to bring the system out of a crisis; a political intervention of "bailout" is not necessary. Moreover, the model leads to the conclusion that any attempt to modify the "natural" levels of equilibrium, either through expansionary policy or wage policies, will be pointless and may even be harmful. Let us take a closer look at these features of the mainstream model.

2.9 EXPANSIONARY POLICY IS NOT ESSENTIAL IN ORDER TO OVERCOME A CRISIS

One of the mainstream model's main achievements concerns the demonstration of the traditional free market thesis that the capitalist system relies on market forces alone: it is therefore self-sufficient. It shows that in the occurrence of an economic crisis, the market economy could get out of it in a spontaneous way: it is not essential to resort to expansionary fiscal or monetary policy. The system can get back autonomously to its "natural" equilibrium, which it had temporarily left due to the crisis. Therefore, according to this model, active economic policies would not be necessary to bring the economy back on track. Figure 2.12 explains how the system always tends to go back to its "natural" equilibrium, even when hit by a crisis.

Let us start from a situation of "natural" equilibrium, as described by point N in the upper chart and by point E in the lower chart. As we know, such a point can be defined as a point of equilibrium, given that the "natural" unemployment rate is precisely that rate at which the demanded wage curve and the offered wage line intersect, that is, workers demand exactly the real wage that firms are willing to give. This means that there is no price–wage spiral, either upwards or downwards: in that point the system is stable.

We suppose that – whatever the reason, fear of international economic turmoils or of a war, and so on – a confidence crisis occurs and spreads among entrepreneurs. The owners of capital suddenly adopt a pessimistic view of the profits they may get from their activity. Hence, they decide to curtail purchases of machinery, plants and equipment, that is, they decide to reduce their demand for investment goods I. The reduction of investment entails a fall in aggregate demand Z (the AD shifts to the left, from AD to AD'). Thus, production reduces from Y_n to Y', whilst unemployment rises from u_n to u': we move from E to A. The unemployment growth weakens workers' bargaining power, making them claim a real wage that is lower than the real wage offered by firms (BC segment), and prompting them to see their monetary wage W reduced. If we assume that firms do

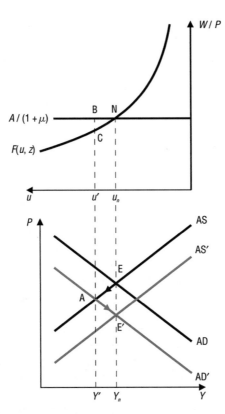

Figure 2.12   Monetary wage and price reduction alone are in principle sufficient to overcome a crisis (expansionary policy is not necessary)

not take advantage of the circumstances and decide to keep the mark-up untouched, it can be stated that the monetary wage reduction will translate into a proportional reduction in prices P, therefore of the expected prices P^e and again of monetary wage, prices, and so on. As a consequence, the AS shifts downwards, from AS to AS'. The race to the bottom involving prices and wages in turn will imply an increase of the real value of the stocks of money held by the population, M/P. The exceeding stocks will be used to purchase assets, bringing about an increase in the price of assets, a fall in the interest rate i, hence an increase in investment I, production Y and eventually a reduction in unemployment u. The process keeps on going until unemployment is back again to its natural level, u_n. At that stage, workers' bargaining power recovers its strength, therefore claiming a real wage matching the real wage offered by firms. The wage–price downward spiral stops: we move from point A to point E′ in the lower chart and we get back to the point N in the upper chart.[2]

According to the mainstream model, the capitalist economy would thus be able to overcome a crisis relying on market forces alone, with no need to resort to any expansionary policy. This theoretical result has brought many free market economists to advocate for the complete inaction of the government and the central bank even in situations of deep political crisis. However, Blanchard does not share such an extreme interpretation of the mainstream AS–AD model. He does not argue in favour of the inaction of political authorities in the event of a crisis. The spontaneous mechanism present in his model is in fact based on workers' willingness to accept a monetary wage reduction, something that depends on many political factors (and on unions' behaviour), and that cannot be taken for granted. Moreover, Blanchard acknowledges that getting back to natural equilibrium through the spontaneous mechanisms of wage and price reduction alone may turn out to be an extremely long and devious pattern, for example due to the possible opposition that unions may set up against the contraction of monetary wages. He does not neglect what the 1929 great crisis has to tell us: then, the late reaction of public authorities – and the belief that market mechanisms alone were going to deal with the crisis – caused a harsh and long economic depression. Blanchard believes the spontaneous adjustment to be a mere textbook hypothesis. In the real world, a crisis such as the one described by point A shall be tackled by public authorities, so as to make the convergence to equilibrium faster. For instance, the central bank could implement an expansionary monetary policy, aimed at increasing the quantity of money M present in the system: aggregate demand would thus get back to its initial position, from AD′ to AD. The real liquid stock M/P would thus grow due to a rise in M instead of a fall in P, and the process would be quicker. This would also spur a faster dynamic, moving from the reduction of the interest rate to the growth in investment and production, and to the subsequent return

---

[2] It is worth stressing that the described dynamic is entirely dependent on the hypothesis that firms do not take advantage of workers' weakness. When monetary wage decreases, firms are said to proportionally reduce prices, leaving the profit margin unchanged. However, it might likely happen that in a similar situation firms leave prices unchanged – or they reduce them less than the fall in wages – in order to obtain an increase in their mark-up. As already shown, prices are in fact given by the cost of each good W/A multiplied by a margin: $P = (1 + \mu)W/A$. The margin is thus $\mu = (AP/W) - 1$. Blanchard's model assumes that a reduction of W is matched by a proportional reduction of P, thus leaving the mark-up unchanged. If firms instead left P untouched, or at least reduced it less than W, then the mark-up would clearly increase. Why should firms not take the chance? We will get back to it: the hypothesis of a constant mark-up – imposed by Blanchard and opposed by critical economists – will be abandoned in the following chapter.

of the system to its natural equilibrium (point E in the lower chart, point N in the upper chart). To sum up, Blanchard does not seem to bring the mainstream model to its furthest logical conclusions. Instead, he apparently mitigates the free market theory conclusions that can be drawn from the mainstream model.

2.10 "NATURAL" EQUILIBRIUM AND THE LIMITS TO EXPANSIONARY POLICY

As we have just seen, Blanchard is prompt to acknowledge the role of expansionary policy, as it will help the system to get back to the natural equilibrium faster. What would then happen if the government used expansionary policy not only to converge towards the equilibrium but also to attempt to go beyond such equilibrium? That is, what would occur if the economic policy instrument was used to pursue a level of production higher than the natural level, hence a rate of unemployment lower than the "natural" equilibrium rate? Blanchard's reply to this question is rather clear-cut: if a scenario of repeatedly rising inflation is to be avoided, expansionary policy cannot reduce unemployment below the "natural" level. This statement is supported by Figure 2.13.

We start from a "natural" equilibrium situation (point N in the upper chart and point E in the lower chart) and we imagine that political authorities are unhappy with the levels of "natural" production and employment: they are willing to implement an expansionary policy which would increase Y and reduce u. For instance, they could increase public spending G; the government could reduce taxes; the central bank could increase the supply of money M; or other measures could be taken to set forth an expansionary policy. Any of these expansionary policy instruments would eventually affect the aggregate demand, which would rise together with employment and production, as indicated by a movement of the AD curve to the right (from AD to AD'). In the graph, the system is now in point A, where production is higher (from Y_n to Y') and unemployment is lower (from u_n to u'). As unemployment goes down, workers enhance their bargaining power and claim a real wage that is higher than the real wage offered by firms (BC segment): the mismatch translates into upward pressure on the monetary wage W and thus on the production costs. Under the hypothesis that firms leave the mark-up untouched, the monetary wage will translate into a proportional price increase, which guarantees that the margin μ is not affected by workers' claims. A run-up spiral is set on, involving monetary wage W, price P, expected price P^e, then wage again, price, and so on, whereas production Y remains constant. In the graph, the AS shifts

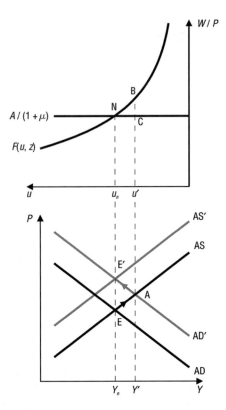

Figure 2.13 *Expansionary policy cannot bring the economy to an unemployment level below the "natural" equilibrium rate*

upwards, from AS to AS'. Furthermore, the price rise will reduce the real value of the monetary stocks M/P in the hand of the population. This lack of liquidity will lead many agents to sell assets in order to purchase money, yielding a decrease in the price of assets, an increase of the interest rate i, a consequent fall in investment I and production Y, and eventually an increase in unemployment u. The process goes on until unemployment reaches again its natural level u_n: there, workers are weaker, and the real wage they demand is again equal to the real wage offered by firms. The race to the top of monetary wage and price reaches an end: we are back to point N, whereas on the AD' we moved from point A to point E' in the lower chart of Figure 2.13.

The effectiveness of expansionary policy is thus only temporary, while the system gets to its natural equilibrium. Is it possible to permanently keep the system on a production level above the natural equilibrium? In theory, the answer is positive. For instance, the central bank could increase M accordingly to the increase of W and P, so as to prevent the fall of M/P back to the initial levels. This will imply continuous injections of liquidity to the system aimed at keeping production above its natural level. It is a political scenario that is considered unfeasible by mainstream economists. For one thing, it would set the economic system on a track of permanent conflict between workers and firms (BC segment), therefore triggering an inflationary wage–price spiral, whose velocity would increase continuously as workers forecast higher and higher expected prices. If we want to avoid setting the economy on an inflationary spiral, we had better stick to the "natural" equilibrium.

2.11 NEUTRALITY OF MONEY, CONTRACTIONARY POLICY, CROWDING OUT AND AUSTERITY

If the expansionary policy is implemented through an increase in the money supply M by the central bank, the final result is the "neutrality of money". It means, according to mainstream economists, that monetary variables (such as M) cannot affect the real ones, that is, those that are "physical" (such as production Y and unemployment u). As we have already mentioned, monetary expansion causes a deviation from the natural equilibrium that is in fact temporary. When the system gets back to its natural position, all the physical variables are back to their initial levels. Moreover, as prices P have risen proportionally to the initial increase in M, the real value M/P of the liquid stocks also gets back to its original value.

Thus, sticking to the thesis of the neutrality of money, the mainstream model reaches the conclusion that monetary expansionary policy only reflects in inflation, in the long run. It causes nothing more than an increase in prices, while it does not affect in any way physical variables (production and unemployment of equilibrium). On top of that, the thesis of the neutrality of money has been raised by some free market economists to promote restrictive monetary policies, by which the central bank reduces the supply of money. Given that money is irrelevant on the levels of production and of other physical variables, they claim that monetary policy should be used to target contraction instead of expansion. As money is neutral, a contractionary monetary policy allows reducing prices with no permanent negative effects on production and unemployment: they will always get back to their "natural" levels in any case. Such an extreme interpretation of the neutrality of money is not shared by Blanchard, who believes instead that a restrictive policy could keep the economic system in a situation of low production and high unemployment for a long time. Nonetheless, it appears as a natural logical consequence of the mainstream model. Moreover, the idea that restrictive policies find their rationale in the neutrality of money seems to be present in the statutes of many central banks. For instance, underlying the treaties of the European Central Bank, there is the idea that monetary policy is helpless in changing the "natural" levels of equilibrium of production and unemployment, while it is decisive in the determination of prices. This is why it is claimed that monetary policy shall target the only goal that it can actually obtain – keeping prices under control to prevent possible inflationary dynamics.

Finally, can we say that public spending and fiscal policy in general are neutral as well? Although it is true that even expansionary public spending in the long run is not able to modify the "natural" equilibrium levels of production and unemployment, on the other hand, contrary to monetary policy, public spending is not neutral on the interest rates and on investment. An increase in G makes production Y rise, so that income rises and with it the purchasing power, but in order to spend more, agents need more money, hence the population is pushed to sell assets. This will imply a fall in the price of assets and an increase in the interest rates, which will lead to a fall in private investment that will compensate the initial growth due to public spending. This dynamic goes under the name of "crowding out" of private investment by public spending. Thus, expansionary policy based on fiscal policy does not modify the natural equilibrium levels of production and unemployment; it causes an increase in interest rates and a reduction in private investment, which are not temporary, so it cannot be defined as thoroughly neutral. By contrast, a restrictive public budget policy, also known as "austerity", causes opposite long-term effects, that is, a reduction in the interest rate and an increase in firms' investment in machinery, plants and equipment. Since such investment is considered crucial for long-term economic development, it can be concluded that for the mainstream model "austerity" policy is welcomed, as it reduces the crowding out caused by public spending and therefore allows for the expansion of private investment.

2.12   CONFLICTS OVER WAGE ARE USELESS AND HARMFUL

As we have shown, according to the mainstream model, expansionary policy is, in principle, not indispensable in order to overcome a crisis; it is indeed completely helpless if the goal is to enhance Y and reduce u beyond their respective levels of "natural" equilibrium. What has the model to say with regard to conflicts over wage? What if workers begin to claim higher wages? The model puts forward an even more drastic thesis on the issue. If workers become more confrontational and strengthen their claims, there will be no effect on wages, while the effect on employment will be negative. The stronger bargaining power does not bring any wage benefit and has the only effect of increasing unemployment. Let us have a look at Figure 2.14 to understand how the mainstream analysis reaches such a result.

The chart in Figure 2.14 describes the following situation. We start from a natural equilibrium situation, expressed by the levels of unemployment and production u_n and Y_n. It should be clear by now that at the natural equilibrium level workers demand exactly what is offered by firms (point N in the upper chart). Let us assume that workers strengthen their claims,

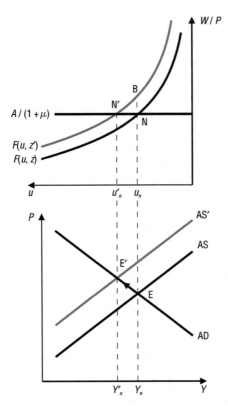

Note: According to the mainstream model a higher degree of workers' bargaining power ($z' > z$) is all but harmful: real wage does not change, whereas unemployment increases.

Figure 2.14   Conflicts over wage

asking for higher wages. It may be due to different reasons: laws may be
enforced protecting them to a higher degree (for example, providing higher
unemployment benefits, stronger protection from unjustified dismissal), or
more conflictual unions may enlarge their membership. Graphically, this
stronger bargaining power is expressed by an increase of the parameter,
from z to z'. This means that the curve of the real wage demanded by workers shifts upwards. As a consequence, u_n and Y_n do not identify equilibria
any longer: now, with the same level of unemployment, workers claim a
real wage exceeding the wage offered by firms (the BN segment in the upper
chart). The monetary wage W is thus pushed up by workers. Firms will in
turn increase prices P so as to defend their profit margin. The increase in
actual prices induces workers to revise upwards the expected prices as well
(P^e) and eventually to ask for further monetary wage increase to compensate; this will lead to a further increase in prices, and so on (upward shift
of the supply curve, from AS to AS').

The upward spiral of wage and price sets up a mechanism that tends to
contract demand. As a matter of fact, when W and P increase, there is a
reduction in the real value of the monetary stocks M/P. Population is thus
brought to increase their money holding by selling assets, so that the price
of assets falls and the rate of interest i rises. The demand for investment
goods I falls, and the same happens to aggregate demand Z, production Y
and employment N, whereas unemployment u increases (movement on the
AD from E to E'). The process goes on until the new "natural" equilibrium
is reached: it is identified by higher unemployment u'_n (therefore by a lower
level of production Y'_n). At the new equilibrium, in fact, unemployment
is so high that workers are pushed to step back and demand once again
exactly the real wage that is offered by firms. It should be noted that the
demanded real wage increases and then falls, whereas the real wage offered
by firms remains at the same level: $A/(1 + \mu)$. This is obvious given that
Blanchard's model considers productivity A and mark-up μ as exogenous,
not subject to be affected by workers' claims or by the outcome of the bargaining process. The conclusion of Blanchard's model is thus that conflict
is not worthwhile: workers would be better off if they did not exercise any
pressure on wages, given that their action will not have any effect on real
wages and will only cause an increase in unemployment.

2.13   VIRTUES OF WAGE MODERATION

So, what should workers do in order to improve their economic conditions,
given that conflict is pointless? The mainstream model suggests the following conclusion: workers should reduce their claims and pursue a wage

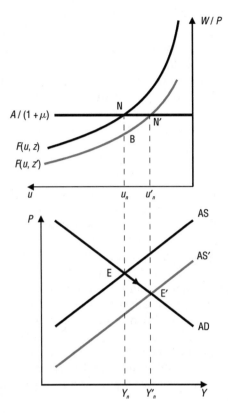

Figure 2.15   Wage moderation (z' < z) leaves wages untouched and brings a fall in unemployment

moderation policy, i.e. the parameter of bargaining power z shall reduce. Figure 2.15 describes the matter.

The promptness of workers to reduce the parameter summarizing their strength ($z' < z$) entails a downward shift of the demanded real wage curve. The demanded real wage becomes lower than the offered wage (NB segment). A fall in monetary wage follows suit. If we still assume that firms do not take advantage of workers' weakness so as to increase the profit margin, then μ remains untouched and the reduction in monetary wage will bring a proportional reduction in prices. Also, expected prices will decrease accordingly, and with them again wage, prices, and so on. This dynamic will take place with a constant level of Y (the supply shifts downward from AS to AS'). Wage and price deflation will bring the usual increase in the real value of monetary stocks (M/P), thus an increase in demand, production, employment and a consequent fall in unemployment (movement on the AD, from point E to point E′). The new equilibrium will be reached in u'_n, where unemployment has reduced as much as to make workers stronger and willing to ask again for the real wage offered by firms $(A/(1 + \mu))$. Again, this has remained unchanged throughout the whole process. According to the mainstream model, then, wage moderation leads to a lower natural rate of unemployment, with a constant level of real wage. If workers are less conflictual, it is possible to reduce unemployment without running the risk of workers asking more than firms are willing to offer.

How, then, can wage moderation – with all these positive effects – be obtained? That is, how can we reduce z? If we bring the mainstream model to its extreme logical consequences, moderation might be obtained by either cooperating with the unions or even playing against them. Ideally, trade unions should be eager to accept a decrease in the effectiveness of their claims. If they are available to restrain their claims on the monetary wage, they will let prices fall so that the stock of money will increase and so will demand, production and employment. However, it may be the case that trade unions are not willing to restrain their claims. Then, harsher measures would have to be adopted. For instance, protection against unjustified dismissal can be lifted or constraints on the rights of unions' assembly and strike may be imposed. A reduction in the z parameter would be obtained this way, thus, their claims would be scaled down. To sum up, the mainstream model could even be used to claim that wage moderation is to be pursued whatever it takes, either with or without the consent of workers.

2.14 OIL, ANTI-TRUST, TECHNOLOGICAL UNEMPLOYMENT

Until now, we have examined Blanchard's mainstream model looking at the possible movements of aggregate demand and of the parameter of workers' bargaining power. The model contains many other variables, so it can describe many other phenomena. We will now spend a few words on some of them.

First, firms' mark-up μ includes not only the profit margin to be paid to entrepreneurs but also all the costs that add up to the cost of labour, for example the cost of raw materials used in the process of production. We can thus say that the mark-up is given by two components:

$$\mu = \text{firms profit margin} + \text{any other cost adding to labour (e.g. oil, etc.)}$$
(2.19)

Then, if we assume that firms are able to preserve their profit margin entirely, it is clear that when extra-labour production costs rise (for instance, when the price of oil goes up), they will increase the mark-up μ accordingly. Sticking to Blanchard's AS–AD model, the consequence of an increase in the oil price – then of the mark-up – will be a reduction of the real wage and an increase in unemployment. This result is shown in Figure 2.16.

The rise of the oil price induces firms to increase their mark-up (from μ to μ'), and thus the selling price $P = (1 + \mu)W/A$. The reason is clear: in order to defend their profit margin, entrepreneurs load the increase in the cost of raw materials on prices. The mark-up and price increase is matched by a reduction of the real wage offered by firms, which determines a downward shift of the horizontal line describing it.

The new real wage that is offered by firms is $A/(1 + \mu)$, and identifies a gap between the wage demanded by workers and that supplied by the firms (NA segment in the upper chart). Workers will try to react to this

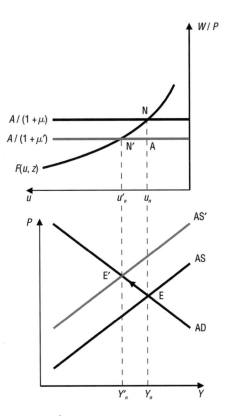

Figure 2.16   Increase in oil price

situation; they will demand a wage increase matching the rise in prices in order to preserve their purchasing power. The usual run-up between monetary wage, price, expected price, monetary wage, price, and so on is then started (the AS curve moves to the left). In addition, the growth in prices brings a decline in the real value of the money stock, inducing the agents to exchange assets for liquidity: asset prices fall, interest rates increase, investment, aggregate demand, production and employment reduce and unemployment rises (movement on the AD, from point E to point E'). The process keeps going until the new "natural" equilibrium is reached. It is characterized by higher unemployment, and workers are so weak that they are forced to accept the lower real wage offered by firms. In the end, according to Blanchard's model, the increase in the oil price falls entirely on workers, both because their real wage falls and because unemployment increases. It is obvious that this result is dependent on a key hypothesis present in Blanchard's model: firms set exogenously the mark-up, and workers are never able to affect it. Thus, any increase in the cost of raw materials will have to be borne by workers. They can only limit the damage by accepting from the very beginning a decrease in their real wage, thus preventing the start of an inflationary run-up that generates unemployment.

Another interesting case is the anti-trust legislation. Although Blanchard rules out that workers' claims can affect firms' profit margin, he concedes that the mark-up may shrink on some occasions. The reason is that the part of the mark-up μ that goes to profits depends on the degree of monopoly present in the economic system. If there are many firms and there is competition between them, they will try to curtail prices as much as they can in order to increase their share of consumers, hence the mark-up will be lower. Vice versa, if there are only a few large firms, presumably competition will be limited: firms retain a large market power that allows them to impose higher prices. The profit margin μ will thus be larger. In this regard, mainstream economists believe it could be possible to reduce the degree of monopoly – hence the level of the mark-up – through a strict anti-trust legal regime. In such a framework, the barriers to competition are eliminated, and collusive behaviour and monopoly positions are subject to punishment. Stricter anti-trust laws increase competition between firms, push prices down and eventually reduce μ. Within Blanchard's model it is shown that this policy increases the natural real wage and decreases natural unemployment: firms are forced to reduce prices and thus μ as they face greater competition. This is represented by an upward shift of the horizontal line describing the wage offered by firms. The student may verify the final result by drawing the graph and explaining the economic sequence it shows.

The mark-up μ, though, does not represent the only variable able to modify the equilibrium in the mainstream model. Technological improvements might increase labour productivity A. Can an increase in productivity generate what is usually defined as technological unemployment? To this regard, let us remember that the unemployment rate is given by $u = 1 - (Y/AL)$; therefore if labour productivity A increases, firms will be able to produce a given quantity of goods Y with a lower number of workers. They will fire workers and unemployment u will increase. Due to technological progress, we will thus face a rise in unemployment. However, the mainstream model rules out the possibility for this phenomenon to last in the long run, the reason being that a higher A implies a fall in the production cost (W/A) as well, and thus determines a reduction in the selling price $P = (1 + \mu)W/A$ provided that μ remains untouched as usual. However, the reduction in prices in turn increases the real value of the money stocks and boosts demand, production and unemployment via the well-known channels, so that the workers fired because of the increase in productivity are re-hired. In conclusion, according to the mainstream model, technological unemployment cannot be in place. On the contrary, technological progress will increase the real wage and bring about a fall in the natural rate of unemployment. The student can validate this conclusion both from the graphical point of view and with a theoretical economic explanation: the process starts from an increase in A, shifting the line of the wage offered by firms upwards and bringing a reduction in prices.

2.15 CONCLUSIONS REACHED BY THE AS–AD MODEL

The AS–AD model had been adopted by Blanchard in editions one to seven of his textbook, and still constitutes the cornerstone of the mainstream treatment of macroeconomics. Its major conclusions are summarized below. The first implication is that economic policies aimed at the expansion of demand are not necessary to overcome an economic crisis. Second, those policies cannot bring the economy beyond the natural equilibrium (said better, they can overtake the natural equilibrium, but this would lead to a permanent conflict between firms and workers, and a consequent continuous rise of inflation). Third, workers' claims are never able to increase the equilibrium real wage, which is in fact determined exclusively by the mark-up set by firms. Instead of claiming higher wages, workers should restrain their wage claims. It is the only way by which unemployment could shrink without giving rise to conflicts and hence to inflationary pressure. To sum up, the mainstream model does not take a positive view of political pressures on the demand side and of social pressure on the side of wages. It is necessary instead that governments' and unions' actions are compatible with the "natural" equilibrium level of unemployment and wage. At best, workers could favour a reduction in natural unemployment only by restraining their claims on wage. The list of results may be continued with other examples. For instance, technological progress and foreign competition can be absorbed by the economic system without severe strains: workers' sacrifices would in fact be only temporary, if necessary at all. In the end, the system will reach a natural equilibrium characterized by unchanged – or even more positive – levels of unemployment and wage.

The mainstream model seems to offer an interpretation of a capitalistic market economy that is largely optimistic. With few limited exceptions, the model argues essentially against public intervention into the economy and denies that unions' conflictual behaviour may be to the advantage of workers.

3. The alternative model

3.1 A DIFFERENT VIEW ON THE ECONOMIC SYSTEM

The AS–AD model, as described in the previous chapter, remains the most important one, both within academia and in economic policy. The model's most extreme liberalist implications were questioned by the onset of the international economic crisis in 2007–2008, but nevertheless, the pillars on which it is built have not significantly changed. Blanchard's "new approach" itself, as we will see in the next chapter, keeps many features of the AS–AD model. However, the so-called schools of "critical" thought have been challenging the dominant paradigm for some time, by highlighting some of its weaknesses. The nature of the challenges posed by economists critical of the mainstream AS–AD model will be the topic of this chapter. These critiques will lead us to an alternative macroeconomic model, which implies different conclusions with respect to the dominant theory. The alternative model denies the harmonious idea of a "natural" equilibrium, replacing it with a conflictual notion of social relations embedded in the dynamics of a capitalist economy.

Blanchard's model rests on two fundamental theoretical tenets:

1. the inverse relationship between prices and aggregate demand (which implies a downward sloping aggregate demand AD);
2. the exogenous nature of the mark-up μ and of the parameter z (workers' bargaining power), which makes the line representing the wage supplied and the curve representing the demanded wage insensitive to the outcome of the bargaining between workers and firms.

Let us consider how schools of thought alternative to the mainstream deal with these two tenets.

3.2 BLANCHARD'S DOWNWARD SLOPING AD CURVE: A CRITIQUE

As we have seen, Blanchard's model shows that economic policies are ineffective in moving the economy away from the natural rate of unemployment.

Such is implied in the hypothesis of a downward sloping AD demand curve, as only a downward sloping AD guarantees that variations in prices allow the economic system to reach the natural level of production Y_n, and hence the natural rate of unemployment u_n. A fiscal expansionary policy might bring unemployment below u_n. However, that would result in an unstable situation, as explained above. Due to the conflict between workers and employers and to the resulting growth in P, money would fall in real terms (M/P), and thus the demand for goods and production would fall as well, until the system is back to the natural equilibrium. On the other hand, if a crisis brought the unemployment rate to $u > u_n$, wages and prices would fall; hence, money would increase in real terms, the demand for goods and production would rise as well, and, eventually, the economic system would spontaneously return to the natural equilibrium. Expansionary fiscal policy in this case would be useless. To sum up, starting either below or above the natural equilibrium, variations in wages, prices, demand and production will bring the system to its equilibrium, and this will happen through movements of the economy on the downward sloping AD.

Why is the demand for goods determined by wage and price dynamics? That is, what is the mechanism that makes the aggregate demand AD downward sloping? The answer to this question lies in the usual sequence: given M, a rising P entails a fall in M/P, an increase in i, a fall in I, in Z, and thus in Y. That is, an inverse relationship between prices on the one hand and demand and production on the other. This inverse relationship has been one of the targets of the controversy fostered by the critical economists, most notably the Keynesians. At the time of the great crisis of the 1930s, those representing the dominant theory claimed that wage reduction – and hence reduction in prices – was sufficient to foster aggregate demand and production, thus reducing unemployment. The economy was as it is represented in Figure 2.12 (point A); they claimed a reduction in wages and prices would move the economy towards point E' and out of the crisis. However, the economic system was apparently stuck in a point such as point A, where unemployment was extremely high. Therefore, the representatives of the dominant theory blamed the unions for the incapacity of the economy to overcome the crisis. Unions were guilty, in their view, of resisting the reduction in wages and hence in prices, therefore preventing a recovery in demand and production.

Inspired by Keynes' work, the proponents of critical theory disputed this interpretation of the crisis. In their opinion, even though the unions had accepted a fall in monetary wage, the subsequent fall in prices would not necessarily have led to an expansion of the demand. Translated into the terms of modern critical theory, this calls into question the very existence of an inverse relationship between prices and aggregate demand, hence the idea of a downward sloping AD. The matter is far from simple: it was in fact the object of a long-lasting controversy throughout the twentieth century. In what follows, we will explore three reasons why critical economists feel skeptical about the downward sloping AD. First, they claim that a fall in P and the resultant rise in M/P do not necessarily imply a fall in the rate of interest i. As a matter of fact, a fall in P entails an increase of M/P, the real value of money, thus causing the agents to buy assets in order to get rid of surplus stocks of money. The purchase of assets would cause their price to rise, with a reduction in the rate of interest following. However, if agents believe that the future price of assets will fall, they will avoid purchasing even if they are holding surplus stocks of money. Professional financial agents are clearly not willing to buy assets that are going to lose value in the future. In conclusion, even though a fall in P causes a surplus of the real money M/P held by the agents, this does not necessarily imply that they will purchase assets, hence we cannot take for granted an increase in the price of assets and a fall in the rate of interest. This situation is known as a "liquidity trap", as agents prefer holding cash instead of other assets.

Second, critical economists claim that even if a fall in P and a rise in M/P were eventually to bring about a fall in the interest rate as well, this would not necessarily bring a rise in investment. As a matter of fact, they claim, firms' investment in new machinery and plants depends more on expectations of future profits than on the rate of interest. If firms lack confidence regarding the profit they are to receive in the future from new plants, they will not invest in the new plants, even if facing an extraordinarily low rate of interest, that is, if the cost of financing the investment is low.[1] Third, and further to the previous points, based on the issue of expectations, it is possible to show that the sign of the relationship between the interest rate and investment is uncertain: a falling rate of interest might imply a reduction in the value of the investment per unit of labour, instead of an increase. In this respect, it is worth mentioning once again that both the analysis made by Blanchard and the analysis put forward in the present work describe an extremely simplified economy, in which only one good is produced. Only by considering that in actual economic systems a huge quantity and variety of goods and means of production are produced is it

---

[1] It is worth mentioning that Blanchard himself has acknowledged that the relationship between interest rate and investment is uncertain, and with no clear empirical confirmation. He commented on the issue: "it is well known that to get the user cost to appear at all in the investment equation, one has to display more than the usual amount of econometric ingenuity, resorting most of the time to choosing a specification that simply forces the effect to be there" (p. 153, comments and discussion by Blanchard attached to the paper by Shapiro: M. Shapiro, O. Blanchard and M. Lovell (1986), "Investment, output, and the cost of capital", *Brookings Papers on Economic Activity 1986(1)*, 111–164.

possible to grasp the critique to the inverse relations between investment and interest rate. We will mention this critique only briefly. The starting point is acknowledging that investment represents firms' expenditure to purchase diverse types of means of production: machinery, equipment, plants, and so on. These various means of production will be multiplied by their respective selling price (expressed, for instance, in unit of labour) in order to get the total value of the investment. Furthermore, the rate of interest may be considered a cost of production, thus concurring to determine the price of the means of production as expressed in units of labour. A fall in the rate of interest has different effects on the cost of the different means of production, to the point of altering the proportions between their prices: in fact, some prices will fall, others will rise. Again, the price of each means of production is multiplied by the quantity used, and the results are added together, thus obtaining the total value in unit of labour of the investment. There is no reason to take for granted that this final value will be higher than the previous one: a fall in the rate of interest may even cause a reduction in the value of investments measured in units of labour (instead of an increase).

The points listed above rule out the existence of a neat inverse relationship between prices and aggregate demand. As an example, we will visualize this theoretical stance as a vertical AD (instead of downward sloping). A vertical AD implies the non-subsistence – or the indeterminacy at least – of an effect of prices on the aggregate demand. The above discussion shows that a falling P, that is an increase in M/P, does not necessarily imply a consequent fall in i; even if this is the case, the reaction of I is not taken for granted. It is an implication of the vertical AD: variations in P do not reflect in variations in the demand – at least, their effect is uncertain, as aggregate demand is influenced by the other variables considered in the system. For instance, if investment reduces following a collapse in confidence, aggregate demand will shrink and the AD curve will shift to the left. However, if the government implements an expansionary fiscal policy, either increasing public spending or cutting taxes, demand will rise and the AD will move to the right.

3.3   CRITIQUE OF THE EXOGENOUS NATURE OF μ AND z

As we have shown, Blanchard's mainstream model assumes both the mark-up μ and workers' bargaining power z to be exogenous. This implies that the supply and demand of wage cannot be influenced by the balance of power between workers and employers, and by the relative bargaining process. On the other hand, a crucial idea in Marx's thought is retrieved by critical economists, that is, the idea that both the way of producing goods and the share of wage and profit depend on the balance of power between social classes, thus subject to change when this balance itself changes. If applied to Blanchard's model, this idea would not stand as it implies that any key variable of the model is in fact shaped by the interests of the parts involved, and by conflicts between them.

For instance, labour productivity A is not a mere technological variable anymore; it becomes the object and outcome of the bargaining process. The level of aggregate demand itself – hence of production Y – becomes something disputed by different social groups: workers would perhaps demand a full employment policy, whereas capitalists would rather prefer some degree of unemployment, in order to weaken workers' claims on wage. Having said that, above all we will focus on two pivotal variables: we will assume that the mark-up and workers' bargaining power are determined by the situation of the balance of power between social classes. The level of z and μ will be socially contended and therefore determined from time to time by the relative bargaining power of firms and workers. As a result, they cannot both be considered exogenous anymore: more precisely, if the balance of power is leaning on the workers' side, then z will be exogenous, and μ endogenous instead. Graphically, the horizontal supplied wage line will move to accommodate to the wage demanded. On the contrary, if the balance of power is favourable to firms, z will be endogenous and μ will be exogenous. Consequently, the demanded wage will adjust to the supplied wage. In this framework, the hypothesis of an exogenous μ, which was taken for granted by Blanchard, makes for just one of the different scenarios. Obviously the two recently mentioned cases are extreme and are raised mostly for teaching purposes. In the real world, each variable will tend to adjust to the value of the other, hence the new levels of μ and z will be situated in a point that is intermediate between the two extremes. The student may assume initially that a social class is dominant over the other, and therefore a variable is exogenous and the other is forced to adjust; this will help to grasp the model and the relative exercises. At any rate, the very notion that z and μ may be subject to continuous adjustment – with at least one of them to be considered endogenous – means that a "natural" equilibrium cannot occur. The system will in fact achieve an equilibrium that is dependent on conflict and on the dynamics of the balance of power between social classes.

3.4   COMPLETE ALTERNATIVE MODEL

Once the AD curve is thought to be vertical instead of downward sloping, and the mark-up μ and the parameter z are not to be considered, both at the same time, exogenous, it is possible to describe the full alternative model (see Figure 3.1).

The alternative model presented is inspired by critical macroeconomic theory. As we will see, this model reaches very different – and sometimes opposite – results with respect to Blanchard's mainstream model. Figure 3.1 illustrates some points of interest.

First of all, the AD is vertical. Second, the line of the supplied real wage and of the demanded wage will now tend to adjust one to the other, depending on the balance of power between classes. Due to the novelties mentioned, the equilibrium level of production and the rate of unemployment cannot be defined as "natural" anymore. As a matter of fact,

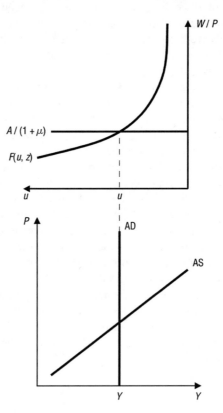

Figure 3.1   Alternative model

within this different theoretical framework, the capitalistic equilibrium is determined from time to time by social forces struggling with each other, hence subject to the pressure that the various social groups and interests will put on economic policy and on wage bargaining. The alleged "natural" character of the equilibrium is therefore denied.

It is worth highlighting that the pattern leading to an equilibrium clearly differs from the one characterizing Blanchard's model. The starting point is now the level of aggregate demand, and thus the position of the AD. The level of demand determines production Y, which in turn determines employment and hence the equilibrium rate of unemployment u. Given the rate of unemployment, the relative strength of firms and workers will decide which of the two groups is going to surrender, therefore which of the two variables μ and z – with their respective lines of wage demanded and supplied – is to make the greater adjustment variation (to accommodate the other). Thus, in the alternative model, the analysis is bottom-up, that is, it starts from demand, moves up to production, then to unemployment, to finally reach the balance of power, which entirely determines the real wage that will prevail at a given level of unemployment. Is it to be set by firms, by workers or at an intermediate level? The logical process is clearly overturned in this model with respect to Blanchard's model. The mainstream analysis is top-down: μ and z are given and they determine the position of the supplied and demanded wage curves. These curves in turn determine the "natural" rate of unemployment, that is, the only one at which workers precisely demand the supplied real wage; in this case, wages and prices are stable. Given the natural rate of unemployment, the natural level of production is straightforward. Finally, the equilibrium will be able to guarantee a level of demand matching natural production.

3.5 MARKET FORCES ALONE CANNOT PUT AN END TO THE CRISIS

Let us take a closer look to the characteristics of the alternative model. As already mentioned, the mainstream model states that public policy is not required to overcome a crisis. The sheer reduction of wages and prices should, in principle, be enough to foster demand and bring the system back to the situation enjoyed before the crisis. The alternative model does not share this view (see Figure 3.2).

We start from an equilibrium situation, as described by point N in the upper side and by point E in the lower chart: notice that the equilibrium is not defined as "natural" anymore. Let us assume that, for whatever reason (fear of an international crisis, a war, and so on), entrepreneurs experience

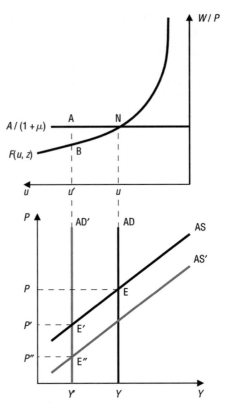

*Figure 3.2   Following a crisis, the economic system gets stuck in a situation
               of low production and high unemployment*

a confidence crisis. They suddenly become pessimistic about the amount
of profit they will be able to get from their activity. Thus, they decide to
cut down the purchase of machinery, plants and equipment, that is, they
decide to scale down investment I. As a consequence, the AD shifts to the
left, aggregate demand Z falls, hence production shrinks as well (from Y to
Y'). Crisis and the following increase in unemployment (from u to u') curb
the power of workers; they in turn appease their claims with respect to
what is offered them (segment AB), and are suddenly prone to a reduction
in monetary wage W.

   For the moment, let us stick to the hypothesis that firms do not exploit
workers' weakness, therefore they do not try to increase their margin μ.
Under this hypothesis, it is obvious that a fall in W will imply a proportional reduction in P. The familiar downward wage–price spiral is then at
work, and it is coincident with a downward shift of the aggregate supply

(from AS to AS'). However, the AD is not downward sloping anymore, it is now a vertical line and this implies that a fall in price does not generate expansionary effects on demand and production. The so-called liquidity trap and a low sensitivity of investment to the rate of interest may hinder the expansionary mechanism Blanchard's model was based on. This is the reason why, according to the alternative model, even in the presence of a further decrease in price and a consequent movement from E' to E'', the system remains stuck at a production level $Y' < Y$. We can even imagine further price reductions and further downward movements of the AS curve. Nonetheless, they will translate into movements along the vertical AD with no effects whatsoever on Y.

Arguably, the wage and price race to the bottom will eventually stop. Such a situation will in fact sooner or later lead firms to exploit this scenario of high unemployment and the consequent workers' weakness. They will thus put an end to the fall in prices by increasing the mark-up μ, which in this theoretical framework is not given anymore but is a function of the balance of power between social classes. The rising mark-up will entail a contraction in the wage supplied by firms $A/(1 + \mu)$, hence a downward shift of the relative horizontal line. Point B is the new equilibrium between what is requested and what is offered, and the fall in wages and prices reaches an end.

It has just been shown that, provided a vertical AD, market forces alone are not able to bring the economic system out of a crisis. Expansionary policy is the only way to boost the economy: a rise in public spending or a tax cut, for instance, could sustain aggregate demand and production until the previous equilibrium level Y is reached again (the AD moves to the right towards the original position).

3.6 EXPANSIONARY POLICY CAN HAVE A PERMANENT EFFECT ON THE EQUILIBRIUM

As already mentioned, Blanchard acknowledges the role expansionary policies can have in bringing the economic system out of a crisis. However, we have also mentioned that he deems such policies to be ineffective in bringing production and unemployment to levels that are stable and respectively higher and lower than the natural equilibrium levels. According to Blanchard, the system tends to get back to its natural level. Expansionary policy, in the long term, is thus ineffective on production and always spurs inflation. It is easy to notice how these conclusions depend on the downward sloping AD hypothesis and on the hypothesis that μ and z are both exogenous. Once these hypotheses are put aside, the effect of expansionary policy is very different indeed (see Figure 3.3).

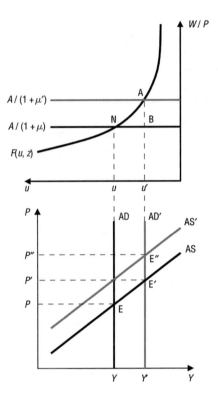

Figure 3.3   Effects of expansionary policy within the alternative model

Starting from an equilibrium situation, described by points N and E, and by production Y and unemployment u, we assume that the government opts for an expansionary policy (for example an increase in public spending), being unsatisfied with the current equilibrium. The aggregate demand Z will rise with production reaching Y' and unemployment u' (that is, a shift of the demand towards the right, to the new position AD'). The fall in unemployment makes workers stronger in their bargaining power, pushing them to demand wages higher than those offered by employers (segment AB). A "race to the top" in monetary wages and prices is set off, with prices reaching the new level P''. Furthermore, a spiral involving prices, expected prices, wages, prices again, and so on, is generated, making the aggregate supply shift upwards to AS', while prices reach P' and possibly even higher levels. Still, the fundamental novelty of this different framework is the vertical AD: as we know, this means that due to the liquidity trap and to the low sensibility of investment to the interest rate, the increase in P does not have a negative effect either on the demand for goods or on production.

The economic system settles in fact on the new levels of production Y' and unemployment u'. Thus, the expansionary policy has a permanent effect on real variables.

However, the gap between demanded and offered real wages (the AB segment) remains, inducing yet more inflationary pressure on monetary wages and prices. In such a situation it is likely that either workers or entrepreneurs will eventually give up and adapt. In Figure 3.3, the example depicts a scenario favourable to workers, where z remains exogenous and the mark-up goes down to the new level $\mu' < \mu$, matching the wage supplied with the demanded wage. The horizontal line (supplied wage) shifts upwards to the new equilibrium A. A different scenario may unfold as well. For instance, the balance of power could remain in favour of the firms, and workers would adapt to the new framework. In that case, the equilibrium would be B, which is reached by a reduction in z and the following downward shift of the demanded wage curve.

We described two extreme scenarios, useful for teaching purposes as they imply that a variable remains exogenous while the other adjusts. Realistically, firms and workers will find an agreement stemming from the new equilibrium u' somewhere in between the points A and B. More likely, then, μ and z will adjust reciprocally, thus determining a new intersection between the demanded wage curve and the line of the wage offered by the employers, along the AB segment.

At any rate, there is no doubt that the expansionary policy had effects thoroughly different from those claimed by Blanchard: both the increase in production and the fall in unemployment are stable results. Moreover, the real equilibrium wage can also increase if the balance of power is in favour of the workers. These results apply to a contractionary policy as well, though in the opposite direction. A reduction in public expenditure, for instance, would have permanent effects on the economic system. The AD would shift to the left, whereas Y would fall with no automatic regress to its initial level.

3.7   CONFLICT VERSUS WAGE MODERATION

Within the mainstream model, wage conflict is ineffective on remuneration, its only result being an increase in unemployment, whereas wage moderation is regarded as positive because it increases employment while leaving the real wage untouched. These results stem from the fact that the mark-up and workers' bargaining power are exogenous, a hypothesis removed in the alternative model, which allows for variations in μ and z. Consequently, the alternative model's results are "open" to various possibilities regarding the outcome of conflict and wage moderation, thus implying that it is not possible to forecast *a priori* the outcome of wage bargaining. This depends on the political–institutional context shaping the balance of power, hence the relative position of workers and firms and its chances of being modified (by movements in μ and z). Let us see what happens when workers' bargaining power increases. The parameter z may increase, for instance, when there is an upsurge in the membership of radical unions, as depicted in Figure 3.4.

Stronger unions and workers' bargaining power imply an upward shift in the demanded wage curve, with the demanded wage exceeding the wage offered by firms (AB segment). Monetary wage W is pushed upwards by the workers. At first, firms will arguably withstand workers' claims, thus trying to leave the mark-up untouched and to pass the increase in wage onto prices. Consequently, the AS curve will shift upwards, and the price

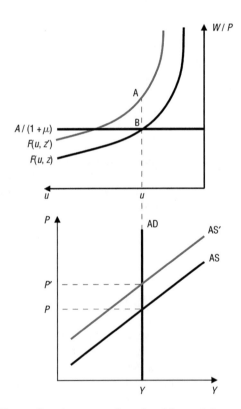

Figure 3.4   Effects of an increase of workers' bargaining power (z' > z) within the alternative model

level will rise from P to P'. This will make the wage grow even more, prices will increase again, and so on. However, given the vertical shape of the AD, the repeated increase in the price level will not entail reductions in demand or in production, nor any increase in unemployment (which sticks at the initial rate u). As there is no increase in unemployment, workers will not lose their strength or renounce their struggle and the race to the top in wages and prices will continue. How will the situation get back to stability? What is needed is clearly that either workers or firms give up and adjust to the new situation.

Let us suppose that firms give up on higher prices and accept a reduction in the mark-up. Formally, this implies that workers' bargaining power is set at the higher level z', whereas the mark-up decreases at $\mu' < \mu$. Thus, the real wage supplied by firms $A/(1 + \mu')$ increases, and the relative horizontal line shifts upwards, making A the new equilibrium point at the interception with the curve of the wage demanded. In A, wage demanded and wage supplied equalize again, hence putting a stop to the wages and prices race to the top. The shift is not drawn in Figure 3.4: it is up to the student to modify the graph following these indications.

In this case, workers were completely successful. Their stronger bargaining power resulted in a higher real wage, with no drawbacks on unemployment. The outcome is therefore opposite to that described by Blanchard. The alternative model is in fact open to the various, different outcomes stemming from the bargaining process, as we have already shown. It may well be that firms withstand workers' claims on wage, eventually causing workers to back down. In that case, on the formal ground, the mark-up level will not change, whereas the parameter of workers' strength will get back to the original level. It might be the result of workers' desertion of more intransigent unions, following a long period of run-up between wage and prices with no increase in real wage; parameter z might decrease once again. Such a situation is depicted by a fixed horizontal line describing the wage supplied and a curve for demanded wage that has to return to its original position (back to the initial point of equilibrium B). This is a situation where conflict is powerless to change the equilibrium real wage – a result like the one presented by Blanchard. This coincidence is due to the assumption made here (shared with Blanchard's model) that μ does not change, so $W/P = A/(1 + \mu)$. However, contrary to Blanchard's claim, the race to the top involving wages and prices did not imply an increase in unemployment, as in the alternative model demand is not sensitive to variation in prices (the student may describe this situation, both in formal and graphical terms).

However, the examples raised describe the two extreme cases: when μ completely adjusts to a rising z, and when μ does not change instead and it is z that must return to its original position. In the actual world, an inter-mediate scenario may occur, with reciprocal adjustments between μ and z leading to a new equilibrium on the segment AB (again, the student may describe this case formally and graphically). The opposite scenario of wage moderation is still to be considered. Imagine a situation where workers and unions agree to a policy of strict wage moderation or where moderation is achieved by the suppression of legal safeguards with a consequent weaken-ing of workers. Moderation is thus the result of either a voluntary strategy implemented by the unions or obtained through coercive actions. In both cases workers' bargaining power z is reduced, hence shifting downwards the demanded wage curve. Demand is lower than offer and the monetary wage tends to fall. Even if we allow for a reduction in P following the decrease in W, we will face the fact that in this theoretical framework the AD is vertical: a fall in prices does not affect the unemployment rate, which does not change. Moreover, in the alternative model the mark-up is not a given anymore: firms may take advantage of workers' weakness and increase μ. Even with falling prices, the real equilibrium wage $A/(1 + \mu)$ will fall, since the reduction in prices will be less than proportional if compared with that in monetary wage. A graphical account may describe a situation where the shift of the demanded wage following a reduction in z is matched by a rise in μ and thus by a downward shift of the supplied wage as well. Wage moderation generates a new equilibrium where unemployment per-sists at the same level while the only reduction is in real wage: moderation is not worthwhile, one could say, as it does not bring beneficial effects to workers. Once again, we have reached a result that is opposite to that put forward by Blanchard (and that can be described by the student, both in formal and graphical terms).

3.8   THE CASE OF THE HORIZONTAL AS

Until now, we have theorized the curve of the real wage demanded by workers as downward sloping relative to unemployment. Such a shape well describes the idea that workers' bargaining power increases with a fall in unemployment, giving rise to more assertive workers' claims. This thesis can be supported in many ways, for example, when the level of employment is high it is easier to get a job, therefore the fear of losing the job is lowered. Besides the variety of claims raised to support and justify this thesis, there is a substantial agreement among economists. The logic of Blanchard's model itself matches the idea, which can be traced back in different schools of thought in economic history (among them, in Marx's own works). The various theoretical approaches allow for different degrees of effectiveness of workers' demand for higher market real wage, but the idea that wage claims become more insistent close to full employment is widespread and widely acknowledged.

At the beginning of Chapter 2, though, we mentioned the fact that the political and institutional framework can shape the slope of the curve for the demanded real wage. In a framework of low legal protection, precarious contracts and low unionization, workers' bargaining power is reduced and thus a fall in unemployment does not necessarily result in workers claiming higher real wages. In this scenario, we might assume the curve for the real wage demanded to be horizontal, in fact overlapping with the curve of the wage offered by firms. Such a situation will be visualized as a unique horizontal line in the labour market, representing both the real demanded wage and the real wage offered by firms. This line describes the performance of the equilibrium real wage as dependent only on the political–institutional framework, hence ultimately on the balance of power between social classes, with no role left to the current rate of unemployment. Formally, the equilibrium real wage is given by the equation $F(z) = A/(1 + \mu)$, where the rate of unemployment plays no role. This level of the equilibrium real wage will thus match accordant levels of monetary wage and prices, and a certain height of the aggregate supply AS. It is worth noting also that the AS line becomes horizontal, as the rate of unemployment does not affect the wage bargaining process. As a consequence, an increase in the aggregate demand, for instance, does not entail a surge in workers' claims or in the price level, or variations in real wage, even though it brings a rightward shift of the AD and a fall in the unemployment rate u (see Figure 3.5).

We have described an extreme, if not unlikely, scenario. However, several contributions to research do consider this situation as realistic. Within the mainstream, for instance, Alan Greenspan, the former Federal Reserve Chairman, claims that, even when the economy is close to full employment, wages' growth may be restrained by "higher workers' insecurity" and by a greater fear of being fired.[2]

Among those belonging to critical schools of thought, some regard the scenario just described as the general case. These scholars advocate the existence of two separate systems of variables: the system of prices and income distribution on the one side; and the system of the quantities produced and of employment on the other side. There is no scope here for a thorough account. To simplify, we can say that the variables determining the position of the horizontal AS, and of the horizontal real wage

[2] A. Greenspan (1997), "The Federal Reserve's semiannual monetary policy report", testimony of Chairman before the Committee on Banking, Housing, and Urban Affairs, US Senate, 26 February.

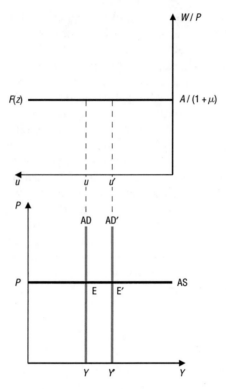

*Figure 3.5   Case of a horizontal AS: A shift in the AD – implying a fall
           in the unemployment rate – does not affect prices or real wage*

line as well, are those defining monetary wages and prices, and therefore
the income share between real wage and profit. On the other hand, the
determinants of aggregate demand, production, employment and unemployment set the position of the vertical AD. Yet the determinants of the
AD and the determinants of the AS are "uncoupled", separated from each
other: the elements affecting aggregate demand and employment do not
affect monetary wage, prices or real wage and vice versa. Is any interaction
between the two groups of variables to be completely excluded? Definitely
not. For instance, the advocates of this theoretical stance do not deny
that a fall in unemployment can in some cases boost workers' claims, thus
affecting the dynamics of monetary wages, prices and real wages. They
oppose, nonetheless, the standard idea that the correlation between the two
groups of variables is to be considered stable and then expressed through
rigid mathematical functions, as is the case with the usual demanded real
wage curve that we used in the previous sections. How general this view

should be considered is a debated issue, but it is clear that it can suggest an explanation for the real world upward movement of the aggregate demand (and thus of employment) with no upward pressure on wages and prices. Similarly, these latter variables may suddenly move with no effect on the aggregate demand or on employment.

3.9 THE CASE OF THE UPWARD SLOPING AD: DEBT DEFLATION

The assumption we have held so far is that the AD is vertical. However, this is just a simplification for didactic purposes. According to critical theory, the inclination of the AD curve is undetermined *a priori*. It can be either downward sloping – as assumed by Blanchard – or vertical, or upward sloping. It can even change its inclination in many points along its path. We have already shown the reasons why the AD may take a downward sloping or vertical shape. Under what circumstances can it become upward sloping? To answer this question, it is necessary to investigate the effects that variations in prices have on the relationships between firms and banks and more generally between debtors and creditors. In this regard, we will consider a situation of crisis where aggregate demand falls, unemployment rises and eventually deflation takes place: a downward tendency in prices and wages. This situation was presented in previous sections. However, we now must consider a further aspect we have neglected so far: price deflation reduces the value of goods produced and sold by firms, hence, it may negatively affect revenues as well. On the contrary, deflation usually does not affect the value of the loans that firms have accessed previously and have to repay (plus interest) to creditors. Deflation can therefore make it more difficult to repay loans borrowed by firms to buy investment goods and finance the production cycle, as it reduces revenues leaving the amount to repay unchanged. In other words, when prices decrease, the monetary value of revenues reduces as well, and therefore firms and debtors in general may become insolvent. In this case, firms and other potentially insolvent debtors will be forced to reduce their expenses, thus making the aggregate demand fall further. Debtors' loss might be balanced by creditors' gain: creditors will in fact have their income enhanced in real terms, given the fall in prices, whereas the value of the repayments remains unchanged. Thus, it could be argued that greater spending by creditors offsets the downsizing of potentially insolvent debtors' expenditure. This is a claim that is hard to uphold: first, due to the fact that creditors have a typically lower spending propensity than debtors; second, as debtors go bankrupt, creditors will get back a lot less than expected. In both cases, even if creditors spend more than before, this will not be sufficient to offset the lower spending by debtors: falling prices will entail a lower aggregate demand. We have thus traced some aspects of the so-called "debt deflation", providing an explanation for the possibility of a positive slope of the AD.

In the presence of a positive slope of the AD, however, not only will a fall in prices be ineffective in tackling an economic crisis, it can even make things worse. Let us go through Figure 3.6.

Starting from 1, let us suppose that a fall in confidence generates a drop in investment by firms, bringing the aggregate demand to the left, from AD to AD′. Hence, production and employment fall, unemployment rises, workers' bargaining power shrinks and monetary wages start to decrease. Assuming that in the beginning firms do not change their profit margin, prices will decrease as well. Expected prices will thus fall, so that prices and wages go through a further reduction (the aggregate supply moves from AS to AS′). Price deflation implies nonetheless a worsening of the conditions of indebted firms – of any creditor, more generally – hence their spending will shrink. The aggregate demand further reduces, rather than having a recovery, and the economy goes to point 2, then to point 3, with further falls in production and employment. The so called "debt deflation" generates a vicious spiral able to aggravate the crisis. Moreover, as time goes by, debtors in troubled waters turn into properly insolvent agents, with side effects for the creditors themselves and for the banking system as a whole. Keynes, among others, believed this dynamic to have worsened the Great Depression back in the 1930s. Similarly, today many economists claim

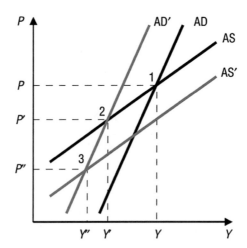

Figure 3.6   Economic crisis with a downward sloping AD

that lacking adequate economic policies, a debt deflation can be a possible outcome. Anyway, it is obvious that allowing for an upward sloping AD drives us even further away from Blanchard's conclusions: here, not only is a fall in wage and prices ineffective in overcoming the crisis but it can even be harmful.

3.10   THE ALTERNATIVE MODEL: OTHER EXAMPLES

The alternative model gets to different results, if compared to Blanchard's analysis, when dealing with other issues as well: an increase in the price of oil or other commodities, anti-trust policy, the effects of unemployment subsidies or legal minimum wage, variations in productivity or in the composition of the labour force, and many others.

For instance, we have already shown that in the mainstream model an increase in the price of oil reflects entirely in a fall in the real wage; if workers oppose such a fall, inflation will come along and the equilibrium unemployment rate will rise. These results are direct consequences of the assumption, typical of the mainstream model, that the share of the mark-up that goes to the owners of capital is an exogenous variable, thus it cannot be eroded by an increase in the cost of commodities. By contrast, in the alternative model, the share of the mark-up captured by capitalists may fluctuate. It is a different perspective, by which the increase in the oil price can ignite a conflict between workers and capitalists, resulting in a wage–price spiral. The latter dynamic may have different results depending on the power relations between social classes. Furthermore, in the context of the alternative model, we can even assume a vertical AD curve: in this case, the spiral will not affect unemployment.

With respect to anti-trust policy, in the mainstream model harsh measures against monopolies – based on market liberalization – determine more competition, hence a contraction of the mark-up and prices, which in turn implies an increase in real wage and a decrease in equilibrium unemployment. The contrary occurs when policy favours market concentration. As a result of different hypotheses on the shape of the AD, the alternative model does not share the same conclusions on the occupational effects of anti-trust policy. Further than that, the very idea that anti-trust policy based on market liberalization is in itself conducive to more competition and hence to decreasing prices and an increasing real wage can be challenged by one of Marx's thesis: market competition generates winners and losers, in the long run "capitals' centralization" in fewer hands, and possibly further dynamics of market monopolization.

If we look at unemployment benefits, when they are set up or increased, the z parameter of workers' conflictuality goes up, with effects that are analogous to those analyzed in the paragraphs devoted to social conflicts and wage moderation in the two models.

If we look at a minimum wage set by the law in monetary terms, this is an obvious measure to tackle wage and price deflation. In the AS–AD model, it may impede the economic system from going back spontaneously to the natural equilibrium after a crisis. In the IS–LM–PC and in the alternative models instead, policies taken to contrast deflation may prevent further negative effects of a crisis.

The possibility that the labour force becomes larger, for instance due to an immigration boost, is dealt with in details in section 5.11. We can nonetheless anticipate here that, even in this case, the two models reach extremely different conclusions.

Labour productivity growth is instead examined closely in section 5.1: the reader will discover that the standard model suggests that it will benefit employment, whereas in the alternative framework higher productivity can generate "technological unemployment", if appropriate measures are not taken.

There are many fields in which to compare the two alternative models, much beyond the examples just mentioned. Students should be able to examine different possibilities, training in the comparison between the models and their different economic policy implications. The exercise can draw on the graphic elaborations of the models contained in the present and previous chapters, and on the algebraic study of the models (section 5.1).

3.11   MAINSTREAM REPLICAS – AND CRITICAL ECONOMISTS' REJOINDER

Two objections might be raised by representatives of the mainstream with respect to the following features of the critical model presented so far:

1.   the vertical AD curve;
2.   the parameters μ and z are no longer exogenous.

The first is supported by the idea that it is possible to trace a downward sloping AD, even in a situation of liquidity trap and insensitiveness of the investment to the interest rate. That would confirm that variations in wages – and hence prices – are able to induce movements in the demand for goods. This objection is based on the "Pigou effect", proposed by the mainstream in an attempt to react to Keynesian critiques in the second half of the twentieth century. Under the name of the Pigou effect goes the idea that a fall in *P*, which implies an increase in *M/P*, may affect the demand for goods through different channels, first, as it is well known, through the reduction of the interest rate and the increase in investment. This was criticized by Keynes and other exponents of critical approaches. There would be a second channel, though, based on the following argument: when the real value of money held by agents (*M/P*) increases, economic agents will not demand assets only – their direct demand of goods will also increase (more consumption). In this case, a fall in *P* and the increase of *M/P* will affect consumption directly – hence demand – and restore the downward sloping character of the AD curve. Critiques would thus be rejected.

Second, mainstream economists deny that the mark-up and workers' bargaining power depend on the balance of power between classes, as advocated by critical economists. According to the mainstream theory, there is instead a very precise reason why the mark-up will be considered insensitive to social pressure: the mark-up stems in an automatic and thoroughly impersonal way from profit maximization decisions implemented by firms in a context of monopolistic competition (also known as imperfect competition). Any attempt to change such an "objective" mark-up by conflictual means would violate the maximization of profits. The rationale rests on the principle that firms need to comply with the condition of maximum profit if they want to stay in the market. Thus, the very fact that μ would not be influenced by workers' demands is a matter of survival for the firms. Based on this idea, the mainstream analysis shows that the mark-up is determined within a model of profit maximization of a firm in monopolistic competition. We define the following variables in order to describe such a model:

R' = firm's marginal revenues;
C' = firm's marginal cost;
Y = quantity produced;
P = price of the produced good;
W = monetary wage;
A = labour productivity.

In monopolistic competition, the profit maximization condition implies that marginal revenues equal marginal cost:

$$R' = C' \tag{3.1}$$

This means that the firm increases its production Y as long as $R' > C'$, whereas it stops producing when $R' = C'$. In a situation of monopolistic competition a firm's marginal cost is given by: $C' = W/A$. When competition is not perfect, production plants may arguably be underutilized; thus, with production Y increasing, labour productivity A holds constant (in perfect competition we would have $C' = W/MLP$, with MLP equal to marginal labour productivity, to be considered decreasing when production increases). With regards to marginal revenues, they are given by:

$$R' = P + Y\left(\frac{\Delta P}{\Delta Y}\right) \tag{3.2}$$

It means that the revenues for any additional unit of good produced and sold are equal to the price of the additional unit, plus the reduction in price of all other units that is required to sell the additional unit (do not forget that $\Delta P/\Delta Y < 0$). Finally, ε represents the elasticity of demand with respect to price, that is, the sensitivity of consumers' demand to variations in P. The elasticity tells us whether consumers are reactive or not to variations in prices, and it is provided by the percentage variation of demand following a given percentage variation in prices:

$$\varepsilon = \frac{\Delta Y / Y}{\Delta P / P} = \frac{\Delta Y}{\Delta P} \cdot \frac{P}{Y} \tag{3.3}$$

Let us set the maximum profit condition, and do some calculations:

$$R' = C' \Rightarrow P + Y\left(\frac{\Delta P}{\Delta Y}\right) = \frac{W}{A} \Rightarrow P\left(1 + \frac{Y\Delta P}{P\Delta Y}\right)$$
$$= \frac{W}{A} \Rightarrow P\left(1 + \frac{1}{\varepsilon}\right) = \frac{W}{A} \Rightarrow P = \left(\frac{1}{1 + 1/\varepsilon}\right)\cdot\frac{W}{A} \tag{3.4}$$

Now, this final equation can be compared to our equation for the determination of prices: $P = (1 + \mu)W/A$. The comparison makes it evident that the term $1/(1 + 1/\varepsilon)$ corresponds to the term $(1 + \mu)$. Then:

$$\mu = \frac{1}{1 + (1/\varepsilon)} - 1 \tag{3.5}$$

It is clear then that μ depends exclusively on the elasticity of demand, that is, it is determined only by the individual preferences of consumers, whereas workers' claims and social pressures do not play any role. If the condition is imposed that to survive firms need to pursue maximum profit, the conclusion will be that the mark-up cannot be influenced by social conflict. The idea that μ and z can be subject to continuous changes is therefore rejected.

Critical economists in turn replied as follows. First of all, they claim, the Pigou effect may be neutralized by the reduction in the quantity of money M that can follow from a fall in prices P. The supply of money is in fact dependent on firms' demand for banks' credit. A reduction in prices will certainly be followed by a lower demand for credit by firms as their productive activities are shrinking, thus reducing the quantity of money present in the system. Therefore, the supply of real money M/P does not increase, and the Pigou effect does not take place. Graphically, the AD can still take a vertical shape. Even more than that, we mentioned earlier that a fall in prices reduces the revenue that firms may get selling goods; they can find it difficult to pay back the loans previously subscribed to buy invest-ment goods and to finance production. In this situation, price deflation can make firms insolvent – and this applies to all debtors in general. Such a situation will thus bring insolvent agents to a decrease in their expenditure, implying a further decline in aggregate demand. This is a scenario of so called "debt deflation", which we have already mentioned: falling prices can even bring about a fall in the aggregate demand. As a consequence, the AD curve may even have a positive slope, which is the opposite of what is conjectured within the mainstream model and by the Pigou effect.

Finally, the idea of a mark-up determined by the impersonal and ineluctable criteria of the maximization of profits, hence insensitive to social pressure, is vulnerable to the following critique. The condition of profit maximization in monopolistic competition requires a downward sloping demand function to be applied. It is the only case that allows for the derivation of a function of marginal revenues (with a negative slope as well) able to determine both the mark-up and the quantity to produce in its intersection with the marginal cost curve. If, on the contrary, the demand curve is vertical instead of being downward sloping, this procedure of mark-up determination becomes inapplicable. As a demonstration, it is sufficient to notice that a vertical AD implies a null elasticity of demand with respect to price ($\varepsilon 50$). Then, if the elasticity is zero, we will get to a meaningless result. Once allowing for the possibility of a positive sloping AD, the marginal revenues curve will have a positive slope as well, so that in some given situations it may well stay systematically above the marginal cost function. In this case, it would be impossible to apply the usual rule of profit maximization in monopolistic competition. To sum up, the only valid criterion to determine the profit margin would be that advocated by critical economists, a criterion related to political–institutional factors that reflect the condition of the balance of power between social classes.

It goes without saying that this is not the only cleavage dividing the rep-resentatives of the mainstream and their opponents. These are just hints of an ongoing debate, which is subject to a continuous evolution, intensified after the beginning of the global crisis in 2007–2008. The examples raised, though, prove that even within a didactic exposition it is possible to show the brilliant dialectic characterizing the confrontation between the approach that is dominant in macroeconomic theory and the critical one.

3.12 ACTUAL LIMITS OF THE ALTERNATIVE MODEL AND PERSPECTIVES FOR FURTHER RESEARCH

As we have seen, the alternative model discussed reaches opposite conclusions with respect to those reached by Blanchard, most notably regarding the effectiveness of expansionary policy and of wage conflict. Sticking to Blanchard, expansionary policies cannot modify the natural equilibrium levels of production and unemployment, whereas within the alternative model they are fundamental. Again, according to Blanchard, not only are workers' claims incapable of changing the equilibrium real wage, they are even detrimental to employment levels. The alternative model instead considers the very claims put forward by the workers – or, more generally, the condition of the balance of power between firms and workers – as the determinant of the equilibrium real wage.

It may be argued that the alternative model reaches conclusions that are way too optimistic with respect to the effectiveness of social pressures and of policies implemented in favour of employment and wage growth. This model seems indeed to suggest that appropriate expansionary fiscal policies could indefinitely increase both employment and production, allowing for an indefinite contraction of unemployment. In other words, the vertical AD curve seems limitless in its movements to the right. Moreover, the model may seem to suggest that workers' wage claims could increase the equilibrium real wage without restrictions, hence reducing indefinitely firms' profit margin. However, such an interpretation would be incorrect. Present within the capitalist mode of production are many constraints to the possibility for public spending and for unions' claims to determine a significant increase in employment and wages. Some examples from the history of the twentieth century are to be considered.

First of all, let us consider the limits to the efficacy of wage claims. Let us suppose the balance of power to be highly biased towards workers: they would succeed in obtaining a fairly high real wage. It is reasonable to imagine that in such circumstances employers would react. For instance, they could threaten a halt to productive investment or to offshore investments to countries where social conflict is under control. They could exert pressure on policymakers, to the point of inducing them to curtail the demand of goods to cool down social pressure. Shrinking demand would be followed by a fall in production and by an increase of unemployment sufficient to weaken unions and force them to scale down their claims. Public spending will face constraints as well: a pure capitalist system leaves the ultimate control over the scale and composition of the social product to private companies. In this context, an expansion of demand boosted by public spending does not necessarily imply an increase in production and employment. Firms may well decide not to increase production, hence, public spending may have the (almost) exclusive result of higher prices.

Within the capitalist production mode, social and political pressure aimed at the increase of wage and employment is limited by the fact that both public decisions concerning demand and economic decisions concerning production are mainly shaped by the hegemon capitalist class and its interests. These remarks lead to the conclusion that pro-labour economic policies could succeed only if targeted directly at the structure of the production mode, by changing those elements that, within the critical approach, are sometimes defined as the "conditions of reproduction" of capital. It is the only way to obtain persistent and significant changes, beneficial to workers, in the balance of power. Some examples of this kind of actions are: a tighter control of the international mobility of capital, in order to prevent a race to the bottom between countries in fiscal policies, wages and safety at work; questioning the efficiency of the financial market and its centrality in the allocation of expenditures; a more developed legislation to protect subordinate employment; public expenditures targeting directly the management of production, and not merely aimed at influencing demand; and a relatively high degree of public planning of investment.

The remarks that have just been raised prevent a naïve and overly optimistic reading of the alternative model. The latter can be considered useful in its didactic purpose and as a first approximation, to be integrated and developed in the light of the recent critical investigation and research.

4. Blanchard's "new approach": the IS–LM–PC model

4.1 FROM THE AS–AD MODEL TO THE IS–LM–PC MODEL

From the seventh edition of his macroeconomics textbook, Olivier Blanchard abandons the traditional aggregate demand and aggregate supply AS–AD mainstream model. In his textbook, he writes that it was "cumbersome and gave too optimistic a view of the return of output to potential". For this reason, Blanchard replaces the AS–AD with an analysis that is defined as IS–LM–PC, which is embedded in last century's macroeconomics, though we call it a "new approach" for the sake of simplicity. In the words of Blanchard, the new IS–LM–PC model "gives a simpler and more accurate description of the role of monetary policy and of output and inflation dynamics".

In this chapter, we will present the pivotal features of Blanchard's new approach, followed by a set of critiques. Most notably, we will discuss how the new IS–LM–PC model is grounded on many of the fundamental theses of the previous AS–AD model, such as the existence of a "natural" equilibrium that is independent from effective demand and from the distributive conflict between social classes, and the thesis that, in almost any case, it is possible to resort uniquely to the central bank's monetary policy to guarantee the convergence of the economic system towards the equilibrium.

4.2 HORIZONTAL LM, REAL INTEREST RATE AND RISK PREMIUM

The first outstanding novelty of Blanchard's new approach to macroeconomics teaching consists in a different formulation of the IS–LM scheme. Two innovations mark the difference: the horizontal LM and the dependency of investment from the real interest rate and the risk premium.

We start from the description of the horizontal LM. We know that the LM relationship describes all the combinations of interest rate and production that put the financial markets into equilibrium. In its traditional formulation, the LM was described by the equation $M/P = YL(i)$. From a graphical point of view, the function was traced sloping upwards from the left to the right, so as to describe a positive relationship between Y and i. In other words, *ceteris paribus*, an increase in production Y was considered to imply a corresponding rise first of income and transactions and then of the quantity of real money M/P desired by economic agents to perform a higher number of transactions. Consequently, an increase in the supply of assets followed by a fall in the price of assets and of the interest rate i will occur. The described dynamic was in fact dependent on the hypothesis that variations in income and demand for money were not matched by variations in the supply of money by the central bank. The argument runs that the central bank decides exogenously the quantity of money M, and it is then for the market to determine the interest rate i able to put agents' demand for money in equilibrium with the supply of money decided autonomously by the central bank.

In Blanchard's new IS–LM model, the traditional hypothesis that the central bank sets the quantity of money exogenously and lets the market determine the equilibrium interest rate is abandoned. This hypothesis, according to Blanchard, is too abstract if confronted with the actual praxis of monetary policy. In fact, central banks act in the financial market by setting the interest rate i as an exogenous given, and then adjust the quantity of money supplied M as a function of the chosen interest rate. In this manner, as the interest rate plays the role of the exogenous variable, whereas the quantity of money is treated as endogenous, central banks keep the financial market at the equilibrium matching the chosen level of the interest rate, even in the case that agents' demand for money does change. It is an interpretation that picks many insights coming from critical approaches to economic theory, and is now shared by Blanchard and various other exponents of the mainstream,[1] among them, John B. Taylor, author of the well-known "Taylor rule", which we will discuss in the next chapter.

Blanchard's new view on monetary policy and banks is therefore described, on the analytical ground, by a LM equation determined by fixing the exogenous rate of interest only, and can be laid down graphically as a horizontal straight line, traced in correspondence to the level of the interest rate chosen.

---

[1] It is definitely worth mentioning the recent opening of the Bank of England to the endogenous theory of money: see M. McLeay, R. Amar and T. Ryland (2014), "Money creation in the modern economy", *Bank of England Quarterly Bulletin 1(2014)* (or the simpler version, "Money in the modern economy: an introduction", *Bank of England Quarterly Bulletin 1(2014)*).

The second innovation included in Blanchard's new IS–LM model concerns the belief that the crucial element in the decision of the purchase of investment goods by firms is not the traditional nominal interest rate i (also known as monetary interest rate). Rather, the decision is dependent on a slightly different variable, which is defined as real interest rate and is usually represented with r. In short, we could say that the nominal interest rate refers to transactions of monetary quantities through time, while the real interest rate expresses the exchange of actual goods through time. This can be clarified through an example directly taken from Blanchard's textbook. Let us suppose that the current price of a kilogram of bread is given by P_t. We assume that we are willing to borrow money at the nominal interest rate i_t to buy the bread. On the following period – when the loan will be due – we will thus have to pay back an amount that is given by $(1 + i_t)P_t$. If we define the expected price of bread in the following period as P_{t+1}^e, the amount of money to pay back will correspond to a quantity of kilograms of bread equal to $(1 + i_t)P_t/P_{t+1}^e$. In other words, to avail ourselves of one kilogram of bread today we will have to forgo a certain quantity of bread tomorrow. The real interest rate expresses exactly this relationship between real goods exchanged through time, hence is given by:

$$1+r_t = \frac{(1+i_t)P_t}{P_{t+1}^e} \tag{4.1}$$

As the expected inflation rate is given by $\pi_{t+1}^e 5(P_{t+1}^e - P_t)/P_t$, then $(1 + \pi_{t+1}^e)$ $= P_{t+1}^e/P_t$. We can thus write the equation for the real interest rate as follows:

$$1+r_t = \frac{1+i_t}{1+\pi_{t+1}^e} \tag{4.2}$$

which can be approximated, when the levels of the rates of interest and inflation are small enough, by the following equation (derived in the mathematical appendix of Blanchard's textbook):

$$r_t \cong i_t - \pi_{t+1}^e \tag{4.3}$$

To sum up, we can state that the real interest rate corresponds to the nominal interest rate net of expected inflation.

In describing the new approach, Blanchard remarks that the real interest rate represents the rate that is actually taken into account by firms and creditors when they have to take decisions on the amount of loans needed to finance the demand of investment goods. The reason why the access to a loan is determined by the real interest rate is simple: variations in the inflation rate affect the real value of the instalments due by debtor firms to their creditors. An increase in inflation will reduce the real value of the payments due, so that debtor firms will be favoured, whereas a reduction will increase the real value and make creditors better off. While the nominal interest rate does not take this aspect into consideration, the real interest rate does as it is obtained precisely taking into account the expected inflation. According to Blanchard, an inflation rate growth causes a reduction of the real interest rate, thus making firms increase their demand for loans to finance a larger demand for investment goods. On the other hand, a fall in inflation increases the real interest rate causing a contraction of firms' investment. The new approach tells us that the demand for investment goods is dependent not only on the performance of aggregate demand and production, as it is usually assumed, but also on the real interest rate, which substitutes the nominal rate.

Furthermore, in the description of the new approach Blanchard underlines that creditors decide to grant loans also according to the risk attached to the loans, which depends first of all on the probability that the debtor might go bankrupt. A risk premium will thus be added to the real interest rate: creditors will require it to be higher, but the higher the chance is that debtors will go bankrupt and will not repay what is due. If we invest a euro on a riskless asset, when it expires we will get a monetary return determined by the nominal interest rate: $(1 + i)$. If we invest a euro on a risky asset instead, and we define with p the probability that the debtor will go bankrupt, assuming that insolvency entails a zero payment to the creditor, we can forecast that we will get $(1 - p)(1 + i + x) + p(0)$ when the asset expires (x is the risk premium we require as an incentive to purchase the asset). How big should the risk premium x be? x will be equal to the value that guarantees the arbitrage condition between risky assets and riskless assets, that is $(1 + i) = (1 - p)(1 + i + x) + p(0)$. Rearranging the equation, we get the equilibrium value of the risk premium: $x = (1 + i)p/(1 - p)$. Blanchard specifies that not only firms that issue assets to finance their investment are subject to the risk of bankruptcy, but also banks and other financial intermediaries collecting investors' savings on one side and granting credits to firms and other agents on the other. Any time the bankruptcy risk of firms, banks and other financial intermediaries rises, the risk premium increases accordingly. However, the growth of the risk premium positively affects the rate of interest required by creditors on the assets and on the loans they grant. This growth in the cost of credit, Blanchard argues, will eventually depress firms' demand for investment goods.

We can conclude that within the new approach firms' demand for investment goods is dependent on the production level Y, on the real interest rate r and on the risk premium x as well. That is:

$$I = I(Y, r + x) \qquad (4.4)$$

Thus, in order to manage the performance of investment, aggregate demand and production, the central bank must guarantee that the nominal interest rate net of expected inflation matches the desired level of the real interest rate. That will also be the level of the horizontal LM:

$$\text{LM)} \qquad \bar{r} = i - \pi^e \qquad (4.5)$$

4.3   THE "EXTENDED" IS–LM MODEL

The new IS–LM model by Blanchard (who defines it as the "extended IS–LM model") is based on the two novelties described in the previous section. According to this model, the central bank considers the expected inflation and manages the nominal interest rate to set a certain level of real interest rate, which is thus defined as "policy rate" r. Furthermore, in this model firms are supposed to take their decisions on the level of investment according to the value of the real interest rate and of the risk premium: the two values add up to the "rate on loans" $r + x$. The extended model IS–LM is then represented by the following equations and by the chart in Figure 4.1.

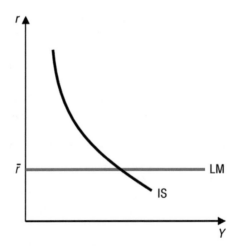

Figure 4.1   "Extended" IS–LM model

$$IS) \quad Y = C(Y - T) + I(Y, r + x) + G$$

$$LM) \quad \bar{r} = i - \pi^e \qquad\qquad (4.6)$$

The IS–LM equilibrium that stems from the equations points to the combination of real interest rate and production (r, Y) that guarantees the macroeconomic equilibrium in the goods market and in financial markets.

Obviously, such equilibrium can change according to the variables exogenous to the model: many examples can be put forward on the matter. Among them, Blanchard focuses on the possibility of what he calls a "financial shock" occurring. This type of shock can be caused by various factors, such as a bank going bankrupt and the consequent worries for the solvency of other banks, which may entail a savers' bank run to withdraw their money.[2] If this happens, savers will require a higher risk premium x to keep on depositing their money, i.e. issuing loans to banks (and eventually to firms). Therefore, the rate on loans $(r + x)$ will grow and firms' demand for investment goods will fall: thus, there is a downward shift of the IS curve, which determines a fall in the equilibrium production Y and employment. Sticking to Blanchard, in normal situations a shock of this type could be solved by an intervention of the central bank, aimed at reducing the real interest rate r and drifting the LM downwards, to get back to the previous level of equilibrium production. However, Blanchard remarks that the shift

---

[2] Why should doubts on the solvency of banks arise and spread? Blanchard singles out one reason, namely a too high financial leverage. To shed light on the concept, let us consider a bank characterized by the following balance sheet: on one side, liabilities composed by 20 units of capital invested by its shareholders and 80 units of loans (money market deposit accounts, time deposits, loans and securities issued by other investors or banks); on the other side, assets worth 100 units and made of cash reserves, loans to households and firms, loans to other banks, residential mortgages, treasury bonds and other financial activities. The financial leverage is given by the ratio between activities and capital: in this case, $100/20 = 5$. If we suppose the bank's assets to yield 5 per cent on average, while it has to pay 4 per cent interest on its liabilities, the total profit expected by shareholders will be: $100 \times 0.5 - 80 \times 0.4 = 1.8$. In percentage terms, it corresponds to a profit rate of $1.8/20 = 0.09$, that is, a 9 per cent margin. In the absence of strict regulations, banks may be induced to enhance their financial leverage to increase shareholders' profit margin, at the same time increasing their exposure to insolvency risks. This can be seen if we imagine that shareholders decide to reduce the invested capital to the value of 10, and to borrow 90. The financial leverage increases to $100/10 = 10$, total profit becomes $100 \times 0.05 - 90 \times 0.04 = 1.4$, and thus the profit margin on the invested capital grows to $1.4/1 = 50.14$, that is a 14 per cent margin. The bank is now much more lucrative but its exposure to insolvency risks also rises. The endowment of capital, that is, the difference between assets and liabilities, is now reduced from 20 to 10, this meaning that the bank is now subject to a higher risk of having its surplus eroded – whatever the reason, for example, due to the presence of nonperforming loans. If capital shrinks too much, doubts on the solvency of the bank can spring up, possibly leading to uncertainty on the financial status of creditor banks. Such a scenario may eventually induce a depositors' bank run.

of the IS and the connected fall in production can be very pronounced. It is a situation where the central bank, in order to restore the previous equilibrium, should set the LM curve below the horizontal axis, that is, a negative real interest rate. As the real interest rate is given by the nominal rate minus expected inflation, a real negative rate could be obtained more easily, the higher inflation is. On the other hand, if inflation is low or even null or negative, getting a negative real interest rate could be impossible. The reason for this is that the central bank cannot set the nominal interest rate markedly below zero: there exists in fact, Blanchard argues, a "zero lower bound", which makes for a floor to the nominal interest rate in correspondence to $i = 0$. This may render the central bank powerless in facing the eventuality of a financial shock, or any other crisis that entails a significant downward shift of the IS. In a similar situation, it would be appropriate to call upon an expansionary fiscal policy by the government, which could, for example, increase public spending to bring the IS back to its initial level. Blanchard does not expand that much on this possible solution, as we will see.

4.4   THE LABOUR MARKET AND THE PHILLIPS CURVE ARE ADDED TO THE MODEL

Blanchard's next step concerns the addition of the labour market analysis and the connected Phillips curve to the extended IS–LM model. In this regard, we recall from Chapter 2 the two fundamental relationships of Blanchard's analysis of the labour market: the equation for wage setting $W = P^e F(u,z)$ and the equation for price setting $P = (1 + \mu)W/A$. For the sake of simplicity we assume now that the function F is linear, for instance: $F(u,z) = 1 - \alpha u + z$, where α is a parameter determining the slope of the linear function and denotes the reactivity of workers' demand on wage to the trend of the unemployment rate. If we substitute this function in the wage equation and then we substitute the wage equation in the price equation and assume for the sake of simplicity that $A = 1$, we get:

$$P = P^e (1 + \mu)(1 - \alpha u + z) \tag{4.7}$$

This equation, expressed in prices, corresponds to the following equation expressed in terms of the rates of variation of prices (the algebraic proof is in Blanchard's textbook):

$$\pi = \pi^e + (\mu + z) - \alpha u \tag{4.8}$$

From which, through a simple step, we get to:

$$\pi - \pi^e = (\mu + z) - \alpha u \qquad (4.9)$$

This equation connects the performance of unemployment to the inflation rate and is called the "Phillips curve", after the economist William Phillips, who verified the existence of a statistic correlation between the two variables. It is a link that can be interpreted in the usual way, already present in the old AS–AD model: the lower unemployment is, the stronger workers will be in their claims on wage, the more the firms will pass wage rises onto prices and hence the higher actual inflation will be in relation to expected inflation.

It is now important to remember a pivotal assumption in Blanchard's analysis of the labour market: at the natural rate of unemployment u_n, workers demand exactly the wage that is offered by firms, implying the absence of a distributive conflict; as the price–wage dynamic is stable, expected prices and actual prices are equal, and expected inflation and actual inflation are coincident ($\pi^e = \pi$). Therefore, when the labour market is at its natural equilibrium level, we can write that $0 = (\mu + z) - \alpha u_n$, from which we get the value of the natural rate of unemployment: $u_n = (\mu + z)/\alpha$. Multiplying and dividing by α the first term on the right-hand side of the equation into the Phillips curve, we get:

$$\pi - \pi^e = \alpha \frac{\mu + z}{\alpha} - \alpha u \qquad (4.10)$$

Finally, as we know the value of the natural rate of unemployment, we can substitute u_n in the formula and, after a simple step, write the equation of the Phillips curve in the following way:

$$\pi - \pi^e = -\alpha(u - u_n) \qquad (4.11)$$

Therefore, actual inflation and expected inflation are coincident only if actual unemployment corresponds to the natural unemployment level.

At this point, recalling some concepts discussed in Chapter 2, we know that the unemployment rate is equal to $u = U/L = (L - N)/L = 1 - (N/L)$ and that the production function is given by $Y = AN$, from which we get that $N = Y/A$. We can thus rewrite the unemployment rate formula in the following way: $u = 1 - Y/AL$. If we substitute the actual production with the natural production, we will get to the natural rate of unemployment:

$u_n = 1 - Y_n/AL$. By substituting these two latter equations in the Phillips curve equation, we obtain:

$$\pi - \pi^e = -\alpha\left(1 - \frac{Y}{AL} - 1 + \frac{Y_n}{AL}\right) \qquad (4.12)$$

By making some further steps, the equation can be written as:

$$\text{PC)} \quad \pi - \pi^e = \frac{\alpha}{AL}(Y - Y_n) \qquad (4.13)$$

This particular formulation of the Phillips curve represents the PC relationship included in Blanchard's new approach. There, the difference $Y-Y_n$ is defined as the "output gap", and identifies the gap between actual production and natural production. The PC equation can be interpreted as follows. When the output gap is positive, i.e. actual production is greater than natural production, it means that actual unemployment is below natural unemployment. In such a situation, the wage demanded by workers is greater than the wage offered by firms; thus, a run-up between wage and price is set off and makes inflation increase with respect to expected inflation. On the contrary, when the output gap is negative, unemployment is higher than its natural equilibrium and therefore workers are weak in their bargaining power. Therefore, we observe a tendency of wage and price to fall, which makes actual inflation smaller than expected inflation. Finally, a null output gap describes a situation where actual production is equal to natural production: then, effective unemployment and natural unemployment are also coincident and thus the wage demanded by workers corresponds to the wage offered by firms. There is no inflationary or deflationary pressure, hence actual inflation is equal to expected inflation.

The reader will easily notice that the logical sequence just described is close to the one outlined in the study of the aggregate supply within the previous AS–AD model. More importantly, this logical sequence sheds light on the existing link between the PC relationship and the labour market. Although Blanchard does not do this, we deem it important to provide a graphical representation of such a connection. In Figure 4.2, the PC relationship and the labour market are drawn jointly. It is only when the labour market is at the natural unemployment equilibrium level that production is at its natural level and the PC relationship shows that there is no difference between actual inflation and expected inflation.

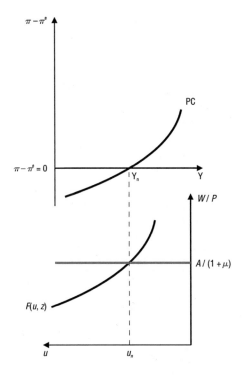

Figure 4.2   Nexus between the labour market and the PC relationship

4.5   THE COMPLETE IS–LM–PC MODEL

The IS–LM–PC model can now be presented in its entirety. The model is composed of three equations: the IS, describing the equilibrium in the goods market; the LM, which describes the equilibrium in the financial markets; and the PC, which shows the link between the output gap and the performance of inflation, which in turn – as we have just shown – relates to the labour market.

$$\text{IS)} \qquad Y = C(Y - T) + I(Y, r + x) + G$$

$$\text{LM)} \qquad \bar{r} = i - \pi^e \tag{4.14}$$

$$\text{PC)} \qquad \pi - \pi^e = \frac{\alpha}{AL}(Y - Y_n)$$

Sticking to Blanchard, we assume expectations on inflation to be static, that is, firms and households expect the rate of inflation at the end of the current period to be equal to the effective rate of inflation of the previous period. This is: $\pi^e = \pi_{t-1}$.

Our purpose is to provide here a brand new graphical representation of the IS–LM–PC model (Figure 4.3). There, together with the equilibrium

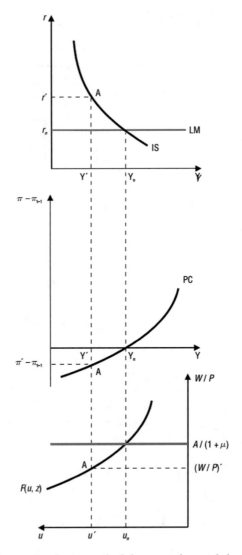

Figure 4.3 *Connection between the labour market and the IS–LM–PC model*

IS–LM and the PC relationship, we also include their link with the labour market, which Blanchard does not make explicit. The goal of this representation is to underline that even in Blanchard's new approach – as was the case in the previous AS–AD model – the labour market has a paramount role in the determination of the so-called "natural" equilibrium. Accordingly, from a logical point of view, the following charts are to be read from the bottom up: first, the natural equilibrium unemployment is determined in the labour market; second, the natural production is determined; and finally, the equilibrium IS–LM is analyzed and the connected PC relationship, in order to assess if and how the aggregate demand can match the natural equilibrium production, and inflation can thus stabilize.

By looking at Figure 4.3 it is noticeable that there is a unique level of the real interest rate able to generate an aggregate demand matching the natural equilibrium level of production. Resorting to an expression coined by the economist Knut Wicksell at the beginning of the previous century, Blanchard defines such a rate with the term "natural interest rate" (r_n). As we will see, according to Blanchard the central bank must pursue a monetary policy targeting such a rate, with the goal of the stabilization of the economic system at its natural equilibrium.

4.6 THE ECONOMIC CRISIS ACCORDING TO THE IS–LM–PC MODEL

How does the new IS–LM–PC model deal with the occurrence of an economic crisis? Let us comment further on Figure 4.3 in order to answer this fundamental question, starting from the supposition that the short-term equilibrium in the goods market is given by point A in the IS–LM graph. At point A, the effective real interest rate r' is higher than the natural interest rate, hence generating a level of demand and production Y' that is smaller than the natural production. If we bring point A to the labour market, we will notice that in correspondence to Y' we also face a level of unemployment u' that is higher than the natural rate. Due to the considerable number of unemployed people, workers are weakened in their bargaining power and induced to demand a real wage $(W/P)'$ that is lower than the equilibrium wage. A downward pressure on wage is thus set off, which, holding the mark-up fixed, should activate a downward tendency in prices as well. This phenomenon can be observed looking at point A in the chart of the PC relationship: the difference between current actual inflation π' and inflation in the previous period π_{t-1} is negative, this meaning that inflation slows down from period to period and, in the long run, may turn into proper deflation.

Can this situation be overturned relying on spontaneous free market forces? Contrary to what was suggested by the previous AS–AD model, within the new IS–LM–PC approach the answer is negative. According to the new model, if we rely on spontaneous market forces the crisis can even get worse.

As a matter of fact, in a situation where $\pi' - \pi < 0$ persists, the real interest rate $r = i - \pi^e$ will tend to grow further as time goes by, reaching even higher levels than r'. In other words, as time goes by the reduction in effective inflation also causes a reduction in expected inflation, thus pushing upwards the real interest rate. Consequently, aggregate demand and effective production fall even further and actual unemployment grows even more. We can see that in the three charts the economy will move along the IS, PC and $F(u, z)$ curves, moving further to the left with respect to point A, hence getting even more distant from natural equilibrium. This way, it could be said that in the IS–LM–PC model the natural equilibrium is unstable: once it is left, the economy will roll further and further away.

In the old AS–AD model, at least in theory, spontaneous market forces were considered able to restore natural equilibrium: an economic policy action was then deemed appropriate, though not necessary, to overcome a crisis. Instead, according to Blanchard's new approach, in order to get out of the crisis described by point A, resorting to economic policy is unavoidable. Any possible movement of the aggregate demand, hence a departure of production, unemployment and inflation from their respective equilibrium levels, will be faced by the central bank with an active and quick intervention to restore the natural interest rate r_n and bring the economy back to its natural equilibrium. Central bankers' monetary policy, within the IS–LM–PC model, is then considered a necessary – and generally sufficient – instrument to overcome a crisis.

Nonetheless there is a situation where the central bank's action may be insufficient to cope with a crisis. Let us consider the occurrence of a financial shock caused by one or more banks going bankrupt or by firms seeing their perspectives for future profits going down. In similar circumstances, the demand for investment goods falls, thus the IS shifts downwards. If the shift of the IS is large in magnitude, the only option available to the central bank to preserve a level of demand and production compatible with the natural equilibrium is to position the horizontal LM in correspondence to a negative real interest rate. This option is available to the central banker if inflation is positive and high enough; it may instead become hard to apply – or even impossible – when inflation shrinks or becomes even negative, that is, it turns into deflation. This is because the minimum monetary interest rate achievable by the central bank is the zero rate. It cannot go below that point, given the existence of what has been called a "zero lower bound", that is, a floor (at zero) to the monetary interest rate. In fact, even with a null monetary interest rate, when inflation is negative the real interest rate remains positive and hence cannot reach a level necessary to bring the economy back to its natural equilibrium. The student can draw the three charts of Figure 4.3 under the hypothesis of a downward shift of the IS so that a negative natural interest rate would be required to restore the equilibrium, but at the same time so that deflation is generated, hence preventing the natural interest rate from being reached.

The situation just described, in which the central bank's monetary policy turns out to be powerless in the face of an economic crisis, is defined by Blanchard with the term "deflationary trap". Blanchard argues that this scenario correctly describes what happened during the Great Depression that started in 1929: in that period, deflation pushed the real interest rate progressively up, contributing to the fall in demand and production. Even the recent crisis since 2008, he claims, has shown a tendency towards deflation, still much less substantial and without the typical characteristics of the "trap". How can the difference between the two crises be explained? A possible answer is that, contrary to what happened in the 1930s, since 2008 most governments have implemented expansionary fiscal policies. In the terms of the IS–LM–PC model, this means that economic policy authorities have not just curtailed the interest rate to bring back the LM to the lowest possible level, they have also increased public spending and cut taxes to push the IS up again. Blanchard's favoured interpretation is different, nonetheless. According to him, the principal innovation characterizing the 2008 crisis as opposed to the 1929 crisis concerns the fact that central banks succeeded in anchoring the expectations of inflation to a given "objective", that is, to the desired level described by the term formally, $\pi^e = \bar{\pi}$. This "anchorage" of expectations to a given "objective" modifies the PC relationship and the connected diagram of Figure 4.3: on the vertical axis of the PC relation we would find the difference $\pi - \bar{\pi}$ instead of the difference $\pi - \pi_{t-1}$. The implication is straightforward: even though following a crisis the effective production becomes lower than the natural production level and thus actual inflation becomes lower than the inflation goal, a deflationary spiral, which would bring the system further away from natural equilibrium, is not activated. In other words, the equilibrium is not unstable. Blanchard argues that in this case recession becomes tameable, even to the point of being solved in the business-as-usual way; that is, simply through the central bank maneuvering the interest rate.

4.7 FROM THE AS–AD MODEL TO THE IS–LM–PC MODEL: CONTINUITY OR BREAK-UP?

We are now able to sketch out some general considerations on the actual importance of the innovations introduced with Blanchard's "new approach" to macroeconomics teaching. The cardinal novelty of the new IS–LM–PC scheme concerns a different conception of the effects of the wage–price dynamic: while the AS–AD model suggested that the movements of those variables contribute to the convergence of production and employment towards the respective levels of "natural" equilibrium, the new analysis focuses on the risk of inflation or wage and price deflation having destabilizing effects, moving the economic system away from its "natural" equilibrium. This mutation of perspective is due to two innovations of the IS–LM–PC model. First, in the new model the LM is horizontal, so there is no explicit reference to the inverse relationship between the price level and the real quantity of money, a feature that was indeed present in the old AS–AD model. Accordingly, in the new approach the eventuality that a reduction of prices could enhance the quantity of real money and thus reduce the interest rate, and stimulate the aggregate demand, is not mentioned. Second, in the new model investment is dependent on the real interest rate. Sticking to this hypothesis, deflation brings the real interest rate up, thus reducing investment and aggregate demand. This latter feature paves the way for the "deflationary trap", as it is called by Blanchard, which is a situation of crisis where the central bank reaches the zero lower bound of the monetary interest rate and is no longer able to balance the rise of the real interest rate, caused by prolonged inflation.

The lack of an analysis of the potentially destabilizing effects of deflation was one of the major shortcomings of Blanchard's textbook. Starting from the seventh edition of his volume, the author partially fills this gap, and this should be welcomed. However, it is worth stressing that the scope of the innovations of the new approach is more limited than it may initially appear. Also, in the IS–LM–PC model the author reiterates the improbable thesis of a mark-up that is utterly insensitive to workers' claims, and the idea of an inverse relationship between interest rate and investment. In so doing, Blanchard chooses to maintain the central logical pillar of the old AS–AD model, that is the existence of a "natural" equilibrium that is independent from effective demand and from the distributive conflict between social classes, and thus the possibility to rely entirely on the central bank's action on the interest rate to guarantee the convergence of the economic system towards that equilibrium. The very case of the "deflationary trap" is considered extreme by Blanchard, historically circumscribed, and in the end solvable if the central bank manages to anchor the expectations of inflation to a given "objective". At a closer look, this thesis requires the anchorage of the inflation rate to be considered the cause and not the effect of the efficacy of the central bank's monetary policy. This logical overturning does raise a set of theoretical issues, but Blanchard does not dig deeper into the matter; he prefers to get straight to economic policy conclusions. In his view, crisis can be solved through inflation anchorage and without resorting to expansionary fiscal policies. In effect, even in the last editions of his model, he insists that a contractionary fiscal policy aimed at "fiscal consolidation" can provide a beneficial stimulus in the long run. It is a thesis that seemingly contrasts with some empirical evidence on the persistence of contractionary effects of budget tightening, which he contributed to elaborating in his role as Chief Economist of the IMF, and which are quoted in his textbook as well (see also Appendix 2 to this volume).

To sum up, even though Blanchard upgraded the previous AS–AD model of aggregate demand and aggregate supply, the theoretical and political spirit of that model is still confirmed in many aspects. The student will be able to work on the new analytical scheme, the IS–LM–PC, to assess which results of the old model are confirmed and which are altered. For instance, starting from the natural equilibrium, one can verify that an expansionary monetary policy that reduces the interest rate and makes the LM shift downwards will provoke an increase in demand and production, but also a continuous growth of inflation. The latter can be stopped only with an opposite monetary policy able to restore the previous equilibrium. There is a major difference with respect to the thesis of the neutrality of money emerging from the AS–AD model: the natural equilibrium is not automatically restored. Nonetheless, it is confirmed that, under the hypothesis of static expectations, expansionary monetary policy could generate a level of production that is higher than the natural level, at the only cost of rising inflation. After all, the hypothesis of an anchorage of expectations to a given rate of inflation would not make much sense either, as an expansionary monetary policy would cause its systematic denial. A similar result is reached by the analysis of expansionary fiscal policy as well: if the IS moves upwards, not only does production grow from its natural equilibrium, but also inflation will constantly grow, until the previous fiscal situation is restored and the IS gets back to the initial level. The student is encouraged to further develop the comparison between the AS–AD and the IS–LM–PC with respect to other issues, among them changes in labour productivity, a rise in the oil price and variations in anti-trust policy. In all these cases, the new approach does confirm the central thesis of the old model: only in correspondence with the natural equilibrium, the stability of price and wage is preserved.

Finally, it is worth mentioning that the IS–LM–PC scheme leads to the old thesis that a wage moderation policy would bring a reduction in natural unemployment and a growth in natural production, with no effects on the real wage. The only novelty with regard to the previous scheme is the following: once wage moderation policy has determined a new natural equilibrium, spontaneous wage and price deflation is not enough to adjust aggregate demand to it, but the central bank shall necessarily implement a policy of interest rate reduction. The student may verify this result by drawing once again the charts of Figure 4.3 and assessing the effects of a reduction of the parameter z of workers' bargaining power.

In conclusion, although Blanchard's new model shows some significant elements of breaking away from the usual approach to mainstream macroeconomics teaching, we find many elements of continuity between the two. To sum up, it could be argued that the new IS–LM–PC puts into question some relevant properties of the natural equilibrium (and its stability among them); nonetheless, it repeats the same theses on its existence, its unicity and, more generally, on the very conception of the natural equilibrium, all of which are typical of the old AS–AD scheme.

4.8   CRITIQUES OF THE IS–LM–PC MODEL FROM THE PERSPECTIVE OF THE ALTERNATIVE APPROACH

It should now be clear why the link with the labour market – tacit in Blanchard's treatment – has been made explicit here and also in the visual representation of the new IS–LM–PC model. As was the case in the old AS–AD model, also in the new model, what happens in the labour market is decisive in determining the natural equilibrium of the economic system. The old and the new model differ with respect to the manner – spontaneous or politically driven – through which the economy may converge to its natural equilibrium. Still, the very existence of such equilibrium and the idea that the economy shall converge towards it persist and actually are the logical fundamental cornerstone of Blanchard's approach to macroeconomics teaching. In this light, it may be useful to compare Blanchard's new approach with the critical approach to macroeconomics that, for didactic purposes, can be represented by the alternative model described in the previous chapter. First, it can be said that the new IS–LM–PC model partially takes up the objections concerning the inverse relationship supposedly present between prices and aggregate demand, expressed by the downward sloping AD of the previous scheme. Such a relationship is substituted by a thesis that is the opposite to some extent, arguing that an increase in inflation reduces the real interest rate and stimulates investment and hence aggregate demand and production. On the contrary, a fall in inflation (and deflation even more so) causes a rise in the real interest rate, thus depressing investment, demand and production. Although in a simplified way, this dynamic shows features of similarity with the more complex case of an upward sloping AD, described in the framework of the alternative model. The new scheme by Blanchard does still stick to the idea that the rate of interest would be able to affect investment, so that the central bank can exploit this relationship to manage aggregate demand. Within the critical approach, as should by now be clear to the reader, the idea of a straightforward inverse link between interest rate and investment is rejected both for empirical and theoretical reasons. In effect, as we have already noted, its statistical relevance was brought into question by Blanchard himself a few years ago.

Second, it may be noted that the new IS–LM–PC model restates the argument of firms' mark-up being independent from wage claims and workers' bargaining power. As was the case in the old aggregate demand and aggregate supply model, in the new approach by Blanchard the hypothesis of a fixed mark-up is at the basis of the determination of the natural equilibrium in the labour market, which in turn affects how the entire economic system works. The critical approach, as it is well known, radically opposes the hypothesis of a mark-up that is insensitive to the conflict between firms and workers. Thus, within the alternative model, the equilibrium of the economic system is constantly altered by the balance of forces between social classes, and by the effects of their conflicts over the repartition of income. To this regard, it is interesting to recall that in Blanchard's new approach, the existence of an inverse relationship between the price level and the demand for goods is *a priori* excluded: therefore, in that context it is impossible to apply the rule of profit maximization we have examined in Chapter 3 (in the section devoted to "mainstream replicas"), which allowed us to determine the mark-up in function of the elasticity of demand relative to price only. With respect to the old AS–AD model, the new IS–LM–PC scheme appears to provide less opportunity of rejoinder to the exponents of the mainstream when challenged with the proposal of considering the mark-up as dependent on the conflict between social classes, put forward by the schools of critical thought.

If we were to graphically represent the differences between Blanchard's IS–LM–PC and the alternative model, we would modify Figure 4.3: the IS would be traced vertically to express the absence of any clear relationship between the interest rate and investment. The three charts would then have to be read top-down: the IS–LM will determine the levels of equilibrium of aggregate demand, production and unemployment; and the labour

market and the connected position of the PC curve would then conform
to that equilibrium through endogenous variations of the mark-up and/or
workers' bargaining power. Sure enough, the equilibrium in question would
be influenced by economic policies and by the conflict between classes: it
would be different from the "natural" equilibrium of Blanchard's model.

The reasons why the alternative model reaches conclusions that are
different not only from the old AS–AD model but also from the new
IS–LM–PC scheme have just been outlined. The alternative model also
differs from Blanchard's new model in its economic policy implications
with respect to wage, technological change, variations in the price of raw
materials, changes in anti-trust legislation and many other typical policy
issues. To take just one example out of the many, while the IS–LM–PC
model proposes once again the idea that a deregulation in the labour market
aimed at reducing workers' bargaining power reduces unemployment and
increases natural production with no effect on the real wage and on income
distribution, the alternative model instead suggests that this deregulation
has negative effects on wage and distribution, and could have no influence
on unemployment and production. As we will see in the next chapter and
in the appendices, these alternative conclusions may be assessed through
the data. Both on the theoretical ground and on the ground of the empirical assessment, the critical paradigm still constitutes a challenge to Olivier
Blanchard and to his new approach to macroeconomics teaching.

5.   The competing approaches: theory and policy

5.1   COMPARING THE TWO MODELS: AN ALGEBRAIC REPRESENTATION

The comparison between Blanchard's AS–AD model and the alternative model can be sketched with the use of a simple mathematical methodology that is described in this section. Let us consider this equation:

$$ax + by + c = 0 \qquad\qquad (5.1)$$

It can be read in two ways, depending on the variable that we consider exogenous (what is known, a "datum" external from the equation), and the variable that we consider endogenous (the unknown, the solution of the equation). For instance, we can imagine x to be the exogenous variable we know beforehand, whereas y is the unknown we want to determine. In this case, the equation can be expressed as such: $y = - (a/b)x - (c/b)$. Alternatively, y can be seen as the exogenous datum, while x becomes the variable to be determined. In this second case, we have: $x = - (b/a)y - (c/a)$. Also, the shift from Blanchard's model to the alternative model that we presented in Chapter 3 can be interpreted through this logic, that is, as a formal procedure of overturning endogenous and exogenous variables, plus the modification of some functional relationships. For instance, let us have a look at the mark-up and workers' bargaining power: in Blanchard's view, both of them are exogenous, whereas in the alternative model they can be considered as mutually dependent, so that at least one of them is to be treated as endogenous. Thus, by overturning the roles of endogenous and exogenous variables and by introducing some changes in the functional relationships, we get to the transformation of the AS–AD model into its logical antagonist.

   The issue can be tackled starting from an algebraic representation of the AS–AD model. To this purpose, from Chapter 2 we recall the aggregate demand and aggregate supply equations representing an economy that is supposed to be closed to foreign trade (for the sake of simplicity):

$$\text{AS)} \quad P = \frac{1+\mu}{A} P^e F\left(1 - \frac{Y}{AL}; z\right)$$

$$\text{AD)} \quad Y = C(Y - T) + I(Y, i) + G \tag{5.2}$$

The following hypotheses are introduced in order to reformulate these equations as linear. We assume the following shape for the function embedded in the aggregate supply equation:

$$F\left(1 - \frac{Y}{AL}; z\right) = 1 - \alpha\left(1 - \frac{Y}{AL}\right) + z \tag{5.3}$$

Moreover, again with the purpose of working with linear equations, we express the equation for the equilibrium between production and demand in the goods market in the following way:

$$Y = c_0 + c_1(Y - T) + I_0 - d_1 i + d_2 Y + G \tag{5.4}$$

The interest rate is then assumed to be dependent on the money supply, expressed in real terms according to the following equation for the equilibrium in the money market:

$$i = f_0 - f_1(M/P) \tag{5.5}$$

By substituting this expression in the equation for the equilibrium in the goods market, we get:

$$Y = c_0 + c_1(Y - T) + I_0 - d_1 f_0 + d_1 f_1(M/P) + d_2 Y + G \tag{5.6}$$

Then, we perform some simple algebraic steps; we define the parameters and we group the expenditure components in a single term, $E = c_0 + I_0 + G - c_1 T - d_1 f_0$. Substituting and reorganizing the aggregate supply and aggregate demand equations we get to:

$$P = \frac{1+\mu}{A} P^e \left[1 - \alpha\left(1 - \frac{Y}{AL}\right) + z\right]$$

$$Y = \beta E + \gamma\left(\frac{M}{P}\right) \tag{5.7}$$

The E term represents the expenditure components inclusive of public spending net of taxation, and of autonomous investment, while β and γ are parameters that stand for, respectively, the multiplier for fiscal policy and the multiplier for monetary policy. Other variables have been described previously in this volume: P is the current price level; P^e stands for the expected price level; μ is firms' mark-up; A is labour productivity, α expresses wage sensitivity to the unemployment rate; Y is the production level; L is the labour force; z is the catchall variable for workers' bargaining power; and M is the money supply of the central bank. The system just described presents the typical characteristics of a "stereogram", that is to say a scheme that can assume the features of either one or the other model examined according to the point of observation, that is according to the different assumptions made regarding exogenous and endogenous variables and the specific forms of the functions considered. Starting from this initial scheme, in what follows we verify how we can transform it into the traditional AS–AD model or into the alternative model.

The distinctive characteristics of the AS–AD model are the following. First, γ is supposed to be greater than 0, in accordance with the idea of an inverse relationship between the price level and the aggregate demand: a deflation should imply an increase in the real money supply, a reduction of the interest rate, an increase of investment, hence of aggregate demand and production. Second, firms' mark-up μ is assumed to be exogenous and independent from the wage bargaining process. Y and P are the only unknowns of the model, while other terms are considered exogenous, as parameters or as variables whose value is decided by the policymakers. We start from a situation characterized by the absence of conflict between supplied wage and demanded wage, thus with no inflation nor deflation in wage and price, implying coincidence between expected price level and effective price level: $P = P^e$. This situation describes a typical "natural" equilibrium. The natural equilibrium levels of production and price will be determined throughout some simple mathematical steps:

$$Y = \frac{AL}{\alpha}\left(\frac{A}{1+\mu} + \alpha - 1 - z\right)$$

$$P = \frac{\alpha\gamma M(1+\mu)}{A^2 L + (1+\mu)[AL(\alpha - 1 - z) - \alpha\beta E]} \tag{5.8}$$

Other variables can be obtained from the model: as already mentioned, the unemployment rate is given by the ratio between unemployed people and the labour force, $u = U/L$; and the labour force is identified by the sum of employed and unemployed people, $L = N + U$, while the production function is given by $Y + AN$. Then some simple steps will lead us to write the unemployment rate as: $u = 1 - Y/AL$. In this equation we can substitute the natural equilibrium value for Y so as to obtain the natural rate of unemployment:

$$u = 1 - \frac{1}{\alpha}\left(\frac{A}{1 + \mu} + \alpha - 1 - z \right) \qquad (5.9)$$

Moreover, as we know that the price level is the natural equilibrium real wage will be:

$$\frac{W}{P} = \frac{A}{1 + \mu} \qquad (5.10)$$

and so on (with A and μ exogenous).

It is worth noticing that expectations on the price level P^e are endogenous in this model, implying that in equilibrium they align with the equilibrium price level P. Most notably, the components of the expenditure E and the quantity of money M only affect the equilibrium price level, while they have no repercussions on the natural equilibrium production Y, which only depends on the exogenous values of L, A, z, α, μ. Nor do E and M affect the natural equilibrium real wage W/P, which depends on the exogenous level of A and μ exclusively. Therefore, and it is only one example among the many possible, it is easy to verify that a fall in confidence that reduces the level of E will only reduce P while leaving Y and W/P untouched. Moreover, a reduction in workers' protection that decreases their bargaining power z will imply a rise in Y and a fall in P, with no effects on W/P, which remains unchanged.

Let us move to the alternative model. Within that framework, γ can be set equal to 0, in order to exclude the existence of a relationship between the price level and the aggregate demand. In graphical terms, this assumption implies the hypothesis of a vertical AD. Furthermore, we may focus on the scenario in which workers' action has prevailed over firms, hence the mark-up μ is determined endogenously by the wage bargaining process. It has been already explained that these are not the only possible options: there are other configurations that can shape the alternative model. There is, for instance, the possibility of an upward sloping AD, describing a debt deflation. In addition, μ can be seen as exogenous as opposed to an endogenous z, pointing to a situation in which workers are obliged to conform to firms' decisions on wage. Here we only deal with just one of the many possible configurations of the alternative model.

As we did for the AS–AD model, also for the description of the alternative model we assume that firms and workers have already reached an agreement, thus wage and price are stable, the effective price level and the expected price level are coincident: $P = P^e$. Some simple steps yield the equilibrium solutions:

$$Y = \beta E$$

$$\mu = \frac{A}{1 - \alpha\left(1 - \dfrac{\beta E}{AL}\right) + z} - 1 \tag{5.11}$$

Finally, it is to be noted that the effective price level is equal to the expected price level, which is to be regarded as exogenous in this model: $P = P^e$. Other variables can be obtained: for instance, the equilibrium rate of unemployment and the equilibrium real wage, which correspond to $u = 1 - Y/AL$ and $W/P = A/(1 + \mu)$. By substituting the equilibrium values of Y and μ in these equations and reorganizing, we get:

$$u = 1 - \beta\left(\frac{E}{AL}\right)$$

$$\frac{W}{P} = 1 + z + \alpha\beta\left(\frac{E}{AL}\right) - \alpha \tag{5.12}$$

Differences with respect to Blanchard's AS–AD model stand out. For instance, according to the alternative model, a decline in confidence and the following fall in expenditure E will imply a decrease in the equilibrium production Y, and an increase of the mark-up μ, with a consequent fall of the equilibrium real wage W/P. Another example would be a reduction in the protection of workers, which would reduce the parameter z, implying an increase of the mark-up and, again, a reduction of the real wage, with no effect instead on production and unemployment. These results are opposite to those emerging from Blanchard's AS–AD model.

The algebraic representation of the competing approaches is helpful in order to further investigate some issues that are addressed at a superficial level by the graphical analysis. Worth mentioning is the case of technological unemployment, that is, an increase in the equilibrium unemployment rate caused by technical change that goes to increase labour productivity. We mentioned in the preceding chapters that the AS–AD model does not allow for technological unemployment in a situation of equilibrium, while this may occur within the alternative framework. These opposing conclusions can now be presented in formal algebraic terms. If we look at the respective equilibrium unemployment rates, we see that an increase in A causes effects that are opposite in the two models: a reduction of u in the AS–AD model, an increase instead in the alternative model. According to the latter, technical innovations that increase labour productivity can actually give rise to technological unemployment, to be counteracted with dedicated public policies, such as an expansionary policy able to cause a rise in E equal, at least, to the exogenous increase of A; or a reduction of the working time so as to compensate for the effects of innovation and thus maintain the level of A unchanged; or a policy mix of the two, and so on and so forth.

It is to be stressed that similar results might have been obtained by comparing the alternative model and the system of equations composing Blanchard's new IS–LM–PC approach. As already mentioned, the IS–LM–PC model allows for the natural equilibrium to be subject to problems of instability; however, the existence, the unicity and the pivotal characteristics of such equilibrium are not called into question. This means that the IS–LM–PC model reaches results that are essentially analogous to those of the AS–AD scheme, when it comes to the determination of the equilibrium. It may thus be subject to the same critiques raised by the alternative model towards the AS–AD.

Obviously, it would be misleading to presume that the differences between the mainstream model and the critical approach can be reduced to a mere question of choice of exogenous and endogenous variables or to a modification of the functional relationships that characterize the didactic formulation. The foundations of mainstream theory as well as the alternative concept of "reproducibility" typical of the critical approach transcend the narrow limits imposed by the simple comparison between the two teaching models exposed in these pages. Nonetheless, the very fact that a simple transposition of endogenous and exogenous variables and the modification of a few parameters force radically different conclusions for economic policy highlights the logical antagonism between existent theoretical paradigms, and thus raises significant ideas for reflection that students can take up.

5.2 TWO COMPETING INTERPRETATIONS OF THE ECONOMIC CRISIS

The global economic crisis begun in 2007–2008 represents a real test bed for economic theory and policy. The exponents of different schools of thought have struggled to provide a coherent interpretation of the crisis from which to derive economic policy. As usual, scholars' conclusions have not been unanimous. Here, we will focus on two alternative explanations of the recession. The first one can be defined as the "financial" interpretation of the crisis: it has been upheld by many exponents of the mainstream, and in effect it is compatible with Blanchard's model. The second interpretation claims instead that the crisis should be considered, at least in part, as a "crisis of a world of low wages", whose causes are thus to be found in structural and social phenomena, not in merely financial and monetary issues. As we will see, from the analytical point of view, the financial interpretation relies on the monetary base multiplier, whereas the low wages interpretation relies on the autonomous expenditure multiplier.

Let us deal with the financial interpretation first: it is the argument that has prevailed within the media and in the political arena. The underlying idea is that the crisis, starting in 2007–2008, is to be interpreted as a crisis originating in the financial sector, which was later transferred to the real economy. According to this view, the only culprit is the misbehaviour of private banks, most notably American ones. Especially in the USA, but also in Great Britain and other European countries, banks had got into large debt and used their leverage to issue mortgages to agents whose solvency was at risk. The debt mechanisms were highly sophisticated but in the long run they collapsed: the debt race was stimulated by easy lending, and vice versa; the race ended when many borrowers were found to be insolvent, so that in turn banks were not able to pay back the debt they had with their clients. Uncertainty suddenly spread all over the world, as depositors were concerned that banks could not honour their debt and would default. Thus, each bank was induced to increase its monetary reserve to deal with possible demand for cash. The result was what the jargon calls a "credit crunch", that is, a rationing of the credit: instead of lending money, banks preferred hoarding in order not to become insolvent to their creditors. The credit crunch caused the interest rates to rise and investment to fall, and so did production and employment. Therefore, the crisis spread from the financial sector to the real sector.

The financial interpretation just described can be examined analytically. In this regard, let us recall the equation of the monetary multiplier described by Blanchard in Chapter 4 of his textbook. The monetary multiplier emerges from the following procedure. As we know, the demand for money consists of the quantity of money that savers want to hold, and it is given by M_d. The total demand is divided into deposits $D = (1 - c)M_d$ and circulating money $CU = cM_d$, with c being the percentage of circulating money that agents want to have in their pocket. Furthermore, as we know, money that clients deposit into private banks is for the greater part used by banks to grant loans. However, banks will keep part of the deposits as a lifebuoy, a precautionary reserve. If we define this reserve as R and the share of reserve desired by banks as θ, we can thus write that $R = uD$, hence $R = \theta(1 - c)M_d$. At this point, we can identify the monetary base with H: it is equal to the quantity of banknotes issued by the central bank. These banknotes, once issued, can be held – physically – only in one of the two following places: in people's pockets as circulating money CU, or in banks' reserves R. Then, $H = CU + R$. Now, a few substitutions are sufficient to clearly see that the total demand for money is given by:

$$M_d = \frac{1}{[c + \theta(1 - c)]} H \qquad (5.13)$$

Provided that in equilibrium the total demand for money is always equal to the total supply of money ($M_d = M$), thus:

$$M = \frac{1}{[c + \theta(1 - c)]} H \qquad (5.14)$$

This ratio is defined as the multiplier of the monetary base or simply monetary multiplier. Therefore, the total supply of money M is given by the monetary base H multiplied by the multiplier. The latter equation sheds light on the importance of private banks within the economic system. In effect, as c and θ are generally smaller than 1, the denominator is then smaller than 1 and the ratio is thus greater than 1. This is why it is defined as "multiplier" of the monetary base: for a given base H issued by the central bank, the total supply of money M will be a multiple of it. The economic interpretation of this multiplicative effect is rather straightforward: the multiplier expresses the capability of banks to bolster the creation and circulation of money. Clearly, when savers deposit money to the bank, the bank will not keep it idle in its safe; instead, it will use the greater part of it to make loans, to get profit out of the interest rate. In this way, a self-sustaining mechanism is set off: those who borrow money will spend it to purchase goods, those who sell those goods in turn will deposit the revenues into their bank, which in its turn will make more loans. It is a spiral of deposits–loans–deposits–loans that creates more money M than the initial base H: a powerful mechanism that benefits the development of credit and of the whole economy, though at the same time being fragile as it is based on clients' trust towards banks. As a matter of fact, the described process guarantees that banks hold in their safe a sufficient number of banknotes to face the normal demand for money made daily by their clients (at the desk or more often at cash machines). If trust vanishes, the banking system goes into crisis. For instance, if doubts on the solvency of banks arise among depositors, they might suddenly opt for a massive cash withdrawal. If this is the case, banks will go bankrupt as they had lent most of the received money and do not hold in their safe an amount of cash sufficient to face a bank run widely spreading among their clients. Therefore, when trust vanishes, agents are brought to increase the percentage of money c they prefer to keep in their pocket instead of banks' deposits. At the same time, banks tend to increase the reserve coefficient U in order to be ready to face possible demand for cash. As a result of this double-sided process, the denominator increases and hence the total quantity of money M shrinks. From this fall in circulating money, we have: an interest rates rise and a fall in investment, in demand, thus in production and employment. Eventually, the propensity to hold money may even reach $c = 1$ (that is, agents withdraw 100 per cent of their deposits to keep everything in their pockets), then it is easy to show that and also the monetary multiplier become equal to 1, hence $M = H$. This is due to the features of this extreme situation in which agents prefer to keep their money "under the mattress", banks disappear completely from the system and the multiplicative effect of the monetary base vanishes altogether.

According to the described financial interpretation, the crisis has unfolded following this scheme: a debt run, coupled with the tendency of banks to grant easy credit to potential insolvent clients; a growing mistrust of the effective capability of banks to collect their credits and to be themselves solvent to their clients; accordingly, banks' clients show an increasing propensity to hold money, while banks' reserve ratio is set at a higher level; this is followed by a fall in the quantity of money, an increase in the interest rates, a fall in loans, investments, demand and the economy as a whole. According to many mainstream economists, both the 1929 great crisis and the current crisis can be explained in the light of the described path. Exponents of the dominant theory usually extract from this interpretation the following political implications:

1. in principle, if workers were prepared to curtail their monetary wage, the economic system could spontaneously get out of the crisis, though it is better to favour the recovery through increases in the monetary base that would compensate for the reduction in the monetary multiplier caused by the loss of confidence;
2. in order to avoid the occurrence of events of this type, it is necessary to put banks' behaviour under stricter control, by introducing norms to prevent banks from incurring excessive debt while granting loans to potentially insolvent agents.

To sum up, according to the financial interpretation, it is necessary to increase the monetary base to overcome a crisis. Moreover, to prevent further crises it is a good idea to introduce stricter financial discipline in credit issuing.

This interpretation can be smoothly described in the framework of Blanchard's mainstream model: it corresponds to a reduction in the amount of money M. Such a reduction implies a shift of the AD towards the left, matched by a decrease in the real value of monetary stocks, an increase in the supply of assets and hence a decrease in their value, a rise in the interest rate, a fall in investment, aggregate expenditure, production and employment, and thus an increase in unemployment. In theory, we could let the system find its equilibrium autonomously. Unemployment should induce workers to curtail their wage claims, therefore prices would go down, the real quantity of money would expand, and demand and production would go up again. Nonetheless, it would be better if authorities intervened with expansionary policies in order to stimulate the recovery of demand. This way, the AD gets back to its initial level and the natural equilibrium is restored.

The crisis finds a different explanation within the framework of the critical schools of thought. Some economists claim that the financial interpretation is true to some extent, but it does not deal with some fundamental aspects of the problem. In particular, the reasons why so many indebted agents have suddenly turned out to be insolvent should be investigated. According to the critics, the answer does not lie in the explosion of the amount of debt, but it also concerns a long-lasting period of modest or even null growth in the income of most of the population, particularly that of employees. The insolvency would thus be explained by the mounting amount of debt attached to a sluggish dynamic of incomes – especially wages. The financial interpretation of the crisis can be considered exhaustive only if it considers the widening gap between rising debt and stagnant income from work.

There is another reason why critical economists suggest moving the focus to wage stagnation. According to their view, low wages in themselves can trigger a crisis, independently from any consideration on debt. This can be shown as follows. Critical economists focus primarily on structural changes that have occurred in many countries in the last 30 years, most notably in social relations and in income distribution. In this time span, they observed the unfolding of a major process of liberalization and deregulation of the financial markets, the goods market and the labour market. Such liberalization and deregulation have increased the freedom of capital movement and the scope for capital operations, thus intensifying international competition between capitals, which has translated into the reduction of legal and contractual protection of workers. Consequently, the owners of capital have got stronger whereas workers and their unions have weakened. The mutation in the balance of power brought an economic growth triggered by technical progress and the intensification of the working pace which was to the exclusive advantage of the owners of capital. Accordingly, income share has moved from wage to profit. The chart in Figure 5.1 shows that the wage share (share of GDP going to wages) plunge happened in some important industrialized countries.

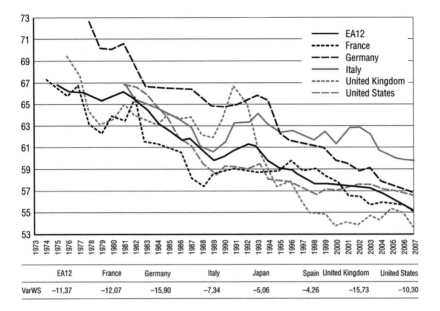

	EA12	France	Germany	Italy	Japan	Spain	United Kingdom	United States
VarWS	−11,37	−12,07	−15,90	−7,34	−5,06	−4,26	−15,73	−10,30

Source: Ameco database, European Commission (https://ec.europa.eu/info/
businesseconomy-euro/indicators-statistics/economic-databases/macro-
economic-database-ameco_en).

Figure 5.1   Drop in the wage share

Empirical evidence is there; how can this phenomenon be explained theoretically? It is worth mentioning that technical progress and the intensification of the working pace have caused an increase in hourly labour productivity A. However, this climb has not been matched by an equivalent rise in hourly real wage W/P: increments in labour productivity of workers have been absorbed for the most part by the profit margin μ. We know that:

$$P = (1 + \mu)\frac{W}{A} \qquad (5.15)$$

From which:

$$\frac{W}{P} = \frac{A}{1 + \mu} \qquad (5.16)$$

Or, if we overturn the terms:

$$1 + \mu = \frac{A}{W/P} \qquad (5.17)$$

Clearly, if productivity A increases while the real wage remains essentially unchanged, the growth in productivity will benefit exclusively the mark-up μ. The wage share is given by the ratio between the total amount of wage paid to workers and the value of production: WN/PY. As national production is given by $Y = AN$, then labour productivity corresponds to $A = Y/N$, and the wage share can also be expressed as that is, the reciprocal of $1 + \mu$. Therefore, an increase in productivity that is not matched by a corresponding rise in real wage implies a surge in the mark-up and a corresponding decrease of the wage share. Empirical evidence finds then a possible theoretical explanation.

It is a low wage scenario. It is also worth noticing that in this scenario the level of real wages does not have to decrease necessarily. The real wage may remain stationary or display a sluggish growth, whilst the profit margin of the owners of capital increases. Capitalists take an almost exclusive advantage from the technical progress and the greater intensity of workers' activity. Why should this low wage scenario lead to a crisis? If workers' productivity increases but wage increases less or it is flat, then the productive capacity of workers steadily grows while their spending capacity does not. We face, therefore, a plunge in the demand for goods, in production and employment. To see this analytically, we can go back to the autonomous expenditure multiplier (described in Chapter 3 by Blanchard) and apply a few variations. First, let us remember that the equilibrium equation between production and aggregate demand is given by $Y = C + I + G$ and consumption is given by $C = c_0 + c(Y - T)$. Production increases or decreases until it matches aggregate expenditure. Moreover, the sale value of what is produced will be distributed between capitalists (owners of firms) and workers, in the form of income: Y does not correspond to production only, but also to the amount of income distributed among capitalists and workers who contributed to its realization. Expressing everything in monetary terms instead of real terms, we can write that revenues PY, i.e. the result of the sale of goods, will go to workers in the amount of WN, that is, the total amount of wages, and will go to capitalists in the amount of μWN, that is, profits expressed as a share of the total amount of wages. Then, we can say that $PY = (1 + \mu)WN$. To get back to real terms, it is sufficient to divide this by P:

$$Y = (1 + \mu)\frac{W}{P}N \qquad (5.18)$$

Although this equation may look like a novelty to the reader, on closer examination it is perfectly equivalent to the price equation, which is not new and is expressed as:

$$P = (1+\mu)W / A \qquad (5.19)^1$$

Until this point, there is nothing new with respect to what is already in Chapters 3 and 4 of Blanchard's textbook. We will now introduce a novelty. We assume that capitalists and workers have different consumption habits: for any marginal euro available in the form of income, we assume that workers will tend to consume a higher percentage than capitalists, who can instead afford saving and accumulation. This hypothesis seems plausible, and is indeed confirmed by empirical investigations. If the income of a blue-collar worker increases by 100 euro, the blue-collar worker will likely consume the most part of this additional income. On the contrary, if the income of a capitalist increases by 100 euro, provided that his/her income is already rather abundant, it may well happen that the capitalist hardly notices the increase: likely, the 100 extra euro will remain in his/her pocket and increase savings even more.[2] Thus, from now on we will not have a single generic propensity to consume c of the population as a whole; instead, we will have two different propensities to consume, a higher one for workers (c_w) and a lower one for capitalists (c_k): $c_w > c_k$. As we know, income is divided as follows:

$$Y = (1+\mu)\frac{W}{P} N \qquad (5.20)$$

with $(W/P)N$ going to workers and $\mu(W/P)N$ going to capitalists. By subtracting taxes T from income, and taking into account that income will be consumed differently by the two groups, we can write again the equation for consumption as follows:

$$C = c_0 + c_w\left(\frac{W}{P}N - T\right) + c_k\left(\mu\frac{W}{P}N - T\right) \qquad (5.21)$$

Only for the sake of simplicity, we now introduce two extreme hypotheses: we assume that the owners of firms only save and accumulate their income, hence do not consume at all, and their propensity to consume becomes $c_k = 0$; on the contrary, we assume workers to entirely consume their wage, hence $c_w = 1$. It is worth stressing that the core of the results is not affected by these assumptions, which are made just for simplicity. The new consumption equation simplifies accordingly:

---

[1] If we start from $Y = (1 + \mu)WN/P$, by multiplying both terms by P we obtain $PY = (1 + \mu)WN$. By dividing both terms by Y we obtain $P + (1 + \mu)WN/Y$. Then, we recall that $Y = AN$ and that N/Y corresponds to $1/A$, so we can write that $P = (1 + \mu)W/A$. We have just shown the equivalence.

[2] Empirical evidence on the matter is conspicuous.

$$C = c_0 + \frac{W}{P} N - T \tag{5.22}$$

How this novelty affects the equation of equilibrium between production and demand – hence the autonomous expenditure multiplier – is now clear. The equilibrium equation $Y = C + I + G$ can now be expressed as follows:

$$Y = c_0 + \frac{W}{P} N - T + I + G \tag{5.23}$$

As we know, production is given by $Y = AN$ and thus $N = Y/A$; by substituting, we obtain:

$$Y = c_0 + \frac{W}{P} \frac{Y}{A} - T + I + G$$

$$Y - \frac{W}{P} \frac{Y}{A} = c_0 + I + G - T$$

$$Y = \frac{1}{1 - \dfrac{W}{P} \dfrac{1}{A}} (c_0 + I + G - T) \tag{5.24}$$

Finally, recalling that $P = (1 + \mu)W/A$, from which $(W/P)(1/A) = 1/(1 + \mu)$, we can thus substitute and write that:

$$Y = \frac{1}{1 - \dfrac{1}{1 + \mu}} (c_0 + I + G - T) \tag{5.25}$$

This is the new equation of the production of equilibrium. The terms in parenthesis represent autonomous expenditure, the ratio outside the parentheses expresses the autonomous expenditure multiplier.

The peculiar characteristic of this multiplier is that it also depends on the profit margin μ, so on income distribution between profit and wage. Let us suppose, for instance, a prominent position of capitalists in the balance of power – within the bargaining process – with respect to workers, so that the increments of labour productivity will be entirely absorbed by the increase of the mark-up μ. It is easy to see that the rise in μ causes a reduction of the term $[1/(1 + \mu)]$, consequently an increase in the denominator $1- [1/(1 + \mu)]$, and eventually a decrease in the ratio representing the multiplier:

$$\mu \uparrow \Rightarrow \frac{1}{1 - \dfrac{1}{1 + \mu}} \downarrow \tag{5.26}$$

It is then clear that for a given autonomous expenditure, the reduction of the multiplier will make production Y and thus employment fall. From an economic viewpoint, the explanation is rather straightforward. Just remember the hypothesis on the different consumption habits: workers show a high propensity to consume their wage, whereas capitalists have a lower (tending to zero) propensity to consume their profit. Therefore, if the mark-up increases, there will be a shift in income: capitalists will be better off, while workers will be worse off. Due to the lower propensity to consume of the former, a higher share of income will remain idle instead of being used. This will imply a reduction of the multiplier, hence production and employment. A world of low wage has a spontaneous tendency towards the crisis.

This result is consistent with the framework inspired by critical theories. Based on the equations of the previous section, it can be assumed that the autonomous expenditure multiplier β is represented by the following equation:

$$\beta = \frac{1}{1 - \dfrac{1}{1 + \mu}} \tag{5.27}$$

Assuming the mark-up to be the outcome of a bargaining process between firms and workers, the multiplier is determined. Then, given the other elements of the autonomous expenditure, we can obtain production, employment and unemployment. Once we know the latter, under the hypothesis that capitalists are stronger in their bargaining power, the parameter expressing workers' bargaining power can be endogenously obtained from the second equilibrium solution of the alternative model, which we recall here from the previous section:

$$\mu = \frac{A}{1 - \alpha\left(1 - \dfrac{\beta E}{AL}\right) + z} - 1 \tag{5.28}$$

Within this framework, if the mark-up increases, the multiplier reduces and the vertical AD moves to the left. The distributive shift to the advantage of capitalists generates crisis and unemployment. It is a situation where the system is not able to get out from the crisis without public intervention. Furthermore, if the recession moves income distribution further to the advantage of capitalists, the recession will get deeper.

At this point, increasing wages might seem to be a policy convenient to everyone in the system, obviously to workers but also to the owners of firms, who could prevent the economic crisis this way. It is a misleading and naïve conclusion nonetheless, due to the following two aspects. First, wages are double-faced: they are a source of demand for firms in general, but at the same time a cost for the single firm. Each single firm cannot have a global view on the issue of wages. As a matter of fact, the single firm does know that increasing the wage of its employees will not push demand up: a contextual and generalized wage rise by all firms would be needed. Accordingly, the single firm is induced to consider the retribution of workers as a cost only; thus, it will do its best to curtail and squeeze it, regardless of the fall in demand that is caused by all firms behaving this way. Second, the owners of firms might not be interested in growth of production and employment. After all, the crisis occurs in concomitance with a surge in the profit margin: it may well be that capitalists are willing to bear the former in exchange for the latter. It could be more important for capitalists to have full control over their capital and the profit margin than to have an economy in expansion where workers get stronger at the same time. In particular, although letting the wage rise and keeping the profit margin constant are necessary conditions to generate a solid growth in production, many capitalists might prefer to have a less dynamic economy, provided that workers' claims are under control and the profit margin can increase more freely.

The two points just described show that:

1. capitalism is first of all an uncoordinated mode of production, in which each agent acts according to their individual rationality, which can easily come into conflict with the overall rationality of the system;
2. capitalism is an intrinsically conflictual mode of production: holders of capital rate maintaining power higher than the growth of social wealth.

Such conclusions rely on the works of the great heterodox thinkers, from Marx to Keynes, and more generally on the contribution of critical economists. These scholars also help us to understand why it is impossible to get out from a crisis by only increasing wages. Structural adjustments should be introduced into the system in order to overcome a crisis of this type, policies such as strengthening unions and the legal protection of workers, enhancing control over capital movements to prevent capital flight and implementing measures of public intervention aimed at creating employment for the direct production of collective goods. Such policies would allow workers to reinforce their position and then to require that increments of productivity translate into wage growth.

In our view, the interpretation of the crisis based on a low wage scenario is effective only to some extent: only some of the aspects that brought about the decline that started in 2007–2008 are captured by this interpretation. Expecting a univocal explanation of such a complex crisis would be a big mistake. Some empirical studies have nonetheless confirmed the existence of a contractionary effect stemming from a distribution of income to the detriment of wage.[3] Moreover, influential institutions such as the IMF and leading exponents of the mainstream have also shared an interpretative key for the explanation of the crisis, which gives paramount relevance to the effects of income inequalities.[4] How far this interpretation can go while still being consistent with the mainstream analysis is still a matter of debate.[5]

It goes without saying that the differences between Blanchard's model and the alternative one relative to the crisis are not limited to the two interpretations just described. A deeper analysis of the topic would show a larger contraposition between the two schools of thought, as it is evident with respect to the issue of the so called "speculative bubbles". This term refers to those typical situations of the contemporary capitalist system, where the price of assets in the financial markets shows explosive increases and sudden drops apparently unrelated to their yields. The intuitive explanation of this phenomenon relies on the fact that prices are made unstable by the behaviour of speculators not concerned with yields and seeking returns on capital instead, just trying to buy cheap and sell dear. The current price of an asset may then be high just because market operators expect it to become even higher tomorrow: they buy it just to sell it and to obtain a return on capital, regardless of the given yield. According to the mainstream model, these speculative oscillations can at most be temporary disturbances: normally, the price of assets must correspond to their "fundamental" value, which depends on yields only, which in turn are anchored to the natural equilibrium levels. Therefore, unless we imagine an exceptional instability in the

---

[3]   Among other examples, see H. Hein and L. Vogel (2007), "Distribution and growth reconsidered: Empirical results for six OECD countries", *Cambridge Journal of Economics 32(3)*, 479–511; E. Stockhammer, O. Onaran and S. Ederer (2008), "Functional income distribution and aggregate demand in the Euro area", *Cambridge Journal of Economics 33(1)*, 139–159.

[4]   J.P. Fitoussi and J. Stiglitz (2009), "The ways out of the crisis and the building of a more cohesive world", Sciences Po Document de travail 2009–2017. See also, International Monetary Fund and International Labour Organization (2010), "The challenges of growth, employment and social cohesion", Joint ILO–IMF conference in cooperation with the office of the Prime Minister of Norway, Oslo, 13 September.

[5]   E. Brancaccio (2011), "Some contradictions in 'mainstream' interpretations of the crisis", in E. Brancaccio and G. Fontana (eds), *The Global Economic Crisis. New Perspectives on the Critique of Economic Theory and Policy*, London, UK: Routledge.

natural equilibrium, it becomes hard for the mainstream to explain the oscillations characteristic of the behaviour of the assets price exchanged in the financial market. Blanchard and other orthodox economists have tried to escape this contradiction in many ways, but, within the adopted theoretical framework, the frequent booms and busts of the financial markets appear as foreign bodies, difficult to explain. The alternative model instead is not touched by this problem, as it denies the concept of natural equilibrium. According to this alternative theoretical view, speculation can heavily affect the performance of financial markets and can even have repercussions on the equilibrium levels of production and income distribution. This happens, for instance, when a speculative bubble bursts and the following fall of prices triggers insolvencies and bankruptcies among those who bought on debt relying on the possibility of selling at a higher price in the future. Such a phenomenon may generate an economic crisis and a resulting rise in unemployment that can weaken workers in the bargaining process, causing a durable increase in the profit margin and a fall in the real wage. Within the alternative model, it may thus happen that variations in the price of assets affect returns and profits, along a logical sequence which is somehow opposite to that of the mainstream model. For further insights, please refer to the section dedicated to the stock market (5.13).

5.3   ALTERNATIVE MONETARY POLICY RULES

Up to now, we have focused on the contrasts between capitalist entrepreneurs and workers. We have shown how, in the mainstream model, "conflict is not worth": workers' claims do not have any effect on real wage, while they increase unemployment. On the contrary, according to the alternative model, the outcome of the struggle between capitalists and workers is decisive for the determination of the wage level, while unemployment is not necessarily affected. In fact, the conflict between entrepreneurs and workers is not the only conflict characterizing a capitalist regime: there are other types of conflict, such as strains between large and small firms or between firms and banks, and so on. In this section, we will focus on a potential conflict that can arise between capitals able to pay back their debt and are thus solvent, and capitals that are in trouble with debt repayment and are thus potentially insolvent. As we will see, according to critical theory, the central bank can influence in a determinant way the outcome of the conflict between capitals, whereas mainstream analyzes attribute a different role to the central bank, to some extent a "neutral" role.

According to the mainstream model:

- in the short run, the central bank's monetary policy can contribute to bring the economy towards the natural equilibrium of employment;
- in the long run, money is neutral, therefore the only task of the central bank is to regulate the price level, hence inflation.

Monetary policy is thus to be interpreted as completely neutral (i.e. it pursues general objectives that do not discriminate between the economic agents) and thus not generating any sort of social conflict. This interpretation is supported also by the most advanced mainstream analyzes, for example by those relying on the so-called "Taylor rule" of monetary policy.[6] The economist John Taylor is known to have elaborated an equation that, in his opinion, should be able to describe the monetary policy "rule" followed by the Federal Reserve (or Fed, the US central bank) when it needs to decide the level of the interest rate. It is worth recalling that within Blanchard's model the central bank sets the quantity of money M to control the rate of interest i. In more recent models, instead, as it is in Taylor's, the central bank is assumed to manage the interest rate directly (something that makes for a closer representation of the actual behaviour of monetary authorities). According to Taylor, central banks tend to set the interest rate with the goal of stabilizing the economic system around a natural equilibrium of unemployment and a given inflation objective. Taylor, as well as Blanchard, considers general objectives, which would not fuel conflicts between social groups.

Let us describe the Taylor "rule" in detail. The term i is the monetary interest rate as set by the central bank; π is the effective inflation rate; $(i-\pi)$ is the real interest rate, that is net of inflation; r^* is the "natural" interest rate, accordant with a situation of "natural" equilibrium for the whole system; π^T is the target inflation pursued by the central bank; Y^* is the "natural" level of production; Y is the actual production; $g_d = (Y-Y^*)/Y^*$ is the deviation of actual production from the "natural" equilibrium path; θ and λ are parameters. The rule can be expressed by the following equation:

$$i - \pi = r^* + \theta(\pi - \pi^T) + \lambda g_d \qquad (5.29)$$

Taylor claims this rule can describe how the central bank manages monetary policy. The idea is that for any given level of actual inflation π and of deviation of actual production g_d, the central bank sets a certain level

---

[6] This is described in Chapter 23 of the eighth edition of Blanchard's textbook (O. Blanchard (2021), *Macroeconomics* (8th edn), Boston, USA: Pearson).

of the interest rate i, which will be either higher or lower than the natural equilibrium value, depending on the situation. For instance, if we are at natural equilibrium and actual inflation is equal to the inflation target, we will have that $g_d = 0$ and $\pi = \pi^T$. If that is the case, the "rule" (Equation 5.29) becomes:

$$i - \pi = r^* + 0 + 0 \qquad (5.30)$$

This means that the central bank will set the monetary interest rate i at a level that in real terms (net of inflation) is perfectly equal to the natural interest rate. The reason is simple: the economy is already at natural equilibrium, so the central bank does not need to generate deviations of the interest rate from its equilibrium value. On the contrary, if $g_d > 0$ and $\pi > \pi^T$, it will be easy to verify from the "rule" (Equation 5.29) that the central bank is going to set a "high" interest rate: $i - \pi > r^*$. At this stage a contractionary monetary policy is needed, able to generate a high interest rate in order to reduce investment, aggregate demand, production and employment, so that workers are made weaker and the race to the top of wage and price, hence inflation, is stopped. The process goes on until production goes down to the natural equilibrium level and inflation decreases to the target rate. Finally, if $g_d < 0$ and $\pi < \pi^T$, the "rule" (Equation 5.29) determines a "low" interest rate: $i - \pi < r^*$. In this scenario, we need an expansionary policy able to reduce the interest rate, and boost investment, demand, production and employment, thus making workers stronger and sustaining the race to the top of wage, prices and hence inflation, until production grows to its natural level and inflation to the target level.

The Taylor rule can be written in a slightly different way, by bringing the inflation rate π to the right and rearranging:

$$i = (r^* - \theta \pi^T) + (1 + \theta)\pi + \lambda g_d \qquad (5.31)$$

Grounded on empirical investigations, Taylor estimated the value of the parameters of his "rule". Analyzing the Fed monetary policy between 1984 and 1992, he reached the conclusion that in this period the US central bank managed the interest rate sticking to a rule based on the following parameters:

$$i = 1 + 1.5\pi + 0.5 g_d \qquad (5.32)$$

Taylor repeated the test on longer lasting periods and confirmed the above values of the parameter to be considered as "optimal". The reason, he claims, is that in those periods in which the central bank perfectly stuck to the "rule" (Equation 5.32), as defined by those parameters, the US economy managed to develop in a regular manner, always remaining close to natural equilibrium, with just a few fluctuations in production and inflation. On the contrary, when the Fed set the interest rate on values different from those suggested by Equation 5.32, the economy went through booms and busts. Most notably, Taylor believes that in the first five years of the new millennium the Fed set an interest rate much lower than the rate identified by the "rule" (Equation 5.32). Consequently, the system overheated, and debt, demand and inflation shot up well beyond the target. These tendencies created the conditions for the outbreak of the crisis in 2007–2008, Taylor claims. Indeed, he maintains that the decision of the Fed to depart from the "optimal rule" and to implement an "easy money" policy contributed to generating an irrecoverable amount of debt that led to the final collapse.[7]

Taylor's analysis can thus be seen as a specification of the "financial" interpretation we have previously discussed: Taylor also focuses on the problem of the debt run. However, he identifies a trigger for this run in the low rate policy implemented by Alan Greenspan, then Chairman of the Fed. Although sophisticated, this interpretation does not modify the role of the central bank. It is conceived as an institution that can behave in either a good or a bad way, which can stabilize the economy or throw it into chaos but does not affect conflicts arising within society, for example between capitalists and workers, or among capitalists.

The Taylor "rule" may, however, be criticized in the light of the alternative model. This "rule" clearly relies on the mainstream idea that maneuvering the interest rate is the way for the central bank to manage the performance of investment, aggregate demand, production, employment and inflation. Critics claim instead the movements of the interest rate to have extremely uncertain effects on investment and aggregate demand. In this view, the cornerstone of Taylor's argument falls. Does this mean that the central bank does not follow any rule at all? It is not obvious. Looking at the contributions of critical theory, it is possible to get a different view on the effective behaviour of central banks and on the "rule" that they follow in setting the interest rates. We describe it starting from a simplified alternative model, based on the following fundamental hypotheses:

- production is determined by demand;
- most savings derive from capitalists' profit.

---

[7]   J.B. Taylor (2009), *Getting off Track*, Stanford, USA: Hoover Institution Press.

For the sake of simplicity, we assume that there is no public expenditure nor taxes, and write down the equation of the macroeconomic equilibrium of the model:

$$Y = C + I \qquad (5.33)$$

As saving is given by the difference between production and consumption: $S = Y - C$, we substitute and rearrange:

$$S = I \qquad (5.34)$$

In the framework of the alternative theory, this equilibrium equation is to be read from right to left. That is, investment determines the demand for goods, hence production, employment, income and, finally, saving. Investment is given by the value of the existing capital $P_t K$ multiplied by the factor of the capital accumulation rate $(1 + g)$. Accordingly, $I = (1 + g) P_t K$. It is to be added that $g = \delta g_d$: for simplicity, we can consider δ as a mere parameter, while g_d corresponds here to the deviation of actual production from the production consistent with the "normal" use of productive forces (the definition is apparently similar to the previous one; in fact, it is based on the denial of the concept of "natural" equilibrium typical of the mainstream approach and of the Taylor rule).[8]

With respect to saving, we can simply assume that workers do not save at all, while capitalists do save all their income. So, saving is equal to the total amount of profits, as computed on the already purchased capital at the price of the precedent period. If we define the rate of profit as ρ, we have that $S = (1 + \rho)P_{t-1}K$. The macroeconomic equilibrium thus becomes:

$$(1 + \rho)P_{t-1}K = (1 + g)P_t K \qquad (5.35)$$

From which, by defining and rearranging, we get:

$$(1 + \rho) = (1 + g)(1 + \pi) \qquad (5.36)$$

Now, we add the solvency condition of firms to the analysis. We define with $(1 + i)P_{t-1}K$ the repayment and the relative interest that firms must give back to banks for the loans obtained in the previous period, used to buy the

---

[8]   For further insights, please look at E. Brancaccio and G. Fontana (2013), "'Solvency rule' versus 'Taylor rule': An alternative interpretation of the relation between monetary policy and the economic crisis", *Cambridge Journal of Economics 37(1)*, 17–33.

needed capital $P_{t-1}K$. Remember that $(1 + \rho)P_{t-1}K$ is equal to firms' profit. It is evident that, on average, firms will be solvent only if the earned profit is enough to cover the due repayments, that is:

$$(1 + i)P_{t-1}K \leq (1 + \rho)P_{t-1}K \qquad (5.37)$$

From which:

$$1 + i \leq 1 + \rho \qquad (5.38)$$

This is the solvency condition of firms. It represents an average, in the sense that ρ is an average profit. For any given i, there will be firms with a profit higher than ρ and thus solvent, whereas other firms will get a profit lower than ρ, hence will be insolvent. Now, we substitute the condition of macroeconomic equilibrium (Equation 5.36) into the inequality (Equation 5.38), and we get:

$$1 + i \leq (1 + g)(1 + \pi) \qquad (5.39)$$

from which, by multiplying and considering πg as negligible, one gets to: $i < \pi + g$. If we recall that $g = \delta g_d$ and impose strict equality, we obtain:

$$i = \pi + \delta g_d \qquad (5.40)$$

Condition 5.40 can be defined as the "solvency rule" of the central banker. If the central bank wants to safeguard the "average" solvency of firms, it must set an interest rate lower or at most equal to the rate emerging from Equation 5.40. This rule is very similar to the equation describing the Taylor "rule" (Equation 5.31). In both, the central bank sets the interest rate i as a function of π and g_d. Nonetheless, beyond this formal similarity, the two rules have very different meanings: the "Taylor rule" describes the central bank as pursuing the general goal of stability of production and inflation close to the natural equilibrium.

The "solvency rule" describes instead the central banker as the "regulator" of a conflict between solvent capitals and potentially insolvent capitals. The right part of the equation clearly describes the "average" profit of firms. Some of them will get a profit higher than average, some others will get a profit lower than average. The "rule" allows the determination of the interest rate that guarantees the solvency "on average". This implies the following: if the central banker sets an interest rate lower than the "average" level identified by Equation 5.40, firms in trouble (characterized by relatively lower profits) will have more possibilities to be solvent. On the contrary, if the interest rate set by the central bank is higher than the level identified by Equation 5.40, there will be more bankruptcies, whereas solvent firms that remain in the market will be greatly advantaged, even being able to acquire their competitors' assets as they are hedging towards insolvency or they are already completely insolvent.

Critical theory thus shows us a monetary policy rule that questions the ability of the central banker to act as a stabilizer of production and inflation, while underlining his or her role as a regulator of social conflict. Most notably, we are referring here to the regulation of those conflicts between solvent firms and potentially insolvent firms, which can give rise to acquisitions (the former buying the latter) generating a process defined by Marx as "centralization of capitals".[9]

5.4   SUSTAINABILITY OF PUBLIC DEBT

In the political arena, a most debated issue concerns the sustainability of public finance, or the assessment of the possibility for the government to finance public spending by borrowing from private citizens. Blanchard deals with the topic in the final part of his textbook. In order to analyze the issue from a critical perspective, we shall start by defining the annual public deficit as the difference between annual public expenditures and annual fiscal revenues. When a government is in a situation of public deficit, it can finance its spending in excess of revenues in two different ways. First, it can borrow money from private agents by selling assets of public debt (a typical example is treasury bonds). In such a situation, new assets will be issued: they are defined here with the term ΔB. On the other hand, it can create money, that is the central bank can mint banknotes; in this case, the supply of money will increase, and this is identified by ΔM. In principle, given a certain level of public deficit, it is possible to finance it either with a corresponding variation of the public debt or of the quantity of money, or with a mix of the two: thus, we can write that $G{-}T = \Delta B + \Delta M$. However, in some countries and in the European Economic and Monetary Union, the central bank is prevented from financing public deficit with a direct emission of

---

[9]   For empirical tests comparing the different rules of monetary policy which have been examined, refer to E. Brancaccio, G. Fontana, M. Lopreite and R. Realfonzo, (2016) "Monetary policy rules and directions of causality: A test for the Euro Area", *Journal of Post Keynesian Economics 38(4)*, 509–531 and E. Brancaccio, A. Califano, M. Lopreite and A. Moneta (2020), "Nonperforming loans and competing rules of monetary policy: A statistical identification approach", *Structural Change and Economic Dynamics 53*, 127–136.

money. In these cases, $\Delta M = 0$ and the only way to finance public debt is through issuing brand new assets: $\Delta B = G - T$.

It is now worth mentioning that public spending is made up of two components. First, the part needed for the public administration to work, for services and defence to be financed, the health service, education, and so on, defined as primary public spending. This is usually labelled by G. The other component corresponds to debt servicing, that is, the amount given by the interest to pay on the stock of debt accumulated so far, which the government must pay to those who purchased assets in the past and now require the payment of the interest. This can be expressed as rB_{t-1}, where B_{t-1} represents the stock of public debt of the preceding period and r is the interest rate that is to be paid to those holding the assets (remember that r is the interest rate net of inflation; here, it is used in the place of the monetary interest rate i since in this section all variables are expressed in real terms). Then, given these premises, we can write again the definition of public deficit as follows:

$$\Delta B_t = G_t - T_t + rB_{t-1} \tag{5.41}$$

If the flow of public deficit ΔB_t is financed by borrowing (with the emission of brand new assets on the market), this will obviously entail an increase of the stock of total public debt accumulated in the previous years, which corresponds to the total amount of circulating assets. If we define with B_t the stock of public debt in the current year t, we can write the following definition of total public debt:

$$B_t = \Delta B_t + B_{t-1} \tag{5.42}$$

This is simple accounting and it tells us that the stock of public debt of the current year is given by the stock of public debt of the previous year plus the flow of new public deficit created this year. As we know, the annual public deficit is given by $\Delta B_t = G_t - T_t + rB_{t-1}$, so by substituting ΔB_t, we can write the accounting expression of public debt as follows:

$$B_t = B_{t-1} + rB_{t-1} + G_t - T_t \tag{5.43}$$

From which:

$$B_t = (1+r)B_{t-1} + G_t - T_t \tag{5.44}$$

where the term $G_t - T_t$ is called primary balance, and corresponds either to a primary deficit if $G_t > T_t$ or to a primary surplus if $G_t < T_t$.

A much debated question concerns the sustainability of public debt. Will the government be able to repay what it borrowed and to pay the relative interest demanded by creditors? Is there a level beyond which public debt is unsustainable and the government has to declare its insolvency? What should the government do to avoid a risk of insolvency? Should it reduce public spending and increase taxation in order to accelerate the repayment to creditors, or would this action generate a recession and make the situation even worse? There are no easy answers. The issue of public debt is a complex one, which should not be addressed through commonplaces. For instance, as we will see, cutting expenditures and raising taxes *per se* does not necessarily make public debt sustainable. Before coming to any sort of conclusion, though, we shall define the concept of sustainability of public debt. Among the possible criteria used by economists there is the comparison of debt with income, that is, to consider the debt sustainable only if it does not grow indefinitely with respect to the level of production, hence income, of the considered country. In other words, public debt can be considered sustainable if the ratio between public debt and GDP tends towards a stationary equilibrium, i.e. if B_t/Y_t tends towards a constant value.

In analytical terms, we must first divide the terms of the equation of public debt by the level of production Y_t. We will have:

$$\frac{B_t}{Y_t} = (1 + r)\frac{B_{t-1}}{Y_t} + \frac{G_t - T_t}{Y_t} \tag{5.45}$$

Then, we multiply and divide the first member of the right side of the equation by Y_{t-1}. This simple step leads us to:

$$\frac{B_t}{Y_t} = (1 + r)\frac{B_{t-1}}{Y_{t-1}}\frac{Y_{t-1}}{Y_t} + \frac{G_t - T_t}{Y_t} \tag{5.46}$$

The relationship between production at time t and production at time $t-1$ corresponds to the real growth rate, that is, $Y_t/Y_{t-1} = 1 + g$. Thus, the equation can be written as follows:

$$\frac{B_t}{Y_t} = \frac{(1 + r)}{(1 + g)}\frac{B_{t-1}}{Y_{t-1}} + \frac{G_t - T_t}{Y_t} \tag{5.47}$$

As we already know, r and g express values that are usually lower than 0.1 (for instance a 5 per cent interest rate net of inflation corresponds to $r = 0.05$ while a 2.5 per cent real growth rate of production corresponds to $g = 0.025$). It means that terms such as rg and g^2 are close to 0. Thus, with a certain degree of approximation,[10] it can be written that:

$$\frac{(1+r)}{(1+g)} = 1 + r - g \tag{5.48}$$

The equation of public debt thus becomes:

$$\frac{B_t}{Y_t} = \frac{(1+r-g)B_{t-1}}{Y_{t-1}} + \frac{G_t - T_t}{Y_t} \tag{5.49}$$

It is worth noting that the ratio between debt and GDP depends on the value that the same ratio assumed in the previous period, multiplied by the term in parentheses, plus a constant represented by the ratio between the primary balance and GDP. In mathematical terms, this is a first order differential equation, which corresponds in general terms to the definition provided by the equation $y_t = \beta y_{t-1} + \alpha$.

A question now arises: which is the stationary equilibrium in the ratio between public debt and GDP? In other words, which value of B_t/Y_t makes the ratio constant? To get the answer, just modify Equation 5.49 by bringing $(1)(B_{t-1}/Y_{t-1})$ on the left-hand side:

$$\frac{B_t}{Y_t} - \frac{B_{t-1}}{Y_{t-1}} = \frac{(r-g)B_{t-1}}{Y_{t-1}} + \frac{G_t - T_t}{Y_t} \tag{5.50}$$

The stationary equilibrium corresponds to a debt over GDP ratio constant in time, or $B_t/Y_t - B_{t-1}/Y_{t-1} = 0$. A further simple step brings to the stationary equilibrium condition of public debt over GDP ratio:

$$\frac{T_t - G_t}{Y_t} = \frac{(r-g)B_{t-1}}{Y_t} \tag{5.51}$$

This latter formulation highlights that a stable stationary equilibrium depends on the difference between the rate of interest net of inflation and the growth rate. If $r > g$ then the right side is positive, meaning that the left side needs to be positive as well if we want the equilibrium condition to hold, that is, $T_t > G_t$. In other words, what is needed is a primary surplus, that is, an excess of fiscal revenues over primary public expenditures. When $r < g$ instead, it is possible to maintain the stationary equilibrium condition even with $T_t < G_t$. It is then possible to have a stationary equilibrium in the public debt over GDP ratio even in a situation of primary deficit, when public expenditures exceed fiscal revenues.

---

[10]   As a matter of fact, $(1 + r - g)(1 + g) = 1 + r - g + g + rg - g^2$. Given that r and g are usually lower than 0.1, we can safely assume rg and g^2 to be negligible. By simplification, we get $(1 + r - g)(1 + g) = (1 + r)$, from which $(1 + r - g) = (1 + r)/(1 + g)$.

The sign of the term $(r - g)$ is thus decisive to assess if a condition of stationary equilibrium requires a primary surplus or can also be obtained in a situation of primary public deficit. Obviously, the total amount of the public debt over GDP ratio (B_{t-1}/Y_{t-1}) plays a role in determining the stationary state. However, it is a limited role, as this ratio is typically positive and therefore cannot modify the sign of the left-hand side of the equation, that is, of the primary balance. By the way, this means that if $r > g$, the stationary equilibrium will always require an excess of fiscal revenues over primary public expenditures, even in the case of a significant "cut-off" of the public debt to GDP ratio.

We have just defined the condition of the stationary equilibrium of public debt to GDP ratio, but the sustainability condition requires this ratio to tend towards equilibrium over time. How can we assess if there actually is a tendency towards equilibrium? This question of dynamic economics can be tackled in many ways. We propose a graphical solution (Figures 5.2 and 5.3). In our chart, we traced the public debt to GDP ratio at time t–1 on the horizontal axis; the same ratio relative to time t has been traced on the vertical axis. The 45-degree line has then been traced, characterized by an angular coefficient equal to 1: it describes all the points where B_t/Y_t matches B_{t-1}/Y_{t-1}, hence where the condition for the stationary equilibrium is satisfied.

The line describing the usual formulation of the public debt equation has also been drawn:

$$\frac{B_t}{Y_t} = \frac{(1+r-g)B_{t-1}}{Y_{t-1}} + \frac{G_t - T_t}{Y_t} \qquad (5.52)$$

The line describing this equation is the public debt line, it will have $(1 + r - g)$ as angular coefficient and the primary balance as its intercept on the vertical axis (point D in Figures 5.2 and 5.3). Point E, where the 45 degree line and the public debt line cross, corresponds to the stationary equilibrium.

Let us first consider a scenario where the interest rate is higher than the rate of growth of production, $r > g$; we also assume the presence of a primary surplus, that is, fiscal revenues greater than primary expenditures: $(G_t - T_t)/Y_t < 0$. The debt equation therefore will be represented by a straight line with an angular coefficient $1 + r - g$ greater than 1, i.e. greater than the coefficient of the 45-degree line. Moreover, because of a primary surplus, the line will cross the vertical axis at negative values (point D in Figure 5.2). In this scenario, it can be easily verified that the equilibrium is unstable, even in the presence of a primary surplus. Starting from the debt to GDP ratio identified by point 1 on the horizontal axis, using the debt line to transpose it on the vertical axis we will get the debt to GDP ratio of the next period, identified by point 2. Moving from there to the

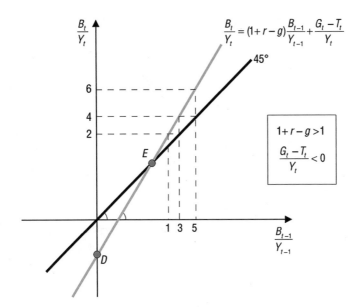

$$\frac{B_t}{Y_t} = (1 + r - g)\frac{B_{t-1}}{Y_{t-1}} + \frac{G_t - T_t}{Y_t}$$

Figure 5.2   Unstable equilibrium even with a primary surplus

45-degree line and using it to transpose on the horizontal axis, we get to point 3, describing the value of the debt in the next period. Repeating the transposition through the debt line we get to point 4, and so on and so forth. Over time, the debt to GDP ratio will clearly move further away from the stationary equilibrium situated in point E. Although taxation exceeds primary public spending, in this scenario the debt to GDP ratio is unstable and it does not converge towards stationary equilibrium: on the contrary, it tends to explode.

Let us consider a different setting. Now the production growth rate is greater than the rate of interest, or $r < g$; we further assume a primary deficit, that is, $(G_t - T_t)/Y_t > 0$. In this situation, the debt equation will have an angular coefficient $(1 + r - g)$ lower than 1, so the slope of the line will be inferior to the slope of the 45-degree line; moreover, the interception on the vertical axis will be positive (point D in Figure 5.3).

In this case, the equilibrium is stable, even if there is a primary deficit. Starting from the debt to GDP ratio identified by point 1, it can be observed that the values assumed in the next periods (2, 3, 4, 5, 6, and so on) tend to the stationary equilibrium. Thus, if economic growth is greater than the interest to pay on the debt, it is possible to have a debt to GDP ratio that tends towards a stable equilibrium even if primary spending is greater than fiscal revenues.

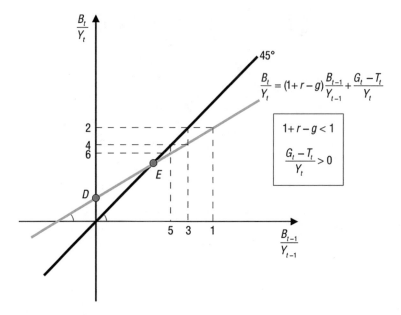

Figure 5.3   Stable equilibrium even with a primary deficit

The student can now verify what happens in other possible scenarios, for instance when the interest rate is greater than the growth rate, and there is a primary deficit at the same time.

We have reached a preliminary conclusion: sacrifices such as public spending cuts and tax rises are not necessarily effective for the sustainability of public debt; it would be better to keep the interest rate lower than the growth rate of production. Would every economist agree to this statement? Blanchard and the mainstream exponents would probably not agree. They claim that, in the long run, the rate of interest r and the growth in production g are determined by the natural equilibrium of the economic system. Such equilibrium, in Blanchard's view, usually corresponds to a situation in which $r > g$: in his book, he describes the case of a negative difference $r - g$ as "exotic". Furthermore, the mainstream exponents insist that once the natural equilibrium level of r and g are reached, these variables cannot be altered by monetary or fiscal policy decisions. Critical economists deny instead the very concept of natural equilibrium: they advocate that fiscal and monetary policies affect g and r respectively, as they could contribute to boosting the first and curtailing the second to make public debt sustainable without necessarily imposing sacrifices connected with primary budget cuts and increases in taxation.

For example, as the reader will remember, the critical approach disputes the idea that the mark-up, the real wage and the rate of interest itself in the long run tend towards defined levels of "natural equilibrium". According to critical theory, if certain conditions occur, the central bank can target a significant reduction of the rate of interest, perhaps with the goal of pushing the difference $r - g$ below zero, this way helping the sustainability of public debt. Accordingly, the exponents of the critical approach claim that a "natural" level of production to be reached in the long run does not exist. This means that government fiscal policy can affect production even in the long run, both on its level Y and its growth rate g. This can be verified by recalling the Keynesian equation for the determination of the equilibrium level of production that can be found on the first pages of Blanchard's textbook. As we know, this equation determines the equilibrium level of production based on the product between the multiplier and autonomous expenditure:

$$Y = \frac{1}{1 - c_1} (c_0 + G + I - c_1 T) \tag{5.53}$$

We assume for the sake of simplicity autonomous consumption and investment to be null, and public spending and taxation to have the same multiplicative effect on production. In addition, we consider that the difference $G_t - T_t$ corresponds to primary public deficit, which can be identified by D_t. Thus, the equation of the equilibrium level of production can be written in these terms:

$$Y_t = \frac{1}{1 - c_1} D_t \tag{5.54}$$

We know that the growth of production is defined by the following expression:

$$g = \frac{Y_t - Y_{t-1}}{Y_{t-1}} AAA \tag{5.55}$$

By substituting the equilibrium production equation and simplifying the term $[1/(1 - c_1)]$, we obtain:

$$g = \frac{D_t - D_{t-1}}{D_{t-1}} \tag{5.56}$$

By defining primary public deficit growth with the term $d = (D_t - D_{t-1})/D_{t-1}$ we reach the conclusion that $g = d$. That is, the annual growth of production corresponds to the annual growth of primary public deficit. This implies that an increase of the deficit d can determine an increase of g able to reduce the term $(r - g)$ and even to make it negative. Although elementary and depending on a set of simplifying hypotheses, this result gives rise to a counterintuitive consideration: a policy that tends to increase public deficit may contribute to increasing production to the point of favouring the sustainability of the ratio between public debt and production.

In conclusion, in the view of the exponents of the critical paradigm, monetary and fiscal policy contribute to determining the long run performance of the term $r - g$, even to the point of making it negative. Therefore, such policies can favour the convergence of public debt towards stationary equilibrium and can turn this equilibrium into a situation where primary public spending is greater than fiscal revenues.[11]

5.5   HYSTERESIS OF UNEMPLOYMENT

The phenomenon of "hysteresis" takes place when the values of a variable depend on the values that the same variable assumed in previous periods: a given value assumed by a variable is therefore persistent over time.

In the framework of the mainstream, hysteresis is mentioned for instance when, following a crisis or a contractionary policy, the rate of unemployment suddenly shoots up and then goes back to its "natural" equilibrium very slowly (or even does not go back). Among the best known studies of this phenomenon we can find the hysteresis model by Blanchard and Summers.[12] Originally, the model was aimed at explaining the persistency of high unemployment in Europe in the 1980s and in the 1990s, then it found other applications as well.

The model by Blanchard and Summers is based on the hypothesis that the labour market is divided into two groups of workers: insiders and outsiders. The former consists of employed, unionized and skilled workers; the latter of non-unionized workers, low skilled, often unemployed. A relevant hypothesis in Blanchard and Summers' treatment of the matter is that outsiders, although unemployed, may not be able to get a job, even if demanding a wage that is lower than that of the insiders. The reason is

---

[11]   On the critical approach to the issues connected with public deficit and debt, see (among the others) L. Pasinetti (1997), "The social 'burden' of high interest rates", in P. Arestis, G. Palma and M. Sawyer (eds), *Capital Controversy, Post-Keynesian Economics and the History of Economic Thought vol. I*, London, UK: Routledge. See also L. Pasinetti (1998), "The myth (or folly) of the 3 per cent deficit-GDP Maastricht 'parameter'", *Cambridge Journal of Economics 22(1)*, 103–116.

[12]   The original paper is O. Blanchard and L. Summers (1986), "Hysteresis and the European unemployment problem", *NBER Macroeconomics Annual 1*, 15–78, and a didactic version was also included in some editions (American and international) of Blanchard's textbook.

that firms might find it unattractive to substitute insiders with outsiders, due to the high cost needed to fire the former and train the latter. The idea at the basis of the model is that, after a shock, unemployment increases and then persists over time, because workers expelled from the productive process rapidly become outsiders: they lose bargaining power, hence become unable to modify the real wage obtained by insiders. Consequently, although unemployment is higher, no process of reduction of wage and prices is activated, therefore demand and production do not recover.

Let us analyze the hysteresis model in detail. To simplify, we assume labour productivity to be $A = 1$ and the mark-up to be $\mu = 0$. We also assume aggregate demand and production Y to linearly depend only on the real quantity of money (we neglect public spending, taxation, and so on). Thus, recalling the equations typical of Blanchard's standard macroeconomic model:

$$Y = AN$$
$$P = \frac{(1+\mu)W}{A} \tag{5.57}$$
$$Y = f\left(G, T, \frac{M}{P}\right)$$

it is noticeable that the hysteresis model uses more elementary equations:

$$Y = N$$
$$P = W \tag{5.58}$$
$$Y = \frac{M}{P}$$

We express the equations in logarithmic terms for the sake of simplicity: the purpose is to change ratios into differences. Just recall that the natural logarithm of a ratio is equal to the difference of the logarithms. For instance, $ln(X/Y) = lnX - lnY$. We identify the logarithms with lowercase letters, $ln(X/Y) = x - y$. The equations can thus be written as follows:

$$y = n \tag{5.59}$$

$$p = w \tag{5.60}$$

$$y = m - p \tag{5.61}$$

As usual, also in this model the equilibrium in the goods market corresponds to the equilibrium between demand and production. Thus, first we substitute Equation 5.60 into Equation 5.61, and then we equalize Equation 5.59 and Equation 5.61:

$$n = m - w \qquad (5.62)$$

The equation is well-known. If monetary wage rises, prices increase as well, the real quantity of money shrinks, the supply of assets grows, their price decreases, the interest rate rises and investment falls and so do demand, production and employment. If the quantity of money increases instead, demand, production and employment rise as well.

Let us assume, for the sake of simplicity, that workers succeed in imposing the desired monetary wage. Which level of w will they choose? As it is clear from Equation 5.62, in the mainstream model by Blanchard and Summers the monetary wage chosen by workers affects prices, the real quantity of money, aggregate demand, production and hence employment. Obviously, when workers set the monetary wage they do not know what the central bank's decision will be with regard to the quantity of money m. Nonetheless, they can formulate an expectation m^e on it. Given this expectation, workers can forecast the level of employment n^e matching each level of monetary wage they can choose:

$$n^e = m^e - w \qquad (5.63)$$

It is necessary to analyze the concept of the target employment for the workers, in order to understand the monetary wage set by workers. The key element is the existence of a conflict between employed insiders and unemployed outsiders concerning the target employment. The former want to set a high wage, even if this implies low demand and production and hence prevents the absorption of unemployed outsiders. The latter prefer instead a lower wage, able to increase demand and production, thus favouring their inclusion. Let us start from the description of two extreme situations: a scenario where unemployed outsiders can exercise a downward pressure on wage so as to determine an increase in demand and production capable of guaranteeing them a job. At the other end of the spectrum, there is a situation where insiders have total control over the determination of wage, so that during the bargaining process they will demand a wage associated with a level of demand and production that guarantees their employment only. In the first scenario, outsiders are absorbed, as wage is such that expected employment is equal to the level of full employment: $n^e = n^*$. In the second, outsiders do not affect the outcome of the bargaining at all. In this case wage will guarantee only the employment of insiders already employed in the previous period ($n^e = n_{t-1}$). The scenarios just described are extreme. Blanchard and Summers argue that outsiders are never able to set the wage, and insiders never have total control of it. A mixed situation is more likely, one in which the monetary wage set by workers is such as to determine an expected employment n^e dependent both on the number of insiders n_{t-1} and on the expected number of outsiders ($n^* - n^e$):

$$n^e = n_{t-1} + \alpha(n^* - n^e) \tag{5.64}$$

The term α is an indicator of the bargaining power of the insiders: the lower α is, the stronger insiders are, and the less influence the outsiders have in the determination of wage and hence of expected employment n^e. Solving for n^e we get:

$$(1 + \alpha)n^e = n_{t-1} + \alpha n^*$$
$$n^e = \left(\frac{1}{1+\alpha}\right)n_{t-1} + \left(\frac{\alpha}{1+\alpha}\right)n^* \tag{5.65}$$

We introduce now the γ parameter, that is $\gamma = 1/(1 + \alpha)$; thus we also have that $(1 - \gamma) = \alpha/(1 + \alpha)$. As it is inversely correlated with α, the parameter γ can be seen as the index of the bargaining power of insiders. Please note that γ represents a share, thus it is always between 0 and 1. If insiders do not have power, then α is very high and γ tends to 0. On the contrary, if insiders are powerful, α tends to 0 and γ tends to 1. The expected employment equation can thus be written as:

$$n^e = \gamma n_{t-1} + (1 - \gamma)n^* \tag{5.66}$$

If $\gamma = 0$, insiders will not have power and outsiders will succeed in lowering wage to the point that expected employment is equal to full employment: $n^e = n^*$. Instead, if $\gamma = 1$, insiders will have total control and will thus impose a wage that determines their employment only, that is, the same employment as the previous period: $n^e = n_{t-1}$.

Now, by substituting Equation 5.66 into Equation 5.63 and solving for w, we get the general equilibrium wage:

$$w = m^e - \gamma n_{t-1} - (1 - \gamma)n^* \tag{5.67}$$

By substituting Equation 5.67 in Equation 5.62, we determine the effective employment of equilibrium n:

$$n = \gamma n_{t-1} + (1-\gamma)n^* + (m - m^e) \tag{5.68}$$

The equation makes clear that the existence (or non-existence) of the hysteresis depends on the bargaining power of insiders, that is, on their capacity to prevent downward pressure of outsiders on monetary wage. Generally, the clash between insiders and outsiders does result in a mixed outcome, with the power of insiders γ in between 0 and 1. Extreme cases help nonetheless in understanding the key features of the model. For instance, if insiders are powerless ($\gamma = 0$), then:

$$n = n^* + (m - m^e) \tag{5.69}$$

It is a situation in which effective employment departs from full employment only following unexpected monetary policy decisions. When the monetary policy shock is absorbed, though, the quantity of expected money will match effective money and employment will suddenly go back to full employment. There is no hysteresis there. If instead $\gamma = 1$ and insiders retain full power, outsiders will have no influence at all on wage, hence:

$$n = n_{t-1} + (m - m^e) \tag{5.70}$$

Wage is completely determined by hysteresis here. In the absence of a monetary policy shock, employment only depends on history. It is worth noticing that in this second scenario "natural" equilibrium loses importance: indeed, there is not a "natural" level of employment towards which the economic system tends to go back. However, the absence of a "natural" equilibrium is not derived from a critique of the theoretical pillars of the mainstream. It is simply explained by the thesis that the power of unionized insiders prevents the market from functioning correctly: it prevents the reduction of monetary wage following an increase of unemployment. As a matter of fact, Blanchard and Summers' model prescribes that the power of insiders should be curtailed to avoid hysteresis, as this would allow outsider unemployed workers to put downward pressure on wage. This model has been largely adopted as an explanation for persistent unemployment through the 1980s and 1990s. The model was used to claim that unemployment would have shrunk and the economy would have got back to the path of full employment, if only the power of European workers' unions had been resized, e.g. through the reduction of workers' protection against dismissals.

Blanchard and Summers' analysis can be criticized. First, one can see that Equation 5.61 of the model assumes the curve of aggregate demand AD to be downward sloping with respect to price: a fall in price brings about a rise in demand for goods and thus in production and employment.

As we have already shown, there may not be a univocal relationship between prices and aggregate demand. This relationship can even be positive instead of negative – decreasing prices may cause a fall in demand instead of a surge. Furthermore, the model's Equation 5.60 assumes that the bargaining of monetary wage will not influence the "natural" equilibrium level of real wage, which in the model is fixed as equal to 1 for simplicity ($P = W$, hence $W/P = 1$). This hypothesis does not hold when the real wage is thought to be influenced by the distributive conflict between firms and workers. A further controversial element of the model is the following: it is argued that the difference between outsiders and insiders is that the latter may set a monetary wage higher than desired by the former. There is no obvious reason for this goal, as a higher monetary wage has no effect whatsoever on real wage by assumption.

5.6 WAGE COMPETITION BETWEEN COUNTRIES IN THE FRAMEWORK OF AN OPEN ECONOMY

Until now we have compared Blanchard's mainstream model and the critical model under the hypothesis of an economy closed to foreign exchanges, which is acceptable only as a first approximation. The analysis would be more complete if we considered the many implications deriving from opening an economy to foreign exchanges, hence to free circulation of international capitals, goods and workers. The topic is extremely relevant: Blanchard devotes a wide section of his book to the issues of the open economy. Here, we will just focus on a few aspects related to the international competition on wages, which is the attempt of each country to curtail wages at home in order to reduce costs and prices, increase national goods competitiveness and thus conquer foreign markets. For this purpose, we will consider an economy that is open but greatly simplified. We consider an economic system made up of two countries only. We assume investments I to be given. Moreover, we rely again on the hypothesis of marginal propensities to consume that are different between social classes (as described in the section devoted to the interpretations of the crisis): for the sake of simplicity, we assume that capitalists save all their profits while workers consume their entire wage. In real terms we will thus have that $C = (W/P)N$. As usual, the production function is given by $Y = AN$ and the total number of workers corresponds to $N = Y/A$; we can thus write that $C = (W/P)(Y/A)$. Finally, we assume net export (the difference between export and import) to be identified by the following expression:

$$NX = X - mY + n/\in \qquad (5.71)$$

where m and n are exogenous parameters. The X term identifies export, which depends on the decisions of the foreign country so can be considered exogenous. Import mY depends instead on domestic income. Lastly, there is the term n/ϵ, which summarizes the relative competitiveness of the given country, which depends on the real exchange rate $\epsilon = EP/P^*$, where P^* is the price level of the foreign country. Let us also assume that the two countries form a monetary union: they have a single currency, so the nominal exchange rate corresponds to $E = 1$. The real exchange rate becomes $\epsilon = P/P^*$. Let us now define the macroeconomic equilibrium of production and demand as $Y = C + I + NX$. We substitute and rearrange and we obtain:

$$Y = \frac{1}{1+m-\left(\dfrac{W/P}{A}\right)}\left(I + X + \frac{nP^*}{P}\right) \tag{5.72}$$

In the light of this equation, let us examine the possible effects of a tougher international competition on wages. The country in question is supposed to implement a set of policies reducing workers' bargaining power (z) to increase its relative competitiveness. As the monetary wage is dependent on z, then W also decreases. Moreover, we know the price level of goods is given by $P = (1 + \mu)W/A$. Assuming that productivity A is constant and firms do not take advantage of the situation and hence leave the mark-up μ untouched, we will see P reducing proportionally with respect to W. In such a situation, the effect of wage competition is positive: W/P remains unaltered, so the multiplier does not change. Furthermore, the fall in P increases the component nP^*/P of demand pushing national production Y up.

However, this result has been obtained assuming that the foreign country does not react to the wage competition policy implemented by the home country. In fact, it is reasonable to expect some sort of reaction. For instance, if we assume that foreign wage W^* and foreign goods price P^* experience a fall equal to that of home wage W and prices P, relative competitiveness will not change, so that nP^*/P remains unchanged and there is no increase in production Y. In this case, wage competition will not affect production. However, we have relied until now on Blanchard's model's hypothesis of a fixed mark-up μ. If we switch to the framework of the alternative model, we can imagine that a reduction of the parameter z, thus of the monetary wage W, would bring firms to take advantage of the situation hence increasing μ: the price level P will decrease less than proportionally with respect to W. The real wage W/P will reduce accordingly. But given that consumption is generated by the total amount of wage, the fall of W/P entails a reduction of the multiplier, a fall in demand and hence in production. Further than that, if we imagine a similar dynamic to take place in the foreign country, then foreign production and income will decrease as well and thus export X towards the foreign country will fall, yielding a further contraction of national production. In this situation, wage competition will have depressive effects on both the home economy and the foreign economy.

For how rudimentary and limited this result may be, it is an interesting outcome: it shows that an international "free market" does not necessarily have positive effects on national economies. Unless the involved countries establish a coordination to avoid a wage race to the bottom, they run the risk of a depression of demand and production. Indeed, a country might be tempted to oppose the contractionary effects of such competition through uncoordinated behaviours or even through a reduction in the degree of openness of its home economy. Uncoordinated behaviour might lead to the collapse of the monetary union. A country subject to a continuous loss of competitiveness towards foreign countries might decide at some point to give up the single currency and devalue its national currency. In this case, the nominal exchange rate E becomes less than 1, so the real exchange rate $\epsilon = E/P^*$ falls, making the home economy more competitive. An even more drastic case may concern the introduction of a certain degree of protectionism in a given country, that is, a reduction in the openness of that country to global exchanges.

5.7 FINANCIAL GLOBALIZATION, TOBIN TAX AND CAPITAL CONTROLS

Still in the framework of an open economy we will now deal with a few issues related to international capital movements. A first element to consider concerns the scope for implementing expansionary monetary policies aimed at reducing interest rates. This possibility, as we shall see, is considerably reduced when there is free international movement of capital. In fact, financial markets agents on the world market are constantly looking for financial assets that ensure the highest returns. In the post-war period, the search for high-yield assets was limited by rules that placed strict limitations on the movement of capital from one country to another. However, over the years these constraints have been gradually removed. Therefore, in most of the world there is today a situation of free movement of capital, sometimes defined with the term "financial globalization". In the extreme hypothesis in which any limitation to free movement is abolished, we speak of perfect international capital mobility. In this scenario, capital holders try to move their wealth to those countries that guarantee the greatest benefits, and, in particular, to those that provide interest rates higher than the others. Capital movements stop only when assets of all countries offer the same return, net of expected changes in the exchange rate. The condition under which capital movements are interrupted, which therefore brings the markets into equilibrium, is called arbitrage condition or uncovered parity condition of interest rates. Blanchard tells us that this condition is given by:

$$1 + i_t = (1 + i_t^*) \frac{E_t}{E_{t+1}^e} \qquad (5.73)$$

in which the left side describes the yield i obtained by purchasing domestic assets, while the right side describes the yield i^* deriving from the purchase of foreign assets. This latter is calculated by including any changes in the nominal exchange rate E.[13] As long as the left side is smaller than the right side of the equation it is better to move capital abroad and buy foreign assets, which yield more. Conversely, if the left side is greater, it is better to keep capital at home. Therefore, if the central bank wants to avoid capital flight abroad, it must always set a domestic interest rate capable of respecting the uncovered parity condition, given the prevailing rate abroad and the expected exchange rate.

We can use a numerical example to clarify the terms of the problem. Assuming that the current exchange rate is given by $E_t = \$1.02/€1$, that the expected exchange rate is $E_{t+1}^e = \$1/€1$, and that the interest rate on the US bond is $i^* = 0.03$ (i.e. 3 per cent), we calculate the interest rate i that the European Central Bank will have to set to avoid capital outflows abroad:

$$1 + i_t = (1 + 0.03) \frac{1.02}{1} \qquad (5.74)$$

It follows that the interest rate necessary in the EU to avoid capital flight to the United States must be at least equal to $i_t = 0.050$ (i.e. 5 per cent). It should be noted that this is a higher interest than the US one, which by hypothesis is equal to 3 per cent. In this example, the reason why the European Central Bank has to set a rate higher than the Fed, if it wants to avoid capital flight, is that market agents expect a depreciation of the euro, that is a loss in value against the dollar. This forecast incentivizes financial agents to move capitals to the United States. To induce them to leave their

---

[13]   The assumption here is that the nominal exchange rate E is defined as the price of the national currency in terms of the foreign currency: also, by "national" or "domestic" we mean the EU, while by "abroad" or "foreign" we mean the United States. That is, from the point of view of us Europeans, we define the exchange rate as the price of one euro in terms of dollars. Newer versions of Blanchard's manual use this convention. If instead the alternative definition of the exchange rate is used (the price of the foreign currency in terms of national currency), then the parity condition must be reversed.

capital in Europe, the European interest rate must therefore be higher than the US one so as to compensate the expected loss due to the depreciation in the exchange rate. The opposite would occur if an appreciation of the euro was expected: in this case the ECB would respect the parity condition even with an interest rate lower than the US one.

Beyond the specific example, the need to respect the condition of uncovered parity of the interest rates constitutes a serious obstacle for national economic policy, and in particular for central banks' monetary policy. If they reduce the interest rate this may cause capital outflows. Thus, on many occasions, the central banks of countries going through economic crises or burdened with growing public debts not only have not been able to reduce interest rates to try to stimulate the economy or stabilize the debt, but even had to increase them to avoid capital flight. Such constraints on expansionary monetary policy caused by the risk of capital flight have taken on dramatic importance in many situations of currency and economic crises. In the 1990s, we had currency crises and capital flight in Europe, Asia and Latin America. This has been happening again in the last two decades, also in Europe. Proposals have been raised to try to give individual countries greater freedom of manoeuvre in monetary policy, and the reintroduction of limits on global circulation of capital was suggested. A well-known proposal in this regard is the so-called Tobin tax, named after the Nobel laureate in economics James Tobin, who proposed it for the first time in 1972. It is a tax on all currency exchanges aimed at making it expensive, hence disincentivizing the movements of capital between countries. According to Tobin, this tax would reduce international speculative movements of capital and would give greater room for manoeuvre to monetary policy.

Here is an example: let us suppose that Europe is going through a phase of crisis and growth in public debt. The European Central Bank may want to intervene with monetary expansion, in order to reduce interest rates. If we assume that the situation is the one described in the previous example, the interest rate needed to avoid capital flight is 5 per cent. However, addressing the crisis and debt problems would require a further reduction of the internal interest rate. Could the introduction of a Tobin tax make this policy viable? We must change the interest rates' uncovered parity condition as follows, in order to contemplate the tax. The purchase of a US bond involves the following steps: first the conversion from euro to dollar, then the purchase of the bond and finally, on the expiry date of it, the conversion from dollar to euro of the profit obtained. The Tobin tax, as a tax on currency transactions, will be applied at the time of the initial conversion from euro to dollar, and at the time of the final conversion from dollar to euro. Given that t is the tax rate applied to each conversion, the uncovered parity condition can be represented in a simplified version as follows:

$$1 + i_t = (1 + i_t^*) \frac{E_t}{E_{t+1}^e} (1 - t) - t \qquad (5.75)$$

We insert now the numeric values of the example into the new parity condition. First imagine that the Tobin tax rate is set by the authorities at the level $t = 0.0075 = 0.75\%$. From the previous example, we also get the values of the US interest rate ($i^* = 0.03$) and the current and expected exchange rates (respectively $E_t = 1.02$ and $E^e_{t+1} = 1$). The only unknown is the domestic interest rate i_t, which represents the minimum rate needed to avoid capital flight.

$$1 + i_t = (1 + 0.03) \frac{1.02}{1} (1 - 0.0075) - 0.0075 \qquad (5.76)$$

Notice that thanks to the introduction of the Tobin tax, the domestic rate that avoids capital flight has been reduced to $i_t = 0.035 = 3.5\%$. Therefore a 0.75 per cent tax on all exchanges of euro against dollar and vice versa would make the movement of capital from one place to another expensive, thus allowing the European Central Bank to reduce the interest rate from the initial level of 5 per cent to the new level of 3.5 per cent, avoiding the risk of capital flight. We can also see it from the opposite perspective: in other words, suppose that the European Central Bank intends to calculate the tax rate t that allows it to keep the domestic rate at exactly the same level as the foreign interest rate of 3 per cent set by the Fed. Using the same data, and setting $i_t = i_t^* = 3\%$, it turns out that to keep the interest rates at the same level despite the expected devaluation of the euro, the Tobin tax rate should be set at $t = 0.01 = 1\%$.

The introduction of a global Tobin tax has been supported by many voices, both in academia and in politics. The European Commission, among others, has proposed its adoption. However, Tobin's original inspiration has been partially forgotten. Today, the introduction of this tax is supported not so much to disincentivize capital movements and therefore give greater autonomy to monetary policy, but rather to obtain tax revenue from financial transactions. Tobin himself was aware of the beneficial effects of using his tax for tax purposes as well, but he specified that this was only a positive side effect. The primary objective was to disincentivize capital movements to give central banks more autonomy in interest rates' policy. Furthermore, there is a potential conflict between disincentivizing capital movements and raising tax revenues: the former goal requires a high tax rate because it aims at reducing transactions, whereas the latter requires a lower rate since more transactions could imply higher tax revenues.[14] However, the Tobin tax has also been contested for other reasons beyond this. Neo-liberal economists have always considered it as an interference with the smooth functioning of free market forces. Some scholars belonging to critical schools of thought, on the other hand, believe that the Tobin tax represents too weak an instrument to counter the ceaseless movements of capital on world markets. According to this view, the simple use of a tax on capital movements is not enough to free monetary policy from the threat of capital flight. Rather, they should be subject to more rigid constraints, and even completely forbidden when it comes to short-term movements, as was already the case at the time of the strict controls in force after the war. Among the reasons why critical economists believe that capital movements should be more tightly constrained is that such shifts not only fuel speculative dynamics and make monetary policy more difficult, but have negative effects in general on the world economy. In fact, if capital can move freely from one country to another, it is obvious that they will move towards those countries that offer them the greatest economic gains. And such economic advantages could come from different sources: in effect, in conditions of free movement of capital, not only are countries forced to keep interest rates high in order to avoid capital flight, but will also compete with each other on many other grounds, especially on fiscal, financial and labour market regimes, in order to attract the maximum amount of financial resources. Governments might, for example, reduce social spending to reduce taxation; they might set low tax rates on capital holders; or guarantee banking secrecy to protect large capitals, introduce softer safety regulations in the workplace so to reduce costs for firms, impose strong constraints on the right to strike and on trade union organizations in order to contain wage claims, etc. – and all of this to induce capital owners to invest in their country. Such measures will tend to increase interest rates and profit margins in general at a global level, while they will probably lead to a reduction in wages and social expenditure.[15] In a nutshell, free movement of capital can induce countries to adopt policies

---

[14] It can be formalized this way: we define the Tobin tax rate with t, the international movement of capitals $M = a{-}bt$, and the tax revenue deriving from the Tobin tax with $G = tM$. Substituting, the revenue becomes: $G = t\,(a{-}bt) = at{-}bt^2$. If the goal is to maximize revenue, the optimal rate will be given by the maximization's first order condition: $dG/dt = 0$, that is $a{-}2bt = 0$, hence $t = a/2b$. If, on the other hand, the purpose is to minimize capital movements, then we impose $M = 0$ thus the rate must be $t = a/b$ (which is greater than $t = a/2b$).

[15] We addressed some of these issues in a direct comparison with controls on the movement of workers (migrations), in a recently published work: E. Brancaccio, A. Califano and F. De Cristofaro (2021), "Migrant inflows, capital outflows, growth and distribution: should we control capital rather than immigration?", *European Journal of Economics and Economic Policies – Intervention 18(3)*, 344–63. DOI: 10.4337/ejeep.2021.0074

favourable to the owners of capital, and often detrimental for workers. This is also why some economists have argued that markets' globalization would have led to some sort of "dictatorship of finance capital", since the interests of the owners of capital have a stronger impact on political decisions than in the past. In this perspective, restoring capital controls is seen as a means to reduce the influence on government decisions exercised by financial lobbies.

5.8   THE DISPUTE OVER THE CRISIS OF THE EUROPEAN ECONOMIC AND MONETARY UNION

The arbitrage condition, or uncovered parity condition of interest rates, also sheds light on the long (and structural) crisis of the European Economic and Monetary Union (EMU) and helps in comparing between two different interpretations: one that focuses on the problem of deficit and public debt, and the other that focuses instead on the different issue of deficit and debt to foreign countries, not only public but also private. The EMU (or "eurozone") crisis has been intense in many of the countries that have adopted the euro as their common currency. In particular, Portugal, Italy, Ireland, Greece and Spain, especially when the crisis hit hardest, recorded a tendency towards growing spreads between the interest rates on treasury bonds issued by these countries and the interest rates on bonds issued by Germany, the strongest country in the Union. Large spreads were recorded especially between 2010 and 2012, but every time that eurozone countries face economic or financial strains the spread with Germany's interest rates gets larger for the weaker countries. According to a widespread opinion, this spread is considered an index of lack of confidence by financial agents, sceptical on the sustainability of the deficit and public debt of these countries. If there is no confidence, investors demand higher interest rates as a form of insurance against the event of governments' bankruptcy.

   On closer inspection, the mentioned troubled countries are not very much alike in terms of public finances. Before the outbreak of the so-called "great recession" of 2008, their finances differed greatly. Taking 2007 as a reference, whereas Greece had a very high public deficit (–6.6 per cent of GDP), Italy and Portugal recorded relatively low public deficits, –1.5 per cent and –2.7 per cent respectively; and other countries such as Ireland and Spain recorded even annual public budget surplus, +0.05 per cent and +1.9 per cent respectively (Eurostat data). Therefore, it seems difficult to attribute the explosion of financial spreads in these countries to a shared problem of messy public finance. These countries, on the other hand, shared a common feature between them: namely the tendency to record deficits towards foreign countries. Taking again 2007 as a reference, the trade balance in relation to GDP is –2.4 per cent for Italy, –5.3 per cent for Ireland, –9.9 per cent for Spain, –10.1 per cent for Portugal and –14.3 per cent for Greece (Eurostat data). These countries were united, in other words, not so much by public spending in excess of tax revenues, but rather by the excess of imports with respect to exports to the rest of the world. That is, these countries tended to buy more than they sold to others, and therefore accumulated debts to foreign countries, not only public but also private.

Some economists predict that it is precisely because of this trend that these countries might at some point be forced to leave the euro. By leaving the euro area and returning to their national currencies, these troubled countries could try to propel production by resorting once again to the instrument of depreciation, which is now precluded by the single currency. The idea is that the return to national currencies and the connected depreciation policy could increase competitiveness, export and income, and therefore help these countries to cope with crises. Other economists cast doubts on the possibility that a return to the national currency and a consequent depreciation policy could increase competitiveness and improve the trade balance, but they think that these countries might still be forced to leave the euro for other reasons: trade deficit translates into foreign debt, hence an increase in the risk of banking crises and a growing need to finance troubled banks with cash. If the European Central Bank is unwilling to provide such cash, at some point each country might want to regain control of its currency, most notably to cover the insolvencies of its own banks.

In any case, both versions of this alternative interpretation of the European crisis see, in the tendency of some countries to accumulate trade deficits towards foreign countries, a possible explanation for the increase in bonds' spreads. This explanation can be presented by resorting again to the uncovered parity condition of the interest rates. As already seen, this is the condition for the yield of domestic bonds be equal to the yield of foreign bonds, hence the stabilization of capital movements as there is no incentive to move capital from one country to another. Such condition, as we have seen, is expressed by the following equation:

$$1 + i_t = (1 + i_t^*) \frac{E_t}{E_{t+1}^e} \tag{5.77}$$

Let us now examine this condition in the context of the relation between eurozone member countries. Among these countries the single currency is in force: a euro issued in Italy is always exchanged for a euro issued in

Germany, and therefore the nominal exchange rate between the countries belonging to the eurozone is given by $E = 1$. Now, if agents in the financial market predict that in the future no country will abandon the euro, then, also, the expected exchange rate is equal to $E^e_{t+1} = 1$. However, if this were the case, according to the uncovered parity condition, the interest rate i of each country should be equal to the interest rate i^* of Germany. In fact, there is a spread between the bonds of troubled countries and German bonds, so: $i > i^*$. How can this differential be explained? In the light of the alternative interpretation of the crisis, we can think that many agents foresee an exit from the euro and a consequent depreciation of national currencies by countries characterized by a tendency to accumulate foreign debts. Suppose that traders expect that Germany will remain in the euro and Italy is instead going to return to a national currency and depreciate it. As the nominal exchange rate represents the price of the national currency in terms of foreign currency, the consequence is that it will take less foreign currency, that is less euro, for each unit of national currency: $E^e_{t+1} < 1$. In this case, as the formula clearly shows, for the parity condition to be met, it is necessary that $i > i^*$ – which is exactly what is happening on the financial markets. In other words, investors fear that Italy will at some point decide to leave the euro, return to the lira and depreciate it. They foresee that Italian bonds will be denominated in lira and will therefore depreciate. For this reason, they are willing to buy Italian bonds only if the uncovered parity is respected, that is, only if Italian bonds yield a higher interest than German ones. If, on the other hand, the uncovered parity is not respected, investors will stop buying Italian bonds, and capital will flow from Italy to Germany. In a nutshell, the parity condition and the relative stabilization of capital flows require that $i > i^*$. According to this interpretation, therefore, the cause of the bonds' spreads lies in investors willing to protect themselves not only and not so much against the risk of bankruptcy of weaker states, but rather against the risk that at some point they decide to abandon the euro. Treasury bonds' yields' spread can be explained by the fact that financial agents contemplate the possibility that Italy will leave the euro, and therefore that Italy's expected nominal exchange rate will decrease accordingly.

As we have seen, this forecast might be based on the idea that Italy and other troubled countries of the eurozone may have an interest in leaving the single currency and depreciating to counter the tendency to accumulate excess imports over exports and consequent trade deficits. But how can this tendency to accumulate trade deficits be explained? A possible answer concerns the different price trends in eurozone countries. Look at the data presented in Table 5.1 on the price patterns in Germany, France and in the countries of the eurozone that are inclined to foreign

Table 5.1   Price levels in selected eurozone countries

COUNTRY	2012	2005	1999
France	112.7	100	89.3
Germany	107	100	95.5
Greece	115.3	100	82.5
Ireland	95.7	100	78.6
Italy	112.4	100	85.9
Portugal	110.5	100	83.3
Spain	111.9	100	78.6

Source: AMECO database.

deficits. From 1999, the year of the introduction of the euro, to 2012, the year of the greatest crisis in the eurozone, the price increase in Germany was equal to: $(107.0 - 95.5) / 95.5 = 0.12 = 12\%$. In all other countries it was significantly higher; for example, in Italy it was 30.8 per cent. In sum, thanks to a greater ability in keeping monetary wages down and increasing labour productivity, Germany recorded lower inflation than its competitors, was more competitive and therefore managed to accumulate excess exports over imports and consequent surplus towards foreign countries. On the contrary, less competitive countries have accumulated foreign deficits.[16]

How is this divergence in inflation rates related to the risk of exiting from the euro and the consequent increase in interest rates' spread? Just recall that the monetary interest rate can be understood as the product between the so-called real interest rate r and the expected inflation rate π^e. That is: $(1 + i) = (1 + r)(1 + \pi^e)$. We can bring this expression into the interest rates uncovered parity condition, which therefore becomes:

$$(1 + r)(1 + \pi^e) = (1 + r^*)(1 + \pi^{e*}) \frac{E_t}{E_{t+1}^e} \qquad (5.78)$$

We assume that real interest rates must be equal between the two countries, that is $r = r^*$. Remember that the hypothesis that both countries remain in the eurozone is described by the condition that they use euro as their currency both today and in the future, that is: $E_t = E_{t+1}^e = 1$. In this case, it is easy to verify that the uncovered parity also requires that expected inflation rates are the same, that is: $\pi_e = \pi_e^*$. However, if inflation rates diverge,

---

[16]   For a few hints on the "competitive spreads" within the EU, see A. Califano and S. Gasperin (2019), "Multi-speed Europe is already there: Catching up and falling behind", *Structural Change and Economic Dynamics 51*, 152–167.

then it becomes impossible to preserve the eurozone. Let us imagine that in our country of interest inflation is higher than abroad, that is $\pi_e > \pi_e{}^*$. In this case, the uncovered parity condition rules that: $E_t = 1 > E^e_{t+1}$. This can imply that the country with higher inflation is expected to be forced to abandon the euro in the future and devalue the new currency. Various exponents of the mainstream believe that economically weaker countries should implement deflationary policies also through wage cuts, in order to increase competitiveness, increase exports and reduce trade deficit to avoid leaving the euro. Blanchard himself has supported this thesis on several occasions.[17]

Scholars supportive of the alternative paradigm, on the other hand, think that the reduction of wages and deflation may deepen the economic crisis, with further falls in employment and income, perverse effects on the ability of the weaker countries to repay their debts and eventually risk of bankruptcies and fire sales of domestic companies to foreign capitals[18] (the upward sloping AD, presented in section 3.9, is useful here). In this different perspective, instead of forcing the countries in deficit to deflate, a mechanism should be adopted to induce Germany and other countries with foreign surplus to increase wages and inflation.[19]

What would happen if a country would leave the eurozone? The prevailing thesis is that going back to the national currency would give rise to a significant depreciation of the nominal exchange rate; this in turn would cause an increase in the cost of imported raw materials and intermediate goods, which at least temporarily would lead to an increase in national prices and a loss of purchasing power of monetary wages. This thesis was also supported by the former President of the European Central Bank Mario Draghi: "leaving the euro area, devaluing your currency, you create a big inflation".[20] Blanchard's textbook seems to hold a similar view. When it considers the effects of a depreciation of the exchange rate in Chapter 18, we read that: "Governments trying to achieve a large depreciation often find themselves with strikes and riots in the streets, as people react to the much higher prices of imported goods". A survey through episodes of the

---

[17] O. Blanchard, "The logic and fairness of Greece's Program", *IMF Direct*, 19 March 2012.
[18] For an in-depth analysis of the reasons why deflation can aggravate a country's debt position and can therefore induce fire sales of national capital in favour of foreign buyers, see E. Brancaccio and G. Fontana (2015), 'Solvency rule' and capital centralization in a monetary union", *Cambridge Journal of Economics 40(4)*, 1055–75.
[19] The proposed "European wage standard" is a possible example in this sense: E. Brancaccio (2012), "Current account imbalances, the eurozone crisis and a proposal for a 'European wage standard'", *International Journal of Political Economy 41(1)*, 47–65.
[20] Transcript of an interview to the Financial Times, published on 18 December 2011.

past, however, does not provide a straightforward confirmation of the idea that exiting from monetary regimes and the connected currency depreciation inexorably causes "big inflation". Looking at such episodes between 1980 and 2013, if it is true that in low per capita income countries the inflationary effect of leaving a monetary regime is on average significant, at least in the early years, on the contrary in high-income countries the inflationary effect appears on average limited and in any case temporary. Above all, it seems that the implications on the purchasing power of wages differ greatly from country to country, probably depending on the different economic and wage policy adopted by each nation in correspondence with currency depreciation.[21] It is obvious that whether a country should leave or remain in the eurozone is too complex an issue to be examined in this context. As always, the student is therefore invited to refer to studies specifically dedicated to the topic. We have seen nonetheless that the uncovered parity condition already provides some preliminary elements for further thoughts, helping in the development of a first understanding of critical issues that the single European currency seems to have caused in the relations between its members.

5.9   SPECULATORS AGAINST CENTRAL BANKS

When a country aims to maintain a fixed exchange rate between its domestic currency and major foreign currencies, the national central bank must have reserves of internationally accepted foreign currencies. These are currencies that are widely used globally as means of payment or as store of value, which are therefore always accepted in exchange (such as, currently, the US dollar, or up to the early twentieth century the British pound). If it does not have enough reserves, the central bank will not be able to purchase the national currency necessary to keep its value stable when it is involved in a wave of market sales. Accordingly, in the event of unmet supply of the national currency on the market, sooner or later it will have to depreciate and the country will therefore be forced to abandon the fixed exchange rate.

This situation can be examined in terms of a game between the central bank and speculators, that is private traders who buy and sell on the market in order to obtain capital gains. We use for the purpose a slightly modified version of an interesting example published in the first edition of

---

[21]   See E. Brancaccio and N. Garbellini (2015), "Currency regime crises, real wages, functional income distribution and production", *European Journal of Economics and Economic Policies: Intervention 12(3)*, 255–76.

Blanchard's macroeconomics manual[22] (sadly taken out from subsequent editions). Consider, for example, the case of Thailand, a country that during the 1997 so-called "Asian crisis" was subject to massive speculative attacks. Suppose that the Thai central bank pursues the goal of defending a fixed exchange rate of 20 Thai baht for 1 US dollar (E = 20BHT / $1). The central bank will aim at defending the fixed exchange rate by using its dollar reserves to buy baht whenever there is an excess of supply on the markets. Speculators, on the other hand, bet on the possibility that Thailand will be forced to abandon the fixed exchange rate and depreciate the national currency: their bet can take the form of a "short sale", an operation that consists in borrowing baht, selling them on the market for dollars and then hope that the baht depreciates so as to buy them back at a favourable exchange rate, return them to the lenders and thus obtain a net gain in dollars. For simplicity, suppose that every speculator willing to bet against the fixed exchange rate borrows a sum of 120 billion baht from a private bank, promising to pay it back at a certain maturity with the payment of an interest of 1 billion dollars. Once the loan is obtained, each speculator will be able to sell the baht on the market at the fixed exchange rate of 20BHT / $1, obtaining $6 billion from the transaction. If this operation is carried out simultaneously by many speculators, the central bank will have to face a massive sale of the national currency and will draw from its dollar reserves to buy baht at the fixed exchange rate. If the central bank runs out of reserves, it will no longer be able to defend the fixed exchange rate: the speculators' sales will lead to an excess supply of baht on the market that will result in their depreciation. Blanchard assumes that the baht depreciates by 50 per cent, so that the new market exchange rate becomes 30BHT / $1. At this point, with just $4 billion, each speculator will be able to repurchase the 120 billion baht he had borrowed and return them to the creditor private bank, to which they will also pay the $1 billion in interests. The result is that each speculator gets a net capital gain of $6 - (4 + 1) = \$1$ billion. If, on the other hand, the central bank has enough reserves to face the mass sales, the exchange rate will remain fixed at the value of 20BHT / $1. In this case, each speculator will have to pay $6 billion to repurchase 120 billion baht on the market, which will then have to return to the private lending bank, with the additional cost of $1 billion in interests. The result is a net loss of capital for the speculator: $6 - (6 + 1) = -1$ billion dollars.

Under what circumstances does the central bank surrender to the massive sales of speculators and the exchange rate depreciates? And when is it

---

O. Blanchard (1996), *Macroeconomics* (1st edn), Boston, USA: Pearson.

Table 5.2   The game between speculators and the central bank

	Soros does not attack	Soros attacks
Livermore does not attack	0; 0	0; –1
Livermore attacks	–1; 0	1; 1

that speculators suffer losses as the central bank manages to preserve the fixed exchange rate? The answer lies in two factors: the ability of speculators to act in a coordinated manner, and, on the other hand, the central bank's availability of reserves. We examine the problem using game theory, a branch of economics that analyzes situations in which the outcome of each agent's behaviour may depend on the behaviour of others. To keep it simple, we suppose that the speculators are only two, Livermore and Soros, after two famous traders. Let us also assume that central bank's reserves amount to $10 billion. The following table, called the "payoff matrix", describes all possible situations depending on whether each speculator does or does not launch the attack on the fixed exchange rate through short sales of baht.

In each box, the left value indicates Livermore's net result, while the right value indicates Soros's net result. The box at the top left shows that if neither of the two attacks, their net result is (obviously) zero. Bottom left and top right point out instead that if the attack is launched by only one of the two speculators, the sale of baht amounts to $6 billion only and therefore can be faced by the central bank, which by hypothesis has reserves of $10 billion: the speculator who does not attack has a zero gain, while the one who carries out the short sale will end up with a net loss of $1 billion, corresponding to the interest payment to the lending private bank. Finally, the box at the bottom right shows that if the two speculators coordinate and attack at the same time, their sales of baht will correspond to a total of $12 billion and will therefore exceed the reserves available to the Thai central bank: the consequence is that the fixed exchange rate will be abandoned and each of the two speculators will get a net capital gain of 1 billion. From the point of view of game theory, it is interesting to note that in the case described the optimal decision of each speculator necessarily depends on the decision of the other: that is, there is no "dominant strategy" that can be pursued independently of the behaviour of the other players. In what circumstances is it likely that speculators coordinate, determining the defeat of the central bank and the eventual end of the fixed exchange rate regime? Blanchard's explanation, contained in the first edition of his manual, is straightforward: when central bank reserves are plentiful, the attack can never succeed. If speculators decide to attack a strong central bank (with a lot of reserves), they are likely to fail, even if they coordinate with each other. Speculation can accelerate a devaluation, but speculation alone is never capable of causing a devaluation. If the central bank is eventually forced to abandon the defence of the exchange rate it is because it was weak anyway.

In support of this thesis Blanchard proposes the following example. If the central bank has only \$5 billion in reserves, each speculator will be able to attack successfully even without coordinating with the other, and therefore the fixed exchange rate will surely collapse. On the contrary, if the central bank has accumulated reserves of \$20 billion, the two speculators will not be able to defeat it even if they coordinate, so they will avoid launching the attack. This thesis seems to match with a very widespread idea among supporters of a liberal view of the financial markets, who oppose any rule aimed at limiting speculative activity. According to this view, the problem does not lie in private traders' speculation, but in public policy instead: speculators' attack must be considered only as a symptom of a problem that has roots elsewhere, most notably in the economic policies that influence the level of reserves of central banks. For example, if a country implements overly expansionary policy, it will end up with an increase in aggregate demand and inflation of such magnitude as to also determine an excess of import over export; this will create a trade deficit. For a certain period, this deficit can be compensated through capital inflows from abroad, but in the long run it will affect the central bank's dollar reserves: the inflow of dollars obtained through export will not be enough to finance import, therefore the importers will ask the central bank to change their baht into dollars to pay for foreign goods. By contrast, if a country keeps aggregate demand and inflation under control, its imports will maintain below exports, implying a trade surplus, hence a net inflow of dollars in the central bank's reserves. According to this interpretation, the cause of a speculative attack must be sought in excessively expansionary policies, which would be inconsistent with the aim of keeping a fixed exchange rate.

At first glance, this view seems to be right. Yet, this understanding of speculative attacks has been subject to many critiques. Some scholars, for example, highlighted that speculators can attack countries that have limited trade deficits or even a balanced trade position, and therefore a large and rather stable amount of international currency reserves. The reason is that in a context of global unrestrained free movement of capitals and large concentration of financial wealth, broad "coalitions" of short sellers can be formed in a more or less coordinated manner, which may have an enormous amount of capital and in principle are capable of putting any central bank in troubles. In other words, whatever the level of reserves of a single central bank, private speculators can still have greater financial force. This alternative interpretation suggests that speculative selling may be a cause in itself of the collapse of fixed exchange rate regimes rather than a mere symptom of inconsistent policies of the country under attack. Other critiques can be added. For example, a country that keeps the trade balance under control and is therefore endowed with large reserves of foreign currency can still suffer the effects of a crisis affecting neighbouring countries with which it has important economic and financial relations. Such a country could, for instance, be net creditor of the other countries in crisis, and scepticism could therefore arise as to the actual possibility of recovering those credits. In this case, a financial contagion effect can take place, inducing speculators to attack the "strong" country as well. These critiques seem to give strength to the call for a coordination in the policies of central banks to counter any coalitions of speculators more effectively, or for the introduction of regulations that limit speculative activity and the free movement of capitals.

5.10 LABOUR FLEXIBILITY, EMPLOYMENT AND UNEMPLOYMENT

The economic policy debate has been focused on the so-called labour flexibility in the set of norms ruling labour relations for many years. A great deal of attention has been paid to employment protection regimes, such as those norms ruling contracts and dismissals. Some mainstream economists have argued that the reduction in the duration of contracts and the loosening of norms regulating dismissals might help to increase labour flexibility and thus obtain a more dynamic labour market: firms would be allowed to better adapt to the business cycle and to variations in technology and in consumers' preferences, and would be induced to increase the number of employees. It is an extremely complex issue, as highlighted by the fact that a thorough investigation on the link between labour flexibility and firms' capacity to adapt to the business cycle would require a modelling able to capture movements of capitals and workers through sectors. Macroeconomic models, in particular didactic ones, are unfit for this type of analysis.

Nonetheless it is worth mentioning that, also in Blanchard's macroeconomic mainstream model, a greater labour flexibility boosts employment and reduces unemployment. For instance, if norms protecting workers from being easily fired are abolished, workers will be weaker in the bargaining process so the catch-all variable z will reduce. We have seen that in the AS–AD model a fall in z generates wage moderation, thus reducing the price level P, increasing real monetary stocks M/P, decreasing the interest rate i, thus stimulating investment I, the demand of goods Z, production Y and employment N, eventually bringing down unemployment u. Moreover, as shown in the previous chapter, a similar result is reached by Blanchard's new IS–LM–PC model.

The thesis of an increase in employment and a fall in unemployment following greater labour flexibility has been dominant for a long time in the political arena as well, giving rise to many variations in the norms ruling labour relations. These changes are reflected in the reduction of labour protection indexes, as computed by the OECD, which have taken place in recent years in various European countries.

Table 5.3 shows the variation that took place in selected countries between 1992 and 2013 in the so-called Employment Protection Legislation (EPL) index, computed by the OECD, and identifying the degree of protection of labour (the lower the index, the lower the normative protection of workers, hence the higher labour flexibility). In Italy, for instance, temporary contracts have spread and protection against easy firing has been reduced: the value of the EPL has decreased significantly.

How has greater labour flexibility concretely affected employment and unemployment? The empirical studies published in the most recent years give results that are somehow in contradiction with mainstream theory's forecasts. There is a well-known example on the matter: the test performed by the OECD and described in Appendix 1 to this volume.

More recently, Boeri and van Ours have published an extended review recording mixed results. First, each of the eight analyzed studies, concerning just the annual flows of unemployed people, points to a reduction of the flows of unemployment because of greater labour flexibility. However, three of the studies show that the effects on the annual flows of employed people are uncertain and two of them even point to a negative effect. Furthermore, if we move from the analysis of annual flows to the analysis of total stock of employed and unemployed people, the results clash even more with mainstream theory. Nine of the 13 investigations on stocks give indefinite results; three show that greater flexibility reduces employment while increasing unemployment; only one points to lower unemployment following an increase in flexibility.[23] The prevailing thesis, according to which flexibility would increase the number of jobs, does not seem to rely on compelling empirical confirmation.

Even Blanchard, going through a wide-reaching review of the empirical works on the issue, reached a clear-cut conclusion: "differences in

---

[23]   T. Boeri and J. van Ours (2008), *The Economics of Imperfect Labor Markets*, Princeton, USA: Princeton University Press.

Table 5.3   Evolution of the OECD Overall Employment Protection Index

Country	1992	2013
Australia	1.02	1.27
Austria	2.03	1.84
Belgium	3.24	2.13
Canada	0.59	0.59
Denmark	1.78	1.79
Finland	1.85	1.86
France	2.98	3.00
Germany	2.92	1.90
Greece	3.78	2.18
Hungary	1.31	1.42
Ireland	0.84	1.01
Italy	3.76	2.34
Japan	1.69	1.12
Korea	3.08	2.25
Mexico	3.10	2.05
Netherlands	2.20	1.88
New Zealand	0.81	1.20
Norway	2.73	2.67
Poland	1.49	1.99
Portugal	3.98	2.50
Spain	3.65	2.31
Sweden	2.78	1.71
Switzerland	1.36	1.36
Turkey	3.63	3.59
United Kingdom	0.67	0.74
United States	0.25	0.25

Notes: The value has been computed with the standard OECD procedure, starting from OECD data (the table includes all OECD countries, excluding those for which the data are not available).

employment protection seem however largely unrelated to differences in unemployment rates across countries".[24] Blanchard himself acknowledges therefore that the data do not confirm the thesis of the link between higher flexibility and lower unemployment, which would be derived from his own teaching model.

On the contrary, the vagueness of the empirical results on labour flexibility, employment and unemployment seems to support the thesis of the critical alternative model. As a matter of fact, we know the alternative

---

[24]   O. Blanchard (2006), "European unemployment: the evolution of facts and ideas", *Economic Policy 21(45)*, 6–59.

model to be characterized by a vertical AD, or at least by an AD that has a slope that is *a priori* undetermined: thus, as already shown, a reduction of employment protection implying a reduction of the z parameter for workers' bargaining power has no effect on employment and unemployment or in any case it is impossible to determine it *a priori*. In effect, this is more in line with the empirical results on the matter. Moreover, it is worth recalling that, according to the mainstream model, a reduction of labour protections that brings the parameter z down does not have an effect on real wage, whereas, within the alternative model, the reduction of z entails a fall in the equilibrium real wage and a shift in income distribution from wage to profit. There is not a great deal of empirical literature on the topic, as also stressed by the OECD. Nonetheless, also in this regard, evidence can be found that is consistent with the relations suggested by the alternative model.[25]

It is obvious that both the set of models used in Blanchard's textbooks and the alternative model are to be considered mainly for teaching purposes: too simplified to be tested directly against empirical results, most notably when complex issues such as labour flexibility are at stake. However, the simple fact that the data do not deny the conclusions reached by the alternative model, while they seem to be inconsistent with the results of the mainstream model, is definitely a notable outcome, worthy of further investigation.[26]

5.11 A FEW NOTES ON IMMIGRATION, UNEMPLOYMENT AND WAGES

Does the inflow of migrant workers spur unemployment among native workers? It is subject to a heated debate. Treating the matter in a scientific way shows that this phenomenon is extremely complex, and results of both theoretical and empirical studies are controversial. As a first step, let us get closer to the issue using the basic analytical tools at our disposal, that is the AS–AD mainstream model and the alternative model in its algebraic structure as described in section 5.1. Let us recall that unemployed people are expressed by U, whereas employed workers are expressed by N; we call "labour force" the sum of two sets, employed and unemployed, given by $L = U + N$. Accordingly, $U = L - N$. From now on, we introduce the

---

[25] See the literature review and the empirical results included in E. Brancaccio, N. Garbellini and R. Giammetti (2018), "Structural labour market reforms, GDP growth and the functional distribution of income", *Structural Change and Economic Dynamics 44*, 34–45.

[26] Further insights on the matter can be found in Appendix 1 to this volume.

assumption that immigrant workers are either employed or actively looking for a job, so they are part of the labour force L. This means that a surge in immigrant workers always implies an increase in the labour force L. As the unemployment rate u is given by the ratio between total employed workers U and the labour force L, we can thus write that $u = U/L = (L-N)/L$. That is, $u = 1 - (N/L)$. Recall that the production function is given by $Y = AN$, from which: $N = Y/A$. We have already shown that we can write the equation for the unemployment rate as follows:

$$u = 1 - \frac{Y}{AL} \tag{5.79}$$

Sticking to what emerged in section 5.1, it is important to highlight once again that the traditional model and the alternative one reach very different results with respect to the equilibrium in production, unemployment, and wage. If we look at the standard theory, the "natural" equilibrium level of production is given by:

$$Y = \frac{AL}{\alpha}\left[\left(\frac{A}{1+\mu}\right) + \alpha - 1 - z\right] \tag{5.80}$$

By substituting this result in the equation of the unemployment rate, we get that:

$$u = 1 - \frac{1}{\alpha}\left[\left(\frac{A}{1+\mu}\right) + \alpha - 1 - z\right] \tag{5.81}$$

By contrast, in the alternative framework, the equilibrium production is:

$$Y = \beta E \tag{5.82}$$

And, accordingly, the unemployment rate is given by:

$$u = 1 - \beta\left(\frac{E}{AL}\right) \tag{5.83}$$

At this point, new migrant workers enter the economy, implying that the labour force L gets larger. The effects can be assessed through a comparative analysis of the different equations for the unemployment rate included in the two models. Differences between the two alternative frameworks are substantial. According to the mainstream model, the labour force does not contribute to the determination of the "natural" unemployment rate of equilibrium, hence a larger L does not affect u. The reason is that in this model both μ and z are exogenous, and together with A and α determine the unique unemployment rate that brings the "natural" equilibrium in the labour market. This is the rate that is accepted by both firms and workers, and thus prevents a race to the bottom or to the top between wage and price. Therefore, for a given A, there will be a unique Y/AL ratio, hence a unique rate of unemployment $u = 1 - Y/AL$ that brings to such equilibrium. Whichever deviation from the equilibrium is destined to be reabsorbed. For instance, if L grows due to a rise in migrant inflows, a temporary increase in the unemployment rate will occur, yielding to a temporary fall of wages and prices. In its turn, this fall will be followed by a higher level of demand and production Y, until the ratio Y/AL reaches the value that determines the unique "natural" unemployment rate, on which firms and workers agree, thus stabilizing price and wage. The opposite happens in the case of an outflow of migrants, which brings L down. To sum up, according to the standard model AS–AD, the way in which immigration affects the labour force L can only have temporary effects on unemployment and production, but cannot modify their "natural" level of equilibrium.

Moving beyond changes in L, a further question arises: what happens if immigrants are willing to accept lower wages than native workers, therefore contributing to the fall of the z parameter of workers' conflictuality? In this scenario, according to the mainstream model, we will see positive effects on the economic system, similar to what happens when wage moderation prevails. Indeed, as it emerges from the equilibrium equations of the AS–AD, when z goes down, u decreases as well, while Y grows. In the mainstream model, if workers are willing to accept lower wages, hence putting a downward pressure on the z parameter, the impact on the "natural" equilibrium of the system will be positive, through the reduction in the natural rate of unemployment and the increase in the natural level of production, the real wage remaining constant at its equilibrium level.

The interpretation of immigration is different within the alternative framework. Here, as we know, μ and z are not necessarily exogenous, and a unique "natural" equilibrium, able to stabilize prices and wages, does not exist. According to this model, the equilibrium levels of unemployment and production depend on the aggregate demand of goods and services, which does not necessarily grow when prices and wages go down. Therefore, as expressed by the relevant equations, for any level of demand and production Y, when there is an inflow of migrants and the labour force L gets larger accordingly, the equilibrium unemployment will set at a higher value. Furthermore, if immigrants contribute to the decrease of the z parameter of conflictuality, there will be a fall in the equilibrium real wage with no positive effects on unemployment and production. Therefore, from the perspective of the alternative model, immigration may affect negatively both unemployment and wage. However, it is possible to counter these dynamics. In order to prevent unemployment u from rising, the trivial solution is stopping migrants' inflows, but more sophisticated solutions exist. For instance, expansionary policy to foster demand for goods E and production Y to match the expansion in the labour force L; or decreasing working hours by law, in order to let productivity per worker A go down to match a growing L caused by immigration; or a combination of these two measures can also be implemented. Then, if avoiding negative effects on the real wage is a desired outcome, all workers, they being native or immigrant, should be encouraged to unionize (together) and to be inserted in a frame of collective bargaining, so that the z parameter of workers conflictuality is not affected.

It is obvious that the described models are useful for teaching purposes only. Their limits are such that they cannot be used for assessing the real effects of immigration. One of the most significant weaknesses is that both assume labour force L to be exogenous, hence not sensitive to variations in effective demand and production. By contrast, several studies suggest that variations of demand and production may affect the inflow of migrants and the connected changes in a given country's labour force: in other words, economic growth in a given country tend to pull immigration, therefore L should be considered non-exogenous, and at least partially endogenous, contrary to what happens in both models. It is worth noting that the two models would change behaviour substantially under this different hypothesis. For instance, if we consider the alternative model, the increase in immigration and in the labour force L would happen only as a consequence of the growth in demand E and production Y, and it will not affect the unemployment rate u.

Dealing with complex issues such as immigration would thus need more sophisticated analytical instruments. However, it is interesting that even in this case the two didactic tools offer contrasting results. Once again, a careful assessment should be made in the light of the available empirical evidence.[27] The problem is that in this case the data do not offer a clear indication. Empirical literature on the effects of immigration on unemployment and wage presents contrasting – and sometimes, ambiguous – results.

---

[27] For a contribution on the empirical question of the economic impact of immigration flows in direct comparison with the effects of capital flows, see the already mentioned E. Brancaccio, A. Califano and F. De Cristofaro (2021), "Migrant inflows, capital outflows, growth and distribution: should we control capital rather than immigration?", *European Journal of Economics and Economic Policies – Intervention 18(3)*, 344–63. DOI: 10.4337/ejeep.2021.0074

5.12 ALTERNATIVE THEORIES OF GROWTH AND INCOME DISTRIBUTION

The comparison between Blanchard's traditional approach and the alternative paradigm can also be made with respect to the so-called theory of growth and income distribution. In a nutshell, the theory of economic growth analyzes the long-term dynamics of the accumulation of capital, that is the accumulation of machines, plants, equipment, means of production which, together with work, contribute to the realization of each year's product. In this regard, it should not be forgotten that so far we have examined only short–medium term macroeconomics, since we have focused on relatively short time spans: usually a year or so. There, capital is considered fixed, a datum, since changes in equipment, plants, means of production, etc. can only happen in the long run. For this reason, in the short–medium term analysis, the function $Y = AN$ is used, in which capital K is implicitly considered exogenous and cannot be changed over the period examined. However, as we move on to the long-term growth theory, K becomes an endogenous variable which is determined by the pace of capital accumulation.

In his manual Blanchard offers a typical mainstream representation of economic growth, inspired by a well-known neoclassical model developed by Robert Solow in 1956. Adopting the same comparative methodology as in previous chapters, we intend to show that even in growth theory it is possible to move from Blanchard's mainstream model to the alternative one by a simple exchange of roles between exogenous and endogenous variables.

To simplify the analysis, we can consider an economy that produces only one good, for example grain, by means of itself used as capital and by means of labour. We define with K the physical quantity of the good available as capital and therefore used as production input. We define with L the quantity of labour employed in production and with Y the physical quantity of the produced good, that is production in real terms. We thus obtain the following generic production function:

$$Y = F(K, L) \tag{5.84}$$

Under a set of assumptions on the existing production technology and defining with α a technological parameter, the specific form of the production function can be the following:

$$Y = \gamma K^\alpha L^{1-\alpha} \tag{5.85}$$

where for simplicity we can set $y = 1$. We also assume that $\alpha < 1$. By dividing the function by L and defining production per capita as $y = Y/L$ and capital per capita as $k = K/L$, the production function can be rewritten accordingly:

$$y = k^\alpha \tag{5.86}$$

$w = W/P$ is the real wage paid to workers and r the rate of profit going to capitalists. Suppose that firms distribute their production as income to capitalists and workers in the following way:

$$Y = wL + (1 + r)K \tag{5.87}$$

This means that Y is both the real value of production and the value of real income distributed to workers and capitalists: that is, when production increases, income distributed increases equally. Dividing everything by L, we obtain the per capita income distribution equation:

$$k^\alpha = w + (1 + r)k \tag{5.88}$$

It is now a matter of finding the optimal production technique, that is the combination $k = K/L$ chosen by the firms to maximize production net of costs. Under given assumptions, the technique k that maximizes the net product can be obtained by deriving Equation 5.88 for k and setting the result equal to zero. By deriving and rearranging, we will have:

$$\alpha k^{\alpha-1} = (1 + r) \tag{5.89}$$

Finally, keeping in mind that Y is the real value of both production and income, defining with C the demand for consumer goods and with I the demand for capital goods and therefore for the accumulation of capital, we can write the equation of the macroeconomic equilibrium between production and aggregate demand:

$$Y = C + I \tag{5.90}$$

The difference between income and consumption corresponds to the saving of the population:

$$Y - C = S = sY \tag{5.91}$$

in which s is the population's propensity to save, that is the percentage of income that families decide to save. Suppose further that the capital used each year in production runs out and must therefore be replenished each year. Therefore, the demand for capital goods each year will be represented by what is necessary to replenish capital K that was used in the previous period to which must be added an additional component gK that represents the accumulation of new capital; g represents the rate of accumulation of capital, that is $I = (1 + g)K$. Substituting, the macroeconomic equilibrium becomes:

$$sY = (1 + g)K \qquad (5.92)$$

Dividing both sides by L, we get $sy = (1 + g)k$, from which:

$$sk^\alpha = (1 + g)k \qquad (5.93)$$

We thus have the following system of equations:

$$k^\alpha = w + (1 + r)k \qquad (5.88)$$

$$\alpha k^{\alpha-1} = (1 + r) \qquad (5.89)$$

$$sk^\alpha = (1 + g)k \qquad (5.93)$$

This system can be considered a sort of "stereogram" of the growth theory. In fact, it is a scheme that can take on different meanings according to the point of view from which one looks at it, that is, according to the different choices that are made about exogenous and endogenous variables of the model. From this system, as we shall see, it is possible to derive both the neoclassical model to which Blanchard refers and an alternative model of growth and distribution. Assuming for simplicity that α is a purely technological exogenous datum, the system is composed of three equations with five unknown variables: k, w, r, s and g. Under given assumptions, the solution of the system requires that two of these unknowns are fixed as exogenous. Depending on the choice of the exogenous variables, the scheme will take on the characteristics of one or the other model.

Let us first consider the solution of the growth model contained in Blanchard's manual. As we mentioned, it is a typical mainstream model, based on the neoclassical theory of growth. As usual in neoclassical theory, this model starts from the hypothesis that there are two fundamental exogenous given: the preferences of individuals and the endowments of scarce resources, in particular capital and labour. It assumes that families offer these endowments of capital and labour to firms at the beginning of each period. Spontaneous market forces determine the rate of profit and the real wage describing the full employment "natural equilibrium": in fact, they induce firms to demand exactly all the endowments of capital and labour offered by families. Using those endowments, firms realize production and distribute an equivalent income to workers' and capitalists' families. Finally, based on their preferences, families decide how much of that income to consume and how much to save. The portion of income that is saved will determine the new amount of accumulated capital that, in the following period, families will offer to firms to realize production, and so on from period to period. This means that for the purpose of the model we must consider exogenous the preferences of individuals that determine the propensity to save s, and the endowments of capital K and labour L that contribute to determining the technique $k = K/L$. Therefore, remembering that α is always an exogenous parameter, we assume that s and k are given, and we solve the system in the following way. Equation 5.89 determines the rate of profit, which corresponds to $r = \alpha k^{\alpha-1}-1$. Equation 5.88 determines the real wage, which (after simple computations) turns out to be $w = (1-\alpha)\, k^{\alpha}$. Finally, the macroeconomic equilibrium Equation 5.93 determines the accumulation rate of capital, described by $g = sk^{\alpha-1}-1$. As typical in neoclassical theory, this latter equation is read from left to right, which is sometimes summarized in the idea that saving determines investment.

The solution just described is generally defined as "non-stationary equilibrium", because in each period K and L can grow at different rates and therefore the ratio $k = K/L$ can change. It can be shown, however, that in the neoclassical growth model the capital accumulation rate g tends to become equal to a hypothetical growth rate of the labour force that is considered exogenous and usually denoted by n. Over time, spontaneous market forces tend to generate saving and a consequent investment which ensures that the growth of capital coincides with the exogenous growth of the labour force. In the end, the equality $g = n$ is obtained, which is the so-called steady state growth equilibrium, in which the proportion $k = K/L$ does not change over time, and therefore neither does per capita production y. This steady state growth equilibrium can be achieved in the following way. Given the exogenous growth of the labour force n, the capital accumulation rate will be $g = n$. Thus g and s are the exogenous variables. The solution is the following. Equation 5.93 determines the equilibrium level of k, after simple steps

$$k = \left[s / (1+g) \right]^{1/(1-\alpha)}. \tag{5.94}$$

Hence, Equation 5.89 determines the equilibrium rate of profit, which corresponds to

$$r = \alpha \left[s / (1+g) \right]^{(\alpha-1)/(1-\alpha)} - 1. \tag{5.95}$$

Finally, with a few calculations, Equation 5.88 determines the real wage

$$w = \left[s / (1 + g) \right]^{\alpha / (1 - \alpha)} - \alpha \left[s / (1 + g) \right]^{(\alpha - 1)/(1 - \alpha)^2}. \qquad (5.96)$$

In the neoclassical perspective, this stationary result must be considered the result of a succession of non-stationary equilibria obtained from the previous solution.

It is not a mere coincidence that Blanchard's long period analysis is grounded on neoclassical theory. The neoclassical growth model represents a fundamental point of reference for all exponents of mainstream macroeconomics. This model shows that for a given exogenous set of scarce productive factors and household preferences, income growth and distribution are determined by a simple process of technical maximization, which, under free market conditions, will determine the balance between supply and demand in each period and will thus ensure a full and efficient use of available labour and capital. Note that this equilibrium is independent of the fluctuations in aggregate demand and policies that influence it; moreover, it is optimal precisely because it is not influenced by the clash between social classes. We could say, in this sense, that the "natural" equilibrium of the short-term macroeconomic model that we have analyzed in previous chapters matches the long-term equilibrium of the neoclassical growth model. In fact, even in the analysis of long-term growth, the typical results of the short-term mainstream model are confirmed and in some way even strengthened: political and social pressures on macroeconomic variables are irrelevant or even harmful.

Not all economists, however, share Blanchard's view of growth and income distribution. Proponents of critical approaches propose alternative interpretations of the mechanism of growth and distribution of income that is typical of a capitalist economy. Obviously, these alternative theories are complex and can be presented here only in a simplified way. Our only purpose is to highlight that the system of Equations 5.88, 5.89 and 5.93 can be interpreted in a radically different way from the conventional one. The different premises from which we can draw the alternative interpretation of the system are the following: the conflict between social classes plays a key role in determining the distribution of income between wages and profits, and aggregate demand and the policies that affect it can influence accumulation and economic growth. These premises, respectively inspired by Sraffa and Keynes, have important implications on the choice of the exogenous variables of the model. We can now assume that the rate of profit r is an exogenous datum determined by the conditions of power relations between social classes, and that the rate of capital accumulation g is also exogenous, determined by the autonomous decisions of entrepreneurs on the demand for capital goods. Thus, in this different scenario we start from the autonomous demand for means of production, which, together with the expenditure for consumer goods, determines the aggregate demand for goods. Accordingly, firms will achieve a certain level of production by adapting the production technique and their requirement of means of production and workers in order to satisfy the aggregate demand. Finally, the distribution of the produced income between capitalists and workers will be affected by the class struggle. Based on these alternative hypotheses, the solution of the system becomes the following. Considering r and g as exogenous, Equation 5.89 determines the technique chosen by firms, which after a few steps turns out to be

$$k = \left[(1+r)/\alpha\right]^{1/(\alpha-1)}. \tag{5.97}$$

Then, from Equation 5.88 in a few steps we determine the real wage

$$w = \left[(1+r)/\alpha\right]^{\alpha/(\alpha-1)} - (1+r)\left[(1+r)/\alpha\right]^{1/(\alpha-1)}. \tag{5.98}$$

Finally, Equation 5.93 determines the share of income which is saved, described by

$$s = (1+g)\left[(1+r)/\alpha\right]^{(1-\alpha)/(\alpha-1)}. \tag{5.99}$$

Note that in this case the latter equation is read from right to left and can be summarized in the typical Keynesian idea that investment determines saving (and in this particular case it also determines the relationship between saving and income).

The description of capitalist growth offered by the alternative model is therefore very different from that proposed by the mainstream analysis. According to the alternative approach, the analysis must start from class conflict instead of the preferences of individuals. Furthermore, there is no scarcity constraint of available capital and labour, since it is assumed that these will adapt to the needs of production and, more generally, of social relations as influenced by the level of aggregate demand and by the state of conflict between classes. It is not surprising then that the neoclassical models are defined as "scarcity models" whereas the alternative models are called "reproduction models", referring to the conditions of reproduction or crisis of capital and of the current social structures. In these alternative models there is no certainty that spontaneous market forces would guarantee the full employment of workers and of productive capacity in general. This means that the goal of full employment can only be pursued with specific economic policies. Furthermore, the distribution of income between wage and profit is not the mere result of a neutral technical maximization but is also influenced by the dialectic between social classes.

The following graph summarizes Equations 5.88, 5.89 and 5.93, from which, as we have seen, it is possible to draw both the neoclassical model and the alternative model of growth and distribution of income.

The graph shall be read in different ways depending on the model examined. Looking at the non-stationary equilibrium of neoclassical analysis we proceed as follows. We start from the k level, which indicates the K/L ratio between scarce endowments of capital and labour. Therefore, in the light of the maximization condition (5.89) given by $\alpha k^{\alpha-1} = (1 + r)$, the rate of profit r is determined. Once the profit rate is known, the slope of the income distribution Equation 5.88 is also determined, as $k^{\alpha} = w + (1 + r) k$. The tangency between the latter and the production function $y = k^{\alpha}$ gives the intercept on the y-axis, which corresponds to the real wage w. Finally, based on the macroeconomic equilibrium condition (5.93), $sk^{\alpha} = (1 + g) k$, we determine the level of capital accumulation g and therefore the angular coefficient $(1 + g)$ that makes the investment curve $(1 + g) k$ rotate until it crosses the saving curve sk^{α} at the given k level. If, on the other hand, we intend to determine the stationary growth equilibrium of the neoclassical model, then we start from a given level of g corresponding to the capital accumulation rate that equals the growth rate of the labour force, which is supposed to be exogenous ($g = n$). From Equation 5.93 we determine the intersection $sk^{\alpha} = (1 + g) k$ hence the level of k that guarantees that equality. Once that k is known, the maximization condition (5.89) $\alpha k^{\alpha-1} = (1 + r)$ allows the determination of the rate of profit r and hence the angle of the income distribution (Equation 5.88) $k^{\alpha} = w + (1 + r) k$, from which we eventually get the intercept on the y-axis

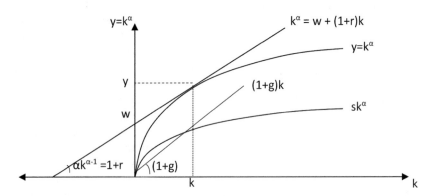

Figure 5.4   Growth and distribution

represented by the real wage w. Finally, if we interpret the graph in terms of the alternative model, we start once again from a given level of the accumulation rate g, but in this case we assume that it is determined by the autonomous decisions of firms, as established by the Keynesian principle of effective demand. The angle of the straight line $(1 + g) k$ is therefore already determined. Accordingly, the rate of profit r is also assumed to be given, based on the Marxian and Sraffian hypothesis that it is determined by the conflict between social classes. Thus, from the maximization condition (5.89), the level of k is also obtained, corresponding to the efficient combination of labour and the only means of production used. Then, as the angle of the income distribution Equation 5.88 is known, from the tangency with the production function we also obtain the intercept on the y-axis that determines the real wage w. The condition (5.93) of equilibrium between saving and investment is eventually met by determining the level of the propensity to save s, which moves the saving curve sk^α until it crosses the investment function $(1 + g) k$ at the level of k previously obtained.

Students should be able to follow the procedures described above to determine the explicit solutions of the endogenous variables of both the analyzed growth models: the equilibrium of the mainstream model in the non-stationary and stationary versions, and the equilibrium of the alternative model. Students may also wonder what happens to equilibrium solutions if further hypotheses are formulated. For example, it can be assumed that workers consume their entire wage wL and instead capitalists save a portion of their profits equal to $s (1 + r) K$. A further hypothesis can concern the term α: instead of an exogenous datum of a purely technological type, it can be determined endogenously by the degree of utilization of the productive capacity. Moreover, alongside consumption and investment, a further item of expenditure independent of income and not directly generating productive capacity can be introduced, for example government spending, and so on.

In short, many variants can be included in the analysis. The take-home message is that even in the context of growth theory, different premises relating to the choice of exogenous and endogenous variables allow us to obtain very different results. As always, then, the assessment of the assumptions and the related models must follow scientific criteria: logical coherence, historical relevance and empirical verification. For example, in the case under examination, looking at logical coherence we should consider that the conceptualization of capital that is typical of some neoclassical models of growth is fraught with contradictions as soon as we move to a world that produces more than one commodity, as shown by Piero Sraffa and his followers. With respect to empirical validation, then, the two different models should be put on the test bench of the data, verifying whether, in the long run, economic growth is independent of patterns of demand or is instead statistically correlated to its fluctuations, and so on. Appendix 2 to this volume offers some preliminary elements for empirical evaluation.

5.13   A COMPARATIVE APPROACH TO THE STOCK MARKET

We can apply the comparison between the mainstream and the alternative paradigm also on the stock market and its interactions with macroeconomic variables. The importance of this analysis stands out if we consider the relevance that stock market trends have assumed in contemporary capitalism.

The prevailing interpretation of the stock market is based on the so-called "Present Value Model" (PVM), which can be traced back to the mainstream concept of "natural" equilibrium and more generally to neoclassical economic theory. According to PVM's assumptions, market agents make optimum use of all available information. This means, among other things, that stock prices cannot be disturbed by speculative phenomena: given that all financial agents make the best use of all existing information, they all derive the exchange value of the shares from the dividends they expect to earn from owning them, and therefore no speculator can gain from price fluctuations. From these theses the PVM draws its fundamental implication: current market price of the shares is determined exclusively by expected future dividends. The model also establishes that stock prices and dividends are in turn grounded on a typical "natural" equilibrium, where every feature is determined by the neoclassical "fundamentals" of technology, scarce resource endowments and individual preferences. Once natural equilibrium is reached, work and other production factors are used fully and efficiently, that is, in such a way as to satisfy preferences to the maximum possible extent. This theoretical framework is the basis of the apologetic view according to which the stock market "is always right" and therefore its forces should be left free to operate without regulatory obstacles or political interference.

The PVM still has many admirers, including the Nobel Prize winner Eugene Fama. Yet this model has been challenged by various empirical tests. For instance, Robert Shiller, also a Nobel laureate, pointed out an outstanding inconsistency in the PVM. He observed that if this model describes reality correctly, then the variance of stock prices determined by expected dividends should be minor in comparison to the variance of what he calls "ex-post prices", calculated on the basis of the dividends actually paid. The reason is simple: in PVM, shares' market price are obtained on the basis of information available today regarding expected future dividends. By definition, such information cannot incorporate unexpected future events such as a war, sudden famine, pandemic or other unforeseen shock. However, as they occur, these shocks affect the dividends that are actually paid over time to the holders of the shares, thus they also affect ex-post prices that are calculated on the basis of these dividends. In other words, while current market prices are computed ex-ante based on mere expectations on future dividends, ex-post prices are based on the dividends that have actually been paid. Therefore PVM determines them in a way that the stock prices should have a variance lower than the variance of the ex-post prices, since the former cannot incorporate unexpected shocks while the latter can.

Shiller performs a series of empirical tests and shows that things are different indeed: the stock prices recorded on the market are characterized by a much greater variance than the variance of ex-post prices calculated on the basis of dividends paid to shareholders (the different pattern of the two variances is illustrated by Figure 5.5). This large variability in shares' market prices constitutes an implicit denial of the PVM. In fact, it indicates that shares' market prices do not depend only on expected dividends but must also be influenced by other factors, such as the "animal spirits" prevailing in the economy, waves of euphoria and panic on the markets, action of speculators, and so on.

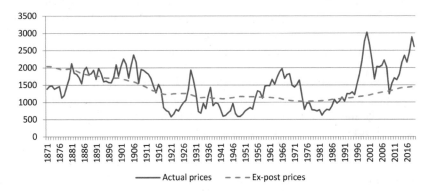

Source: Our elaboration based on 1871–2019 New York Stock Exchange data provided by Shiller.

Figure 5.5 *The variance of the stock market prices is greater than the variance of the ex-post prices obtained from the dividends actually paid*

Following Shiller's tests, the validity of the PVM has been questioned by various scholars, even within the mainstream. Both in his research and his manual, Blanchard suggested that stock market prices are possibly determined not only by expected dividends but also by other factors, including "speculative bubbles", to which he himself has devoted several studies. For Blanchard and other exponents of the mainstream, speculation can therefore explain the strong fluctuations in stock market prices with respect to the "natural" equilibrium values described by the PVM. This view recognizes that the stock market can be subject to speculative waves and can move on trends that are not perfectly rational. However, this does not imply a rejection of the relevance of PVM. In the opinion of these scholars, the "natural" equilibrium described by the PVM is still to be seen as an ideal reference point towards which the stock market should hopefully tend, but from which it is diverted due to a series of disturbances caused by speculation or other "imperfections". To these mainstream scholars willing to recognize the influence of such imperfections, PVM does not exactly describe the reality of the stock market but still represents a point of reference we should expect reality to tend to.

On the other hand, there is a more radical way of interpreting Shiller's tests. That is, moving a critique to the root of the neoclassical bases of PVM and proposing a conception of equilibrium based on the alternative paradigm. In what follows, a comparative approach to two competing theories of the stock market is presented. For this purpose, we adopt a simple stock market diagram that presents the typical features of the "stereogram". Depending on the point of view from which it is observed, it may reflect one or the other theory examined. We will see that this scheme can assume the neoclassical characteristics of the PVM or the typical features of the alternative paradigm depending on the initial choice of the exogenous variables.

Let us take a cue from section 5.12, dedicated to growth and distribution theories, and make some substantial changes. We consider a simplified economy that produces only a commodity by means of the same commodity and work. We define with L and K respectively the quantities of labour and the commodity used as capital, with g the capital accumulation rate, with w the real wage, with r the rate of profit, with C the consumption of capitalists, with P the current price of shares and with D the dividends. The terms $\alpha, \beta, \gamma, \delta$ take various meanings depending on the model considered. For simplicity, let us set the quantity of shares traded in the current period and the share price of the previous period equal to one. The technology is represented by the following production function, which we assume continuous and differentiable to facilitate the comparison between the theories: $Y = (K)^{\alpha}(\gamma L)^{1-\alpha}$. We assume that society is divided into classes:

workers and shareholder owners of the companies. For simplicity, assume that workers consume their wage entirely, whereas shareholders consume the portion of profit corresponding to dividends and use the remaining income to buy shares. The starting scheme is therefore made up of the following six equations:

$$(1)\ (K)^{\alpha}(\gamma L)^{1-\alpha} = w\gamma L + (1 + \delta r) \tag{5.100}$$

$$(2)\ aK^{\alpha-1}\,L^{1-\alpha} = 1 + r \tag{5.101}$$

$$(3)\ 1 + \delta r = P + D \tag{5.102}$$

$$(4)\ P = D\beta/(1 - \beta) \tag{5.103}$$

$$(5)\ P + D = C + P \tag{5.104}$$

$$(6)\ (1 + g)K + C + w\gamma L = P + D + w\gamma L \tag{5.105}$$

Equation 5.100 describes the balance between production and income distributed in the form of wage to workers and profit to businesses. Equation 5.101 shows the optimal technical choice in equilibrium conditions. Equation 5.102 establishes that companies pay profits to the owners by repurchasing their shares at market price and distributing dividends to them. Equation 5.103 determines the price at which shareholders buy new shares on the market. Equation 5.104 indicates income that companies have provided to shareholders and how they spend it in consumption and purchase of shares. Finally, Equation 5.105 describes the macroeconomic equilibrium between the aggregate demand on the one hand, composed by consumption of workers and shareholders and investment of firms, and the value of production, hence income distributed to workers and shareholders, on the other.

First, we go through the solution of the system reflecting the neoclassical PVM. In this case, the assumption is that the exogenous variables are given by the scarce endowments of capital K and labour L and by the parameters α, β, γ, δ; moreover, we set $\gamma = \delta = 1$. The parameter β indicates the intertemporal preference of individuals between present and future income. This means that in this model, stock price depends only on dividends and preferences, in line with the PVM. Through a few steps and simplifications, the solution of the model is as follows. Equation 5.101 determines the rate of profit r. Equation 5.100 gives the real wage w. Equations 5.102 and 5.103 jointly determine the share price P and dividends D. Equation 5.104

gives shareholders' consumption C. Equation 5.105 determines capital accumulation rate g.

It can be easily noticed that we are facing a typical "natural" equilibrium where all the endogenous variables are determined according to the neoclassical fundamentals of technology, preferences of individuals and the endowment of scarce productive factors. In particular, it is easy to verify that price's equilibrium value is given by $P = \alpha\beta K^{\alpha-1}L^{1-\alpha}$ while dividends' equilibrium value is given by $D = \alpha(1 - \beta)\, K^{\alpha-1}L^{1-\alpha}$. The Keynesian issue of effective demand plays no role in the solution of the system. It is worth noticing that Equation 5.105 must be read from right to left: that is, capital accumulation resulting from the investment decisions of companies is determined by households' saving choices, as typical in neoclassical analysis. Furthermore, there is no trace of the Marxian and Sraffian struggle between classes for the distribution of income: in fact, both wages and profits are determined endogenously on the basis of neoclassical fundamentals alone.

However, the stock market model can also give rise to a radically different solution, which follows the logic of the alternative paradigm. In this conceptual framework the exogenous variables change. In addition to K and α, the exogenous rate of capital accumulation g is included, which depends, in a usual Keynesian way, on the "animal spirits" of entrepreneurs. The "normal" levels of the real wage w and the rate of profit r are exogenous as well, as they result from the struggle between classes. In turn, the level of dividends is determined in exogenous terms as well, as a function of the "normal" rate of profit and an exogenous parameter ω, determined by this equation external to the model: $D = \omega(1 + r)$. Thus, the endogenous variables of the model change accordingly. Among these there is now the term β, which is considered here as an index of the extent to which any "bubble" tends to affect stock prices, which means that in this model prices can be uncoupled from dividends. Also, the terms γ and δ are now determined endogenously by demand and contribute to determining respectively the actual degree of utilization of productive capacity and therefore the actual quantity of labour γL employed in production, and the deviation of the market profit rate δr from the normal profit rate r.

The solution of the model is the following. Equation 5.101 determines the level of employment L matching the "normal" profit rate. Equation 5.104 gives shareholders' consumption C. Equation 5.105 gives the stock price level P. Equation 5.103 determines the β indicator of the presence of any "bubbles". Equation 5.102 determines the factor δ that helps to define the market profit rate δr. Equation 5.100 gives the actual degree of utilization of the production capacity γ and the related level of employment.

In this case we are faced with a "conflictual" equilibrium typical of the alternative paradigm. The "normal" levels of the distributive variables are determined exogenously on the basis of the power relations between social classes, in line with the Sraffian approach and more generally with Marx's methodology. Furthermore, the accumulation of capital that determines the demand for new capital goods is also considered exogenous, in line with the Keynesian principle of effective demand. Worth noticing that, in this case, Equation 5.105 must be read from left to right: the accumulation of capital, which is equal to firms' investment, determines production and income and therefore households' saving as well. Finally, through simple steps it is easy to verify that in equilibrium the level of share prices is given by $P = (1 + g) K$ while the level of dividends remains anchored to the "normal" distribution based on the equation outlined above: $D = \omega(1 + r)$. Note that neoclassical fundamentals of technology, preferences and scarce production factor endowments no longer play a role. Indeed, dividends are determined by the "normal" rate of profit and therefore by the struggle between classes, while share prices are determined by the pace of new investment, that is by the "animal spirits".

Finally, it is possible to make the analysis more realistic by assuming that share prices are influenced also by the portfolio choices of shareholders and by their possible "speculative" positions: for this purpose, the exogenous term λ alongside prices can be inserted in Equations 5.104 and 5.105, hence λP and therefore $P = (1 + g)K/\lambda$. Further changes can be made to account for the solvency conditions of the players involved, and so on.

It is evident that we are facing two very different ways of interpreting the manner in which the stock market works. But how to choose between the two models? Which of them is most accurate for the analysis of real market trends? As always, the choice between competing theories also depends on their empirical verification. Thus, it may be interesting to verify which of the two models is better able to incorporate the results of Shiller's test. Recall that the test shows a much greater variance of shares' market prices compared to ex-post prices calculated on the basis of the dividends actually paid. If we look at the solutions of the neoclassical model, we notice that the determinants of both stock prices and dividends are traceable to the same neoclassical fundamentals of technology, preferences and scarce factor endowments. Sharing the same determinants makes it very difficult to have in the model such different variances between stock prices and ex-post prices calculated on the basis of dividends. By contrast, in the alternative model the determinants are very different: whereas dividends are linked to the balance of power between social classes, share prices are driven by firms' investment choices and by possible shareholders' speculation. Since the determinants are different, it is reasonable to assume that they may have different variances. Even from this very preliminary observation it seems legitimate to state that the alternative model appears more capable of accounting for the greater variance in prices than in dividends detected by the Shiller's test.[28]

5.14   GROWTH AND CLIMATE CHANGE

Climate change with the related ecological crisis represents another crucial area in which there are significant differences between the alternative approaches of economic theory and policy. To highlight these differences, we will focus on the theses of William Nordhaus, a mainstream economist expert on environmental issues who received the Nobel Prize in 2018.

In his research, Nordhaus acknowledges that climate change is influenced at least in part by human activity: emissions of carbon dioxide and other pollutants contribute to Earth's temperature rising, and this can harm the well-being of everyone. Therefore, he tries to calculate the cost of ecological transition policies necessary to reduce polluting emissions and verifies whether this cost is higher or lower than the damage of climate change caused by the emissions. His goal is to find the optimal balance between the cost of ecological policies and the damage of climate change, that is, the cost that is worthwhile to bear to reduce this damage. More specifically, Nordhaus assesses how cost and damage should be shared over time between the present generation and future generations. In the light of his research, Nordhaus reaches controversial conclusions. In his opinion, it is wrong to require the current generation alone to bear the cost of the reduction of polluting emissions as soon as possible. Rather, emissions should be reduced at a gradual and increasing pace over time, that is, more at the expense of future generations, according to what has been called the "climate-policy ramp". The reason why Nordhaus argues that future generations should bear a larger share of the cost necessary to reduce emissions is that they will be richer than the present generation, thanks to the effects of technical progress and economic growth, and therefore be able to deal with the expenses necessary for the ecological transition more easily.

Simplifying as much as possible, we can present Nordhaus' thesis by making a few changes to the neoclassical model of growth described in previous pages of the present book. By defining with ΔT the variation of

---

[28]   Also refer to: E. Brancaccio and D. Buonaguidi (2019), "Stock Market Volatility Tests: A Classical–Keynesian Alternative to Mainstream Interpretations", *International Journal of Political Economy 48(3)*, 253–274; B. Algieri, E. Brancaccio and D. Buonaguidi (2020), "Stock market volatility, speculation and unemployment: a Granger-causality analysis", *PSL Quarterly Review 73(293)*, 137–160.

Earth's temperature with respect to a given "normal" level at the beginning of the century, with θ_1 and θ_2 two exogenous parameters and with D the economic damage deriving from the increase in temperature and the consequent climate change, it is possible to write down the following damage function:

$$D = 1/(1 + \theta_1 \Delta T^{\theta_2}) \tag{5.106}$$

Note that if $\Delta T = 0$ then $D = 1$: if temperature remains at its normal level there is no damage. On the other hand, if ΔT is greater than zero then D is less than one, and damage is caused at the macroeconomic level. Then we insert the climatic damage D in the usual production function of the neoclassical growth model; we also add a variable A, which describes technological progress:

$$y = ADk^\alpha \tag{5.107}$$

Assuming that A is between one and a number greater than one, while D is between one and a number less than one, it becomes clear that production can be increased by technical progress while it can be depressed by climate damage.

Using Equations 5.88, 5.89 and 5.93 of the growth model described in section 5.12, we can reach the stationary growth equilibrium of the neoclassical model. That is, assuming that s and g are both exogenous (with the latter equal to the exogenous growth rate n of the labour force), we can write Equation 5.93 as follows:

$$sADk^\alpha = (1 + g)k. \tag{5.108}$$

By rearranging the equation we will obtain the equilibrium level of k, or

$$k = [sAD/(1 + g)]^{1/1 - \alpha}. \tag{5.109}$$

Using it into Equation 5.89 we can then calculate the equilibrium level of the rate of profit, which corresponds to

$$r = \alpha AD[sAD/(1 + g)]^{(\alpha - 1)/(1 - \alpha)} - 1. \tag{5.110}$$

Finally, by using these equations in 5.88, we obtain the real equilibrium wage, equal to:

$$w = AD[sAD/(1 + g)]^{\alpha/(1 - \alpha)} - \alpha AD \, [sAD/(1 + g)]^{(\alpha - 1)/1 - \alpha)^2} \tag{5.111}$$

Let us compare two different steady-state growth equilibria, one for the current generation and another for the future generation. If we assume that the parameter α is constant and that the growth of the workforce and the propensity to save s do not change between one generation and the next, the two equilibria differ only in the respective levels of technical progress A and the resulting economic damage from climate change D. Let us assume for simplicity that the present generation starts from levels of A and D both approximately equal to one. We also suppose that future generations will record a greater increase in Earth's temperature, which makes D less than one, but at the same time they will enjoy technical progress such that A becomes greater than one. The future generation will therefore enjoy a per capita capital k, a per capita production y and an income distributed in the form of wages and profits that may be higher or lower than the current generation, depending whether climatic damage or technical progress prevails. Nordhaus argues that technical progress systematically tends to prevail over climate damage, so future generations will be richer than the current one. Therefore, in his opinion, the cost of reducing temperatures and limiting climate damage should be borne mostly by future generations.

Nordhaus's conclusions have been disputed from many sides. Environmental associations have argued against the idea that technical progress certainly outweighs the damage that derives from climate change: it may be that the second tends to overwhelm the first, thus making future generations poorer than the current one. For these reasons, environmentalists have accused Nordhaus of supporting poorly founded theses, which only serve to provide an alibi for those who oppose the immediate reduction of polluting emissions. Indeed, if we look at the climatic damage equation D, we notice that if parameters θ_1 and θ_2 are set high enough, then even small variations in temperature can bring the term D far below one, that is at a level that exceeds even an impetuous growth of technical progress A. In this case, future generations would actually be poorer, and it would not be fair to burden them with the larger part of the cost of the ecological transition. Furthermore, if the damage of climate change was particularly pervasive, it could itself jeopardize technical progress, thus making the economic decline of next generations inexorable. This does not seem to have occurred so far, but it cannot be excluded from our future horizons.

However, this critique is not the only or most effective that can be made to Nordhaus. Further objections can be raised from the alternative growth and distribution perspective. Recall that this model draws on the Keynesian principle of effective demand, according to which capital accumulation rate g is determined exogenously by autonomous decisions of the entrepreneurs, influenced by the optimistic or pessimistic view that pervades the economy. This means that g can be highly unstable compared to what Nordhaus' neoclassical model supposes: there, this variable depends on forces that move in a decidedly more predictable way, that is, the growth of the workforce, which ultimately matches population growth. Given that in the real world g is more unstable than in Nordhaus' and neoclassical assumptions, it becomes much more complicated to predict future generations' economic equilibrium, and therefore more questionable to assume that it will be richer than the present one and rich enough to be able to bear the higher costs of the ecological transition.

More than that, it is worth noting that Nordhaus' model endogenously determines both profit and wages, as typical in neoclassical theory. Therefore, these variables cannot be changed, because their equilibrium levels are given by the maximum and efficient use of labour and capital. This explains why Nordhaus and neoclassical scholars in general deal with redistributive problems only with respect to the relation between different generations, while avoiding any issue concerning the conflictual distribution of income between social classes. By contrast, the alternative model draws on Marxian and Sraffian hypothesis, according to which the profit rate r is determined exogenously by power relations between social classes, thus is subject to variations according to the outcome of their struggle. For example, social conflict could force capital owners to carry the burden of the ecological transition through a reduction in the rate of profit. In effect, the alternative model sheds light on a crucial aspect of climate change: the ecological transition needed to reduce polluting emissions raises a problem of cost distribution that generates not only a conflict between generations but also between social classes.

Students can go back to section 5.12 on alternative theories of growth and distribution and elaborate the critiques to Nordhaus based on the alternative model in both algebraic and graphical form.

5.15   THE ECONOMIC CONSEQUENCES OF COVID-19

In the latest edition of their manual, Blanchard and his co-authors include some thoughts on the coronavirus pandemic and the possible economic consequences. The analysis is carried out using the new IS–LM–PC model, but we will see that its fundamental features can also be described using the traditional AS–AD model.

We start from a usual situation of natural equilibrium, as described for example starting from section 2.8 of this volume. Blanchard's central thesis is that the crisis triggered by the virus causes changes not only on the demand side but also, primarily, on the supply side. The reason is that the lockdown and other social distancing measures aimed at containing the spread of the virus also result in a reduction in workers able to reach workplaces, continue their activities, etc. In other words, the amount of work available is reduced. The consequences of this situation affect primarily the way in which Blanchard represents the labour market. In fact, the equation of the real wage offered by firms is no longer horizontal but becomes vertical, representing what we could define the "social distancing unemployment rate", which we indicate here with u_d and which, according to Blanchard, is higher than the natural rate of unemployment we started from: $u_d < u_n$. Furthermore, Blanchard assumes that government's income support measures create a wage floor that prevents real wages from falling even if unemployment rises, so that the equilibrium real wage remains at the usual level $W/P = A/(1 + \mu)$. This implies that the equation of the real wage requested by workers is no longer decreasing but is horizontal at the ante-virus level. The new equilibrium on the labour market is therefore represented by the cross made by the vertical line of the wage offered and the horizontal line of the required wage, with a real equilibrium wage that remains unchanged and an unemployment rate that becomes higher. This new equilibrium on the labour market, of course, will also have repercussions on the respective AS–AD chart, where a new level of "social distancing production" must be traced. We indicate it here with Y_d and it will be lower than the natural production level: $Y_d < Y_n$.

The effect of social distancing on the demand side shall be added: the decline in employment in fact means a fall in income and therefore in consumption, as well as entrepreneurs' uncertainty about the future and thus a fall in investment. The AD, therefore, shifts to the left. According to Blanchard, the decline in consumption and investment is likely to be so large as to place aggregate demand even below the new Y_d equilibrium. In this case, at least according to the AS–AD model, mass unemployment should spontaneously lead to the usual deflation of wages and prices, which would yield an expansion in the quantity of real money, reduce the interest rate and thus foster investment again, demand and production until the new equilibrium Y_d is reached. However, Blanchard excludes this possibility, both because he assumes that income support measures will prevent wages from falling, and because he has come to believe that deflation does more harm than good to the economy. He therefore suggests implementing expansionary policies, both monetary and fiscal, to bring the AD upwards to the new Y_d equilibrium. In no case, however, can these policies lead the economy to the old natural equilibrium Y_n, which remains unattainable as long as the employment constraint caused by social distancing measures exists. In this regard, Blanchard even argues that monetary and fiscal expansion beyond the Y_d limit would only end up fuelling an inflationary trend.

The following thesis can thus be drawn from Blanchard's model: as long as social distancing is implemented, the pandemic determines a decline in production and equilibrium income while it should leave income distribution substantially unchanged. Expansive policies can mitigate the decline in production and employment but as long as the distancing lasts, they cannot restore the natural equilibrium. Let us now see if we can reach different conclusions based on the alternative approach. This approach, as we shall see, formulates three objections to Blanchard's interpretation of the pandemic.

We begin with the limit on production caused by social distancing and represented by the vertical line of the real wage offered and the corresponding levels of unemployment u_d and production Y_d. This limit can be safely accepted also in the alternative model. After all, this is a constraint caused by social distancing only, which is unrelated to any specific assumptions about income distribution and therefore has nothing to do with the controversial idea of a natural equilibrium. But are we sure that this constraint is necessary? The fact that the alternative model denies the existence of a natural equilibrium has implications for the relevance of the limit imposed by u_d and Y_d. As a matter of fact, in this model we usually start from a Keynesian equilibrium, whose constraint is generally given by a level of effective demand lower than the maximum potential production. This means that this alternative analysis describes a situation in which there is a systematic excess of available work and unused production capacity. This difference is crucial for analyzing the effects of the pandemic. If the system is already below the maximum potential level of production, then the roof imposed by social distancing is less likely to become binding on the growth of production. In fact, even accepting that the lockdown and other public health measures prevent many people from working, we should take into account that there are many unemployed workers and unused production capacity, which may become available for productive activity. In other words, some will choose or be forced to stay at home due to the virus, but others who were previously unemployed may instead be available to work. It is obvious that the pandemic could give rise to bottlenecks that could limit production in various sectors for a while, but if we start from low levels of aggregate demand, it becomes less likely that these production troubles generalize and become binding on the general macroeconomic equilibrium. Therefore, if we start from a Keynesian equilibrium with low demand, it becomes less likely that the measures to contrast the pandemic cause such a shortage of workers as to place the roof indicated by u_d and

Y_d below the ante-virus equilibrium. This has two implications. From a theoretical point of view, the labour market can be analyzed in the usual way, without the need to consider the curve of the offered real wage vertical. And from the point of view of economic policy, expansive monetary and fiscal manoeuvres can be implemented more decisively, as there is less risk of encountering a general production constraint and therefore creating inflationary tensions.

The second objection that can be raised to Blanchard concerns the productivity of labour, representing the quantity of goods and services produced on average by each worker in a year, and indicated with the term A. It is reasonable to assume that, at least initially, measures to contrast the pandemic may lead to difficulties and slowdowns in the production and distribution processes of goods and services, and therefore to a decline in labour productivity, at least temporarily. But if A decreases, as it is well known, then there is a risk of an increase in prices $P = (1 + \mu)W/A$, unless a reduction in the monetary wage W or in the mark-up μ occurs. However, in the mainstream model this issue cannot be examined: to simplify the analysis, Blanchard sets productivity $A = 1$ and therefore implicitly assumes that it is not affected by policy to contrast the pandemic. This is a relevant limitation of his model.

Finally, we examine Blanchard's hypothesis that, after the pandemic, the real equilibrium wage $W/P = A/(1 + \mu)$ remains unchanged at the ante-virus level. The reason he gives is that income support measures prevent wages from falling despite unemployment. From a theoretical point of view, here the hypothesis is necessary because the line of the offered real wage is drawn vertically, and therefore cannot help in determining the mark-up μ and the connected real wage. Claiming that the mark-up remains at the ante-virus level is thus a way to fix it as an exogenous variable once again. However, explaining this invariance of the mark-up through income support policy is an unprecedented fact for Blanchard and his co-authors. The reader of the present textbook is aware that up to this point a policy of subsidy and income support could at most intervene on the parameter z and in this way affect the real wages requested by workers, hence natural unemployment. But the option that these policies could affect the mark-up and thus the real equilibrium wage and the related distribution of income was excluded. With this novelty, albeit implicitly, Blanchard seems to recognize that subsidies can affect the profit margin. Apart from anti-trust measures, it is the first time that it is admitted in the mainstream model that policy that interferes with the conflict between social classes can influence the mark-up.

If we instead follow the logic of the alternative model, the question does not apply. In fact, in the alternative approach the Marxian and Sraffian idea, according to which the mark-up and other distributive variables are determined by the conflict between social classes, is generally accepted. In the alternative scenario, however, there is no reason to believe that the pandemic will leave the real equilibrium wage unchanged. Income support policies will certainly be able to curb the decline in wages, as Blanchard says, but we can guess that if the crisis persists, workers will be contractually weakened and therefore real wages will eventually fall. The factors that influence the distribution of income are many more than what Blanchard's model suggests.

The conclusion of the alternative model is that the economic consequences of the pandemic may be more complex than those described by Blanchard's analysis. In the first place, if we start from an equilibrium with low demand, the constraint on production caused by social distancing measures does not necessarily become relevant, thus it is even possible that appropriate expansionary policies allow the restoration of the ante-virus equilibrium without inflationary risk. Moreover, distancing measures may also lead to a decline in labour productivity. Finally, the pandemic is likely to induce significant changes in real wages and in the distribution of income across social classes.

Of course, like all major events of historic relevance, the coronavirus crisis is so articulated and complex that it cannot be analyzed through the simple tools of the didactic models examined here. The hints contained in these paragraphs can nonetheless be useful for a preliminary investigation of the phenomenon. Students are invited to derive graphical representations.

5.16 MARKET VERSUS PLANNING: THE COVID-19 PANDEMIC

In this textbook, the comparative approach has been applied to different macroeconomic theories so as to deal with two issues concerning a capitalist economy either left to market forces or influenced by public policy: (i) what determines the aggregate level of production and employment; and (ii) how the income produced is distributed between workers' wages and capital owners' profit. We gave some preliminary answers to these questions, using mostly short-term macroeconomic models, mentioning on few occasions long-term growth models. The comparison between the mainstream and the alternative method has been framed within this methodological and theoretic perimeter. The comparative approach, however, can be applied to further issues in economic theory, anytime that controversies arise. With the aim of broadening the scope of the analysis, in this section we cope with a more general matter with respect to those previously presented. It concerns the controversy in the organization of a modern economy as a whole.

In extremely simplified terms, we can distinguish two extreme cases. On the one hand, there are capitalist market systems in which the property of the means of production is predominantly private, and the organization of production is largely determined by decentralized decisions taken by a multiplicity of private owners acting in the market. At the other end of the spectrum, we can find systems based on public planning in which the principal decisions on the organization of the production of goods and on income distribution do not take place in the market, but are taken predominantly by the state, and thus are centralized. If the planning system is also characterized by collective property on the principal means of production, then, more precisely, we are facing a socialist planning system. It is obvious that these extreme cases combine in various forms in the real world (and through history).

Olivier Blanchard, in the debate that has been included in this volume, took a stance on the matter, and it is worth raising a few notes on this. Although Blanchard expressed his favour towards the idea of government's agency in economic policy, he also specified that such policy should operate in a free-market capitalist system. In his opinion, it does not exist as an alternative to the capitalist mode of production. Relying on alternative organizing principles of the economy, such as planning, would be a mistake. The vast majority of economists share this view. Planning tends to be associated with the historical experience of "real socialism", that is the Soviet Union and other countries of the "socialist bloc", unfolding between the Bolshevik Revolution in 1917 and the fall of the Berlin Wall in 1989. For many people, the dissolution of the Soviet world that followed represents still today factual proof that would demonstrate the inefficiency of systems based on planning. Using the lens of history, however, China should be considered part of the "socialist bloc", and it is going through a long phase of impressive development. But its economy is nowadays seen as a complex mixture between public planning and capitalist market, therefore it does not seem to represent an example clearly in favour of one of the two systems. It is worth mentioning nonetheless that the concept of planning has been evoked in different situations beyond the socialist experience. In 1974, during the first oil crisis, even in the United States, the symbol of capitalism and free market, a debate on planning took place. Inspired by the economist and Nobel prize winner Wassily Leontief, the discussion focussed on the existence of "failures" in the decentralized market system and on the possibility of broadening the scope for decisions taken at a centralized level by the government. The debate was put aside a few years later, with the advent of the *Reaganomics* liberalist doctrine.

But today, after the so-called global great recession of 2008 and the critiques raised against the current accumulation regime, based on free market and private finance, occasionally the debate on possible alternatives comes to the surface. In this regard, defendants of the current market system insist on the idea that alternatives such as planning would be based on a state bureaucracy characterized by opaque, slow and cumbersome decisions, and on the impossible claim of assigning to a single central body of the state the task of determining the prices of the economic system. This would give rise to a whole series of inefficiencies and errors, usually referred to as "failures of the state". Furthermore, critics of planning are also convinced that individual, civil and political freedoms would not be adequately protected in a system where the state centralizes the main economic levers. The proponents of a modern take on planning, however, argue that "market failures" can be even more serious and more pervasive than those attributed to state bodies. In their opinion, the free capitalist market more easily generates unemployment and underutilization of productive capacity, recurrent crises, inequalities, waste of natural resources, unsolved negative externalities such as climate emergencies, and more generally causes problems of coordination of decisions. Furthermore, the market would be characterized only in appearance by the free decisions of a multiplicity of decentralized and independent private subjects: the trend towards centralization of capital means that it is, in reality, increasingly dominated by "economic giants", which concentrate the power to take decisions. In this sense, even in a capitalist market system there is the risk that economic, and therefore also political, power will concentrate in so few hands that even individual freedom and rights can be jeopardized.

Obviously, these few lines do not cover exhaustively the complex comparison between the capitalist market system and its possible alternatives. The debate remains open and goes beyond the purposes of this manual. Here we only mention two theories that are often evoked in the discussion on the subject. On the one hand we will examine Smith's so-called "invisible hand theorem", in defence of the capitalist system based on decentralized market decision. On the other hand, we will briefly deal with game theory and, in particular, an example of Nash's non-cooperative game, which can be useful in highlighting the social benefit of centralized planning of certain decisions.

Among the arguments in favour of the free capitalist market, the best known is the so-called "invisible hand theorem" developed by Adam Smith, one of the founding fathers of economic science and author of *The Wealth of Nations* in 1776. According to this "theorem" each individual acts in the free market guided by its own selfishness, but precisely by following their own particular interest they will contribute to general economic development and therefore will unwittingly end up serving the interest of the community. Smith writes that "everyone is led by an invisible hand to promote an end that was not part of his intention". The impersonal forces of supply and demand in the free market thus represent an "invisible hand" that causes a heterogony of ends, in the sense that it is precisely by pursuing their selfish objectives that single individuals are indirectly led to accomplish the common good. Smith adds that "it is not from the benevolence of the butcher, the brewer, or the baker that we expect our dinner, but from their regard to their own self-interest". The reason why the "theorem" works, according to Smith, is that those who run a business, competing with each other, will try to prevail by producing exactly the commodities that consumers want. Furthermore, capitalists will try to adopt the most efficient production methods in order to minimize costs, and thus be more competitive than their direct competitors. The reduction in costs implies that goods are sold at the lowest possible price. Therefore, as production constantly adapts to the wishes of consumers and sale prices become lower and lower, the development and widespread well-being of the entire community is guaranteed. Broadly speaking, these are the reasons why, according to Smith, it is good to let market forces and competition free to operate. And this is, after all, the best-known theoretical basis of the economic policy of the so-called "laissez-faire", also called "liberalism".

Smith's theorem, therefore, says that only from the action of a myriad of selfish, independent individuals competing with each other on the market can the collective good arise. This idea represented a shocking novelty for those moral theories of society, often of religious origin, according to which only the redemption of individuals can induce them to charity and thus promote the common good. Even Smith's thesis, however, was challenged on its own ground: efficiency. Critics of the free capitalist market argue that the latter can give rise to faults, wastes and situations of social malaise that can only be resolved through coordination of decisions based on public planning mechanisms.

An example in this regard comes from the so-called game theory, a method of analysis that examines situations in which there are problems of "strategy", that is, cases in which the decision of each subject depends on their expectations about the actions of the other participants in the game. If we look at strategy in this way, it is a concept that is typical not only of economics but also of other areas, from chess to team sports, to diplomatic disputes and military conflicts between different countries. Now we apply game theory to a typical case of free market efficiency. To this end, we will examine the case of a "non-cooperative Nash equilibrium", named after John Nash, the Nobel Prize-winning economist who greatly contributed in elaborating it.

Let us consider a problem of the greatest relevance and typical of modern production processes: the choice between private or public management of scientific research and technological development activities. These activities have two contrasting characteristics: on the one hand, the agents who carry them out have huge costs and thus try to draw the maximum profit out of them selling the results achieved in the market; on the other hand, if the results of these activities were made available to everyone, this would result in a more rapid dissemination of knowledge capable of further increasing the collective well-being. In other words, scientific research and technological development are expensive but also yield a positive externality: they generate positive social effects that escape the usual mechanism based on the exchange of private goods at prices set by the market. To this regard, scientific research and technical development activities in the fields of energy, environmental protection, aerospace, artificial intelligence, etc., are relevant examples. But perhaps the most emblematic case concerns research in the medical and pharmaceutical fields: we can raise here the specific situation of Covid-19 and on the measures to defeat it.

Let us make an example inspired by research on the virus. We consider two large private companies, A and B, which operate in the production of vaccines, drugs and therapies in general in the fight against the pandemic. These companies have to choose whether to adopt a conflictive or a cooperative strategy. The conflicting strategy occurs when each company retains private ownership of its scientific and technical discoveries, preventing the other from learning about them or patenting the discoveries and demanding very high prices for their use. The cooperative strategy occurs when the two companies decide to make their respective scientific and technical discoveries available to each other. Now imagine that A and B find themselves in the situation described by the following table.

The numbers – which in the jargon of game theory are called "payoffs" – indicate the respective profits of the two companies according to the strategies adopted, while the term in brackets indicates the level of

Table 5.4   An example of non-cooperative Nash equilibrium and inefficiency of market mechanism

	B cooperates	B defects
A cooperates	3; 3 (high collective benefit)	–1; 4 (medium collective benefit)
A defects	4; –1 (medium collective benefit)	1; 1 (low collective benefit)

scientific and technological progress that the community as a whole can enjoy according to different situations.

For example, let us assume that A and B both defect, that is, they keep their respective technical-scientific discoveries for themselves or demand very high prices to disseminate them: in this case they will obtain profits equal to 1 billion each but the scientific and technical progress of the community will be low, since knowledge does not spread (bottom right box). Instead, if the two companies cooperate and make their discoveries available to each other at no cost, then they will obtain 3 billion in profits each and the community will be able to benefit from a high technical-scientific progress generated by the dissemination of knowledge (top left box). Finally, if one of the two companies cooperates by making its technical-scientific discoveries available while the other defects by keeping its discoveries secret or demanding very high prices to make them available, then the first company will obtain negative profits equal to –1 billion, since it will run into costs to obtain results and will not be able to benefit from the discoveries of the other firm, while the latter will obtain positive profits of 4 billion since it will be able to use its discoveries in an exclusive way and enjoy the discoveries of the competitor for free. In this case, the overall scientific progress for the community lies in between the two other cases, given that one of the two companies retains its knowledge but the other disseminates it (boxes at the bottom left and top right).

Well, it is easy to verify that defect, under these conditions, is the dominant strategy, that is, it is the strategy that will be preferred by each company regardless of the choice of the other. Let us compare the profits that can be obtained in different circumstances from company A:

- if B defects then A is better off fighting (A gets 1 billion profit instead of –1);
- but even if B cooperates, for A it is still worthwhile to defect (A gets 4 billion instead of 3).

It is easy to verify by looking at the table that the same is true for B. The final result is that both firms will choose to defect. The system will thus be in equilibrium only in the box at the bottom right, in which each company obtains 1 billion in profits and technical-scientific progress is low for the community as a whole, being limited by the fact that discoveries remain private. This is called Nash's non-cooperative equilibrium. It is interesting to note that this equilibrium is reached despite the fact that it generates a worse result than cooperation, both for individual companies and for the community as a whole. One might wonder why the two companies do not find a cooperation agreement, reaching the equilibrium in the box at the top left. The problem is that such an agreement between them would be fragile: the payoffs show that the temptation for each one to defect from the agreement, or even just the fear of the defection of the competitor, pushes both to defect. It could be assumed that if the game is "repeated" something changes, as repetition of inefficient outcomes could favour cooperation. However, it is evident that we are faced with a situation in which the selfish free behaviour of each player in the market determines an inefficient result for all. To this respect we can say that Nash's non-cooperative equilibrium contains an implicit criticism of the liberal view that was typical of Smith's old invisible hand theorem. As we have seen, this conclusion also applies to the scientific research devoted to the fight against Covid-19, thus showing how relevant this critique can be.

How can we push the economic system towards the cooperative equilibrium and maintain it in the box at the top left? A solution could be assigning to the state a relevant role in scientific research and technological development, for example by giving significant resources to an office for public planning of investment in research and development. The public authority would assume the costs of carrying out the research, and also make the results obtained available. The dissemination of knowledge would thus determine both an increase in the profits of private companies themselves and a general increase in technical-scientific progress for the well-being of the community. In the specific case of Covid-19, if such a solution was adopted we could then speak of some sort of "scientific communism in the fight against the virus": that is to say, a central public authority acquires the private knowledge of individual companies to make them available for free to the entire scientific community engaged in the search for effective therapies against the virus. More generally, in any area in which there are externalities, under given conditions it may happen that a centralized planning system gives more satisfactory results than the usual decentralized mechanisms typical of the capitalist market system.

Appendix 1   Labour flexibility and unemployment

Domenico Suppa

A1.1   INTRODUCTION

In order to assess some of the policy implications of the two alternative macroeconomic models presented in the previous pages, it would be important to check the existence of a relationship between the *Employment Protection Legislation* (EPL) and the *unemployment rate*. Among the many works that have been devoted to the relationship between these two variables, we want to replicate here a famous test carried out on several occasions by the OECD.[1] This way, students will be able to reproduce some research results in the field of employment protection. The proposed exercise, based on the OECD analysis, constitutes a first approach to the empirical research and therefore constitutes an attempt to satisfy, even though at an elementary level, the increasing need to validate propositions designed within a theoretical system not only by their logical coherence, but also on the ground of their congruence with the data.

Next, we will introduce the procedure to collect statistical data used into the final calculation of the so-called correlation index, with some hints on the regression analysis. From the operational point of view, and in the author's intention, this is the track for a simple exercise to be performed in a two-hour class. Of course, a theoretical discussion on the proposed statistical and econometric methodologies is beyond the scope of these few pages: relevant references will be provided in the footnotes. Therefore, in the next section, an intuitive approach is adopted to present the statistical concepts involved in this exercise.

---

[1]   A survey of these works is contained in OECD (2013), *OECD Employment Outlook 2013*, Paris: OECD Publishing. Results obtained directly by the OECD (since 1999) have been published in several OECD Outlooks available at http://www.oecd.org, topics: Employment.

A1.2 CORRELATION INDEX AND SIMPLE REGRESSION IN BRIEF

In economics, as in other disciplines, statistical methods are used intensively with many research objectives: from the measurement of elementary phenomena to the verification of complex theoretical models. On the other hand, each model, though sophisticated, always represents a stylized simplification of real phenomena and of their correlations. Moreover, the measurement of any phenomenon, even of the most elementary, always comes from an approximation that is inevitably affected by errors. Statistics and probability calculus – on which the so-called *statistical inference* is based – may be able to "control" the various, always present, sources of error, thus constituting an indispensable support in every scientific field, including that of economics.

A typical goal of statistical sciences is to verify whether there is a *probabilistic* dependence between two phenomena, for example *x* and *y*, and measure its strength, if this dependence exists. In the calculus of probabilities two events (such as, for example: (a) the introduction of a law reducing workers' protection from layoffs; and (b) the change in the unemployment rate) are mutually independent if the occurrence of one does not modify the probability that the other might occur; otherwise the two events are mutually dependent in probabilistic terms.

Of course, this probabilistic dependence can take different forms or it may be completely absent (if the events are mutually independent). It should be pointed out that the definition of probabilistic dependence in general does not describe a *cause–effect* relationship: the identification of relations of causality is the primary task of theoretical analysis, and only subsequently the causal links may be verified by the use of advanced statistical techniques (which will not be treated here). It is clear, however, that, given certain conditions, if the variables taken into account appear to be mutually independent, even the theoretical hypothesis on the causality link cannot be considered valid (or, using the terminology of statistical inference, significant) on the basis of its empirical verification. On the other hand, if there is some form of regular and systematic dependence between the variables, this should emerge from the methodologies of statistical analysis applied to empirical data.

The propositions of a theoretical paradigm specify at least the sign of a precise functional link: for example, "*y* is a growing function of *x*" or "the unemployment rate decreases as labour flexibility increases". We can thus state a theoretical hypothesis that can and must be evaluated, that is, submitted to empirical verification.

As a first approximation, the *correlation index* can be used to verify the presence of a functional link between two variables. This is an index that expresses *the strength of the linear link* between two variables. The so-called

Table A1.1   Some statistics for X and Y

N	X	Y	X−E(X)	Y−E(Y)	[X−E(X)]^2	[Y−E(Y)]^2	[X−E(X)]*[Y−E(Y)]
1	20	35	−32.14	−15.71	1033.163	246.939	505.102
2	30	20	−22.14	−30.71	490.306	943.367	680.102
3	40	80	−12.14	29.29	147.449	857.653	−355.612
4	60	90	7.86	39.29	61.735	1543.367	308.673
5	65	30	12.86	−20.71	165.306	429.082	−266.327
6	70	60	17.86	9.29	318.878	86.224	165.816
7	80	40	27.86	−10.71	776.020	114.796	−298.469
Sum	**365**	**355**	0	0	**2992.857**	**4221.429**	**739.286**
Mean	52.1429	50.7143					

linear approximation, for its computational simplicity (since it is constructed only with operations of sum and multiplication), is the first step in the study of a functional link. In some cases, linear approximation also leads to satisfactory results: it is able to capture the relationship between the variables of interest in a rather accurate way. Let us see now how the correlation coefficient is calculated by using a simple numerical example with the aid of a spreadsheet. In Table A1.1, the terms $E(X)$ and $E(Y)$ indicate the arithmetic mean of the X and Y variables respectively. In this table the columns report: the observation unit number; the values of the variable X; the values of the variable Y; deviations of each value of X and Y from the respective average (note that the sum of such deviations is always equal to zero); the square of deviations; and the product of deviations.

Table A1.1 contains all the information needed to calculate the correlation index with the formula:[2]

$$\rho(X,Y) = \frac{\sum_{i=1}^{N}\{[X_i - E(X)][Y_i - E(Y)]\}}{\sqrt{\sum_{i=1}^{N}[X_i - E(X)]^2}\sqrt{\sum_{i=1}^{N}[Y_i - E(Y)]^2}}$$

$$= \frac{739.286}{\sqrt{2992.857}\sqrt{4221.429}}$$

$$\rho(X,Y) = 0.208 \tag{A1.1}$$

---

[2]   To compute the correlation index, a perfectly equivalent formula more efficient in computational terms can be used (since it drastically reduces the number of differences that can cause underflow errors): $\rho(X,Y) = \frac{E(XY) - E(X)E(Y)}{\sqrt{E(X^2) - [E(X)]^2}\sqrt{E(Y^2) - [E(Y)]^2}}$

This formula defines the correlation index $\rho(X, Y)$ and shows that it is the result of the ratio between the *covariance* (the numerator) and the product of *standard deviations* of the two variables (the denominator).[3] The denominator of the ratio that defines ρ is always greater than zero (if X and Y are not constant) and it is necessary in order to make the measurement expressed by ρ an absolute number, that is, independent from the unit of measurement of the two variables and therefore suitable for comparisons. The numerator, being the sum of products of the deviations from the average of the two variables, reflects the congruence or the discordance of their signs and the magnitude of such differences, determining the sign and the magnitude of the correlation index. The following charts (Figure A1.1) are helpful in understanding the gist of the previous considerations. The two graphs at the top represent in sequence the X and Y variables of the previous table. The graph at the bottom left is the scatter plot of the two variables, and the graph at the bottom right shows, through dashed segments, deviations from average (or residuals).

The correlation coefficient tends to assume positive values if deviations fall, on average, between the first and the third quadrant (relative to the perpendicular lines that pass through the average values $\bar{X} = E(X)$ and $\bar{Y} = E(Y)$). Conversely, the numerator tends to assume negative values if deviations fall mainly in the second and fourth quadrant originated by the lines perpendicular to $\bar{X}$ and $\bar{Y}$.

In the example above, ρ assumes a very low positive value (0.208), indicating that the variables X and Y are essentially uncorrelated.

The following important properties of the correlation coefficient can be drawn from its formula:[4]

1. symmetry: $\rho(X, Y) = \rho(Y, X)$;
2. the correlation of a variable with itself is equal to one: $\rho(X, X) = 1$;
3. the correlation index assumes values between -1 and 1;
4. the correlation index is invariant (except the sign) if the two variables are modified by linear transformations;

---

[3] This can be shown by multiplying and dividing the formula by the number of observations.
[4] The properties of the correlation coefficient will be easily memorized considering that it is the cosine of the angle between the X and Y vectors (belonging to the N-dimensions Euclidean space, where N is the number of observations). For a rigorous introduction to statistical methods and their theoretical foundations: F.M. Dekking, C. Kraaikamp, H.P. Lopuhaä and L.E. Meester (2005), *A Modern Introduction to Probability and Statistics: Understanding Why and How*, London, UK: Springer; or the classic G. Casella and R.L. Berger (2002), *Statistical Inference*, Pacific Grove, USA: Duxbury. For an introduction to econometrics at an intermediate level see J.H. Stock and M.W. Watson (2011), *Introduction to Econometrics* (3rd edn), Boston, USA: Pearson; or, at a more advanced level, W.H. Green (2012), *Econometric Analysis* (7th edn), Upper Saddle River, USA: Prentice Hall.

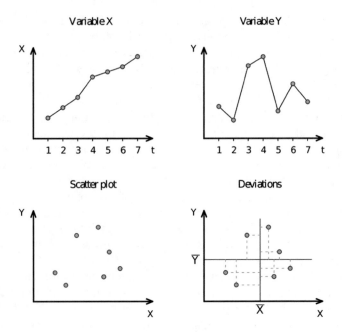

Figure A1.1 A graphical description of the two variables

5. the correlation index is 1 or –1 only if there is a perfect linear link (respectively positive or negative) between the two variables;
6. if the variables X and Y are independent (*in the probabilistic sense*), the correlation index $\rho\,(X,\,Y)$ is null.

The last proposition is not invertible: uncorrelated variables ($\rho = 0$) are not always independent, while property number 6 states that independent variables are always uncorrelated.

When the correlation index shows a *significant* linear link, the next step is to estimate this functional relationship by determining its parameters, that is, by performing a *regression analysis*. Indeed, a high correlation indicates that there is a relationship between variables x and y of the type:[5]

---

[5] The validity of a regression model requires that all standard assumptions on which its formulation is based are satisfied and, where necessary and possible, econometric techniques are applied to remove the assumptions which are not satisfied. For a complete discussion of regression model theory students can refer to the literature cited in the previous footnote. It is also worth emphasizing that, for obvious reasons of space, in this hyper-simplified exposition we do not distinguish between random variables, sample and sample realization, between parameter, estimator and estimated value, although it would be required for a correct

$$y_i = a + bx_i + e_i \qquad (A1.2)$$

where a and b are respectively the intercept and the angular coefficient (the slope) of the line that approximates the points of the scatter plot and $e_i = y_i - a - bx_i$ represents the *error* made with such approximation. The method used to estimate the parameters a and b of the regression line $y_i = a + bx_i$ is to *minimize the sum of the squares of residuals (errors* in our simplified terminology) $Dev(e) = \Sigma_{i=1}^{N} e_i^2$. Following this analytical procedure, we obtain the parameters:

$$b = \frac{\sqrt{\sum_{i=1}^{N} [y_i - E(y)]^2}}{\sqrt{\sum_{i=1}^{N} [x_i - E(x)]^2}} \, \rho(x,y) \quad a = \bar{y} - b\bar{x} \qquad (A1.3)$$

In the numeric example above, we get the following estimated parameters:

$$b = \frac{\sqrt{4221.429}}{\sqrt{2992.857}} \, 0.208 = 0.247$$

$$a = 50.7143 - 0.247 \times 52.1429 = 37.835 \qquad (A1.4)$$

A preliminary criterion to evaluate the *fitness* of the *regression line* to the points of the scatter plot is the ratio between the variability explained by the estimated regression line and the variability of the y variable. This ratio is called *coefficient of determination* and is indicated by the symbol (*R-squared*). The calculation of R^2 derives from the definition recalled above and it can be demonstrated that it is equal to the square of the correlation index:

$$R^2 = [\rho(x,y)]^2 = 1 - \frac{Dev(e)}{Dev(y)} \qquad (A1.5)$$

where is the deviance of the y variable (that is, the sum of squared residuals of y from its mean). In our numerical example we get:

$$R^2 = 0.208^2 = 0.04326 \qquad (A1.6)$$

---

inferential approach. For example, we should have differentiated random variables (r. v.) like *error terms* (by definition unknown) from their *estimator* (which also are r. v.) and from the *residuals* (which are particular realizations of error terms).

Normally, the correct version of R^2 computed by means of correct variances is also used. In any case, the R^2 index indicates how much of the total variance (*total sum of squares*, TSS) of y is explained by the regression line. This is the result of a *variance decomposition*: the TSS equals the sum of the regression's variance (ESS: *explained sum of squares*) plus the *residual sum of squares* (RSS).

An important criterion to test the validity of a regression model is the statistical test on the angular coefficient b. This test formulates the *null hypothesis* H0: "coefficient b is zero" against the *alternative hypothesis* H1: "coefficient b is not zero", and compares the test statistic t_c, the ratio between the estimated parameter b and its standard deviation, with the theoretical value assumed by the Student random variable t in correspondence of N-2 degrees of freedom (where N is the number of observations) and an assigned level of significance α (this *test size* is the probability of rejecting H0 when it is true, that is, the probability of committing the *error of the first kind*; conventionally a is generally fixed at 0.001, 0.01 or 0.05).[6] When N assumes a high value, in practice, it can be taken into account that for a level of significance α of 5 per cent, the theoretical t takes the value ±1.96 and therefore H0 can be rejected (at the level of significance of 5 per cent), if the value of t_c (in absolute value) exceeds this threshold.[7]

The interpretation of the probability (called *p-value*) that the theoretical t (in absolute value) takes a value greater than $|t_c|$ is more immediate. In this case, once we define α, it will be enough to check that the *p-value* $< \alpha$ in order to reject H0 with a probability of error of the first kind less than α. If we know the *p-value* we can avoid using probability distribution tables of the *t-Student random variable* to decide whether to accept or reject H0.

The first step in the analysis of the relationship between two quantitative variables is the graphical analysis of their scatter plot (a very useful but sometimes neglected analytical tool). In the graphs in Figure A1.2, we thus propose some simulations and express for each of them the correlation coefficient and the determination index among x and y.

The graphs show how the distribution of points in the plan is related to the value of the indicators we are dealing with. Both ρ and R^2 provide clear information on the fact that there is a particular type of probabilistic dependence between the variables: a linear relationship that can be well

---

[6]   When appropriate conditions are satisfied, the ratio between the b parameter and its standard deviation is in fact distributed as a *t-Student random variable*.

[7]   As any change to the state of affairs generally represents an expensive operation, the *statistical hypothesis test* assumes a conservative perspective by assigning small values to the probability of committing the *error of the first kind* (having identified with H0 the *null hypothesis*), preserving in such way the *status quo*.

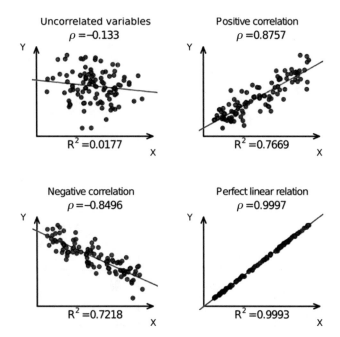

Figure A1.2   Correlations between variables

approximated by a straight line. One has to be careful, because in many cases the variables studied are linked by relations that are not linear. The graphs in Figure A1.3 show some of these circumstances, pointing out that even when linear correlation is absent, there may be very strong functional links between the variables. These relations are detectable through the scatter plot examination.

In cases similar to those shown in Figure A1.3, parabolic, sinusoidal, logarithmic and exponential functional forms may be more appropriate than a straight line to approximate and describe the probabilistic dependence between x and y variables.

A1.3   THE RELATIONSHIP BETWEEN EPL AND UNEMPLOYMENT RATE

Let us apply the tools described in the previous paragraphs to the relationship between the labour protection index and unemployment rates. The OECD database provides a large amount of economic data that can be selected and downloaded by anyone who has access to the web. The labour

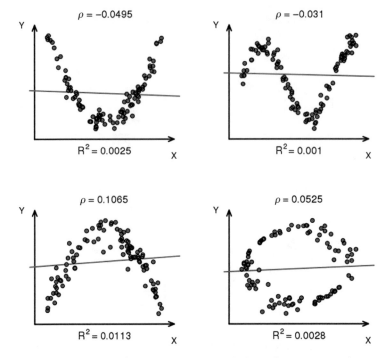

Figure A1.3   Scatter plot examination can help in detecting non-linear strong functional relation between the variables

protection index and the unemployment rate can be obtained from the website http://stats.oecd.org at:

1. Labour → Employment Protection
2. Labour → Labour Force Statistics → Annual Labour Force Statistics → Population and Labour Force

Data can be obtained even in the form of spreadsheets. Variable names can vary, the unemployment rate may be denominated by the OECD as "Unemployment rate as % civilian labour force" and the labour protection index (EPL) may be "Strictness of employment protection – individual and collective dismissals (regular contracts)". The OECD, for specific economic and statistical reasons, makes available different versions of these indicators. In order to complete the current exercise, we have chosen to rebuild the index called *Overall EPL version 1*, a comprehensive and synthetic indicator based on the average of the two versions currently made available by the OECD: the "Strictness of employment protection – individual and

Table A1.2   Employment Protection Legislation and Harmonized Unemployment Rate, average values (1985–2015), OECD data

Country	Code	Overall EPL Version 1	Harmonized Unemployment Rate
Australia	AUS	1.10	6.89
Austria	AUT	1.96	4.77
Belgium	BEL	2.63	8.26
Canada	CAN	0.59	8.19
Chile	CHL	2.81	8.16
Czech Republic	CZE	2.01	6.41
Denmark	DNK	1.95	6.03
Estonia	EST	2.09	9.91
Finland	FIN	1.91	9.26
France	FRA	2.95	10.03
Germany	DEU	2.44	7.85
Greece	GRC	3.38	14.33
Hungary	HUN	1.42	8.08
Iceland	ISL	1.18	4.57
Ireland	IRL	0.89	10.73
Israel	ISR	1.46	7.76
Italy	ITA	3.14	9.40
Japan	JPN	1.45	3.71
Korea	KOR	2.55	3.43
Luxembourg	LUX	3.00	3.49
Mexico	MEX	3.05	3.88
Netherlands	NLD	2.03	5.87
New Zealand	NZL	1.06	6.21
Norway	NOR	2.68	4.04
Poland	POL	1.69	12.67
Portugal	PRT	3.67	8.26
Slovak Republic	SVK	1.81	14.79
Slovenia	SVN	2.16	7.09
Spain	ESP	3.03	16.72
Sweden	SWE	2.39	6.37
Switzerland	CHE	1.36	4.37
Turkey	TUR	3.62	9.61
United Kingdom	GBR	0.73	7.26
United States	USA	0.25	6.12

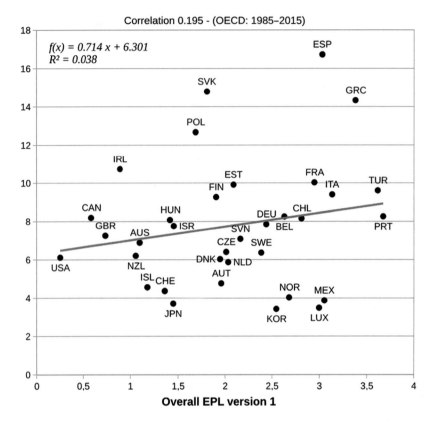

Figure A1.4   The correlation between Employment Protection Legislation and the Harmonized Unemployment Rate

collective dismissals (regular contracts)" and the "Strictness of employment protection – temporary contracts".[8] The unemployment rate we have used is the "harmonized unemployment rate", as it is suitable for

[8]   The Calculation procedure for the *Overall EPL version 1* is described at p. 102 of OECD (2004), *OECD Employment Outlook*, OECD Publishing (in addition, the second chapter of the book contains a detailed description of the methodology that, starting with the detection of 21 fundamental variables, comes to the construction of different synthetic indicators of the EPL). Although the OECD does not publish the Overall *EPL indicator* online any longer but only the elements needed for its calculation, the index is still useful. Specifically, the *Overall EPL version 1* allows the student to have an overall employment protection indicator for many countries and with a long enough time span. Of course, the same statistical test was also carried out on individual components of the *Overall EPL version 1* without obtaining appreciable differences in results. Additionally, it is always a good idea for students to use different variables to practice calculating and interpreting correlation and simple regression models.

comparison between countries. Both time series, EPL and unemployment rate cover a fairly long time span (from 1985 to 2015).

According to the "OECD Employment Outlooks" methodology, we use a cross-sectional analysis of the average value of the EPL and of the unemployment rate throughout the time span and for all countries for which data are available. There are, in particular, for both indicators, data for 34 countries over 31 years. Table A1.2 summarizes the averages computed for each country over the entire 31-year time span.

Students can retrieve the data directly from the OECD website or can use the data already prepared and available.[9] The graph in Figure A1.4 shows the scatter plot of the two variables, reporting the index of determination and the results of the regression analysis.

The coefficient of correlation between the EPL and the unemployment rate is very low – less than 0.2. Thus, the results show that there is no significant relationship between EPL and the unemployment rate. The exercise can be repeated by introducing time lags or it can be done on the average variations of the two indicators, without a significant change in results. Of course, the test must be considered nothing more than a simple didactic exercise. However, it is worth noticing that the results, albeit rudimentary, appear in line with OECD analyzes and, more generally, with the scepticism expressed within economic literature on the possibility of finding precise relations between labour protection indices and unemployment rates.[10]

---

[9] See http://www.emilianobrancaccio.it/didattica/ where all the data and the instructions needed to replicate step-by-step the OECD test are available.

[10] In various studies conducted by the OECD on the relationship between the various versions of the EPL and the unemployment rate, no significant correlations emerge. See: OECD (1999), *OECD Employment Outlook 1999*, Paris: OECD Publishing; OECD (2004), *OECD Employment Outlook 2004*, Paris: OECD Publishing. OECD has based its first EPL studies on version 1 and then switched to version 2. In this test, we use version 1 of the EPL, essentially finding the same results obtained by OECD in 1999 and 2004. Our study has also used a more advanced model for econometric analysis of panel data that we do not present here, but it may still be interesting to briefly summarize those results: the estimation of *fixed effects panel model*, which takes into account the heterogeneity between countries, shows that there is a significant negative linear relationship between the unemployment rate and the EPL indicators in their various versions (in addition, this formulation is preferable, in terms of statistical significance, than a random effect specification).

Appendix 2 Contractionary fiscal policy and fiscal multipliers

Andrea Califano and Fabiana De Cristofaro

A2.1 INTRODUCTION

The aim of this appendix is to reproduce a test proposed by Blanchard and Leigh[1] on the effects of "contractionary" policies – or "fiscal consolidation" policies – on the dynamics of GDP after the international great recession of 2008–2009. The results of this test will be commented on in light of the debate on the existence and magnitude of the so-called "fiscal multipliers", which represent a specification of the typical Keynesian autonomous expenditure multipliers. In particular, Blanchard and Leigh's test shows that the multiplier effect is relevant and the possibility that it lasts no less than two years is taken into account: any given cut in government expenditure, indeed, is associated with a larger fall in GDP for more than one year. As we shall see, this result will provide further insights into the evolution of Blanchard's thought and the comparison between his mainstream macroeconomic models and the alternative model.

A2.2 AUSTERITY AND FISCAL MULTIPLIERS

Up to the onset of the international great recession, estimates of the fiscal multipliers were relatively low: 0.5 per cent approximately in a range between 0.4 and 1.2 per cent.[2] According to these estimates, a reduction in

---

[1] O. Blanchard and D. Leigh (2012), "Are we underestimating short-term fiscal multipliers?", in International Monetary Fund (IMF), *World Economic Outlook*, Washington, USA: IMF; and O. Blanchard and D. Leigh (2013), "Growth forecast errors and fiscal multipliers", *American Economic Review 103(3)*, 117–120.

[2] A. Spilimbergo, S. Symansky and M. Schindler (2009), "Fiscal Multipliers", International Monetary Fund Staff Position Note, no. 9/11.

public expenditure by 1 per cent would imply a fall in GDP of 0.5 per cent only. Even more, some authors upheld the so-called "expansionary austerity" thesis, according to which public spending cuts would stimulate GDP growth rather than inducing recessive effects.[3] Influential dissenting voices within the mainstream started to emerge in 2010, when the IMF claimed that fiscal consolidation policies can bring relevant contractionary effects on production and employment.[4] However, the most important turning point in the debate on multipliers occurred with the notorious "box" by Blanchard and Leigh included in the October 2012 IMF *World Economic Outlook*, and with their subsequent paper published in the *American Economic Review* in 2013.[5] Within the latter work, the authors claim the usual estimates of fiscal multipliers implicitly accepted by the IMF, the European Commission and other institutes providing forecasts to be underestimated by about one percentage point on average. This meaning that for any percentage point of cut in public spending, the forecast for the growth of the GDP was overly optimistic, on average one percentage point higher than what actually happened. Blanchard and Leigh's contribution was not welcomed with universal agreement: while many authors praised it, the European Commission and the European Central Bank, among others, criticized it.[6] It is unquestionable, however, that the two authors' test has played a pivotal role in the further development of the debate. This appendix aims at closely replicating the 2013 Blanchard and Leigh test and discussing it in the light of the comparison between mainstream and alternative models.

---

[3] See, among others: F. Giavazzi and M. Pagano (1990), "Can severe fiscal contractions be expansionary? Tales of two small European countries", in O. Blanchard and S. Fischer (eds), *NBER Macroeconomics Annual, vol. 5*, Boston, USA: MIT Press; F. Giavazzi and M. Pagano (1996), "Non-Keynesian effects of fiscal policy changes: International evidence and the Swedish experience", *Swedish Economic Policy Review 3(1)*, 67–103; A. Alesina and R. Perotti (1995), "Fiscal expansions and fiscal adjustments in OECD countries", *Economic Policy 10(21)*, 205–248; A. Alesina and R. Perotti (1997), "Fiscal adjustments in OECD countries: Composition and macroeconomic effects", International Monetary Fund Staff Papers, no. 44; A. Alesina and S. Ardagna (2010), "Large changes in fiscal policy: Taxes versus spending", in Jeffrey R. Brown (ed.), *Tax Policy and the Economy, vol. 24*, Cambridge, USA: NBER.

[4] International Monetary Fund (2010), *World Economic Outlook*, Washington, USA: IMF.

[5] See footnote 1 of this appendix.

[6] European Central Bank (2012), *Monthly Bulletin – December 2012*, Frankfurt, Germany: ECB; and European Commission (2012), *European Economic Forecast – Autumn 2012*, Luxembourg: EC.

A2.3   BLANCHARD AND LEIGH'S TEST

The idea on which Blanchard and Leigh's test is based is that of investigating the relationship between the planned amount of fiscal consolidation – that is, spending cuts and tax hikes – and the forecast errors in GDP growth estimate. So, if larger fiscal contractions are related to an increase in GDP growth forecast errors, this might mean that the effect of the fiscal multiplier has not been correctly estimated. More specifically, a negative correlation between fiscal consolidation and GDP forecast errors would highlight an underestimation of fiscal multipliers.

The data needed in order to replicate the test are reported in Table A2.1. They represent the cross-sectional dataset of the 26 European economies considered by Blanchard and Leigh.

With the use of some simple statistical tools, we can picture the relationship between the two variables in a scatter plot (or dispersion diagram). We plot the data of fiscal contraction policies on the horizontal axis and the forecast error on the vertical axis for every country examined. Any couple of values representing a country is recorded by a point in the chart.

A regression analysis is performed in order to estimate the magnitude of the variation of the forecast error that occurs in correspondence with a change in fiscal policy. In accordance with the graph pictured in Figure A2.1, Blanchard and Leigh estimate a linear regression model with the Ordinary Least Squares (OLS) method. The procedure consists in finding the straight regression line that best approximates the relationship between the points pictured in the scatter plot, according to the criterion of distance. This is the line that minimizes the distance from the observed points. The estimated regression model can be expressed by the following equation:

$$Error\ g_{i,t:t+1} = \alpha + \beta\ Fiscal\ Consolidation_{i,t:t+1|t} + \epsilon_{i,t:t+1} \quad (A2.1)$$

where *Error* $g_{i,t:t+1}$ is the dependent variable, which measures the forecast error of the cumulative real GDP growth computed on a biannual basis, that is, in the time span that goes from period t to period $t + 1$. The error is thus given by the difference between the cumulative growth rate actually observed $g_{i,t:t+1}$ and the cumulative growth rate forecast on the basis of the information available at time t : $g_{i,t:t+1}$. *Fiscal consolidation*$_{i,t:t+1|t}$ is the explanatory variable and represents the forecast change of the fiscal balance in percentage of potential GDP: when positive, we are facing fiscal consolidation; if negative, it is the case of a stimulus to the economy. It is interesting noticing that the authors have chosen a time span of two years, so as to examine possible lagged effects of fiscal policy.

Table A2.1   *Forecast errors and planned fiscal consolidation cumulative growth rates over the two-year period 2010–11*

Country	Code	Growth forecast error	Forecast of fiscal consolidation
Austria	AUT	1.74	−1.13
Belgium	BEL	1.74	1.36
Bulgaria	BGR	−0.14	0.17
Cyprus	CYP	0.41	−1.73
Czech Republic	CZE	0.10	0.24
Denmark	DNK	−0.70	−1.53
Finland	FIN	2.68	−0.97
France	FRA	0.08	0.40
Germany	DEU	4.27	−2.64
Greece	GRC	−7.15	5.30
Hungary	HUN	−0.04	0.71
Iceland	ISL	−0.28	2.17
Ireland	IRL	0.29	3.17
Italy	ITA	0.23	0.55
Malta	MLT	2.71	−0.54
Netherlands	NLD	0.06	−0.02
Norway	NOR	−0.75	0.05
Poland	POL	2.28	0.11
Portugal	PRT	−1.24	1.30
Romania	ROM	−5.15	2.52
Slovak Republic	SVK	−1.11	1.09
Slovenia	SVN	−1.34	1.66
Spain	ESP	−0.39	1.19
Sweden	SWE	6.32	−0.06
Switzerland	CHE	1.70	−1.20
United Kingdom	GBR	−1.30	1.67

In what follows, we reproduce the baseline model, which is the principal test performed by Blanchard and Leigh using the data relative to the errors made by the IMF only, based on the forecast published in the *World Economic Outlook* (WEO) issued in April 2010, concerning GDP growth of the 2010–2011 interval.

The parameter we are interested in is β. This term represents the change in the forecast error associated with a variation of one unit in the fiscal balance as a ratio to GDP. If the error is negative, this means that forecasters have been too optimistic. If the error is null, there is no linear relationship between the examined variables. From a graphical point of view, the term β represents the angular coefficient of the regression line associated

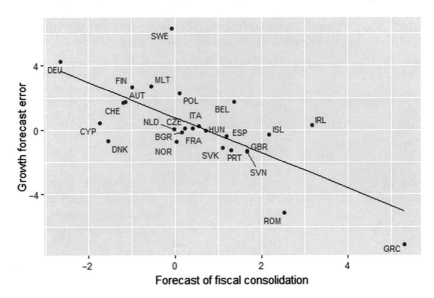

Figure A2.1   Scatter plot and regression line of Blanchard and Leigh's test

with the estimated parameters. The regression line resulting from the estimation of the previous equation is traced in Figure A2.1.

Such a straight line describes the relationship existent on average
between the forecast error and fiscal policies applied in the 2010–2011
period by European advanced economies. It has a positive intercept and a
negative slope, as described by the estimates of the parameters, reported
in Table A2.2.

The estimate of the regression coefficient is –1.095: it means that for
any additional percentage point of fiscal consolidation, the effective GDP

*Table A2.2   OLS estimation results of the relation between forecast errors
and planned fiscal consolidation over the period 2010–11. IMF
cross-sectional data of 26 European Advanced Economies.
The R^2 of the regression is estimated to be 0.496*

Blanchard and Leigh's test

	Coefficient	Standard error	t-statistic	p-value
α	0.775	(0.383)	2.02	0.0541
β	–1.095	(0.255)	–4.29	0.0003

growth has been at least one percentage point lower than the forecast value. As the intercept α has no strong economic interpretation in this exercise, we shall discuss only the inference on the parameter β.

As already discussed in Appendix 1, an important criterion to test the validity of a regression model is the so-called t-test of significance. This test is based on the statistic t, computed using the estimated standard error, which represents a measure of the variability of the estimate. Recalling the null hypothesis $\beta = 0$ and the interpretation of the p-value we are able to comment on the results presented in Table A2.2. According to the results obtained we can thus conclude that the estimated regression coefficient is statistically significant and that the null hypothesis is rejected at the 1 per cent confidence level (when the first three decimals of the p-value are 0, the significance is generally approximated to 1 per cent). A more practical interpretation of the p-value can be the following: assuming the null hypothesis is true, the probability of observing our sample would be equal to 0.03 per cent. It is then clear how the p-value provides evidence contrary to the null hypothesis.

Let us conclude the interpretation of the estimation results by discussing a well used measure of the goodness of fit of the model to the observed data: the coefficient of linear determination R^2. The value derived by computing the index is fairly encouraging: the R^2 associated with Blanchard and Leigh's test is 0.496, meaning that almost 50 per cent of the variability of the GDP growth forecast error is explained by the variability in the fiscal policy plans.

A2.4   DEBATE AROUND THE TEST

Blanchard and Leigh's test has been the subject of lively discussions. Some of the major criticisms of the "box" published by Blanchard and Leigh in the IMF WEO of 2012 have been raised by the European Commission and the European Central Bank, as already mentioned. According to these institutions, once increases in sovereign bond yields are taken into account, the correlation between forecast errors and fiscal consolidation breaks down, leading to lower estimates of fiscal multipliers. In the paper published in 2013 in the *American Economic Review* Blanchard and Leigh reply to these criticisms. They evaluate the possible impact of unobserved relevant variables by looking at, among others, sovereign borrowing costs and sovereign credit default swap (CDS) spreads. The new results of the two authors largely confirm the estimates of the regression coefficient that were published in the "box" of 2012. Finally, in a more recent note published by the European Commission, Blanchard and Leigh's theses seem to be getting a more positive and widespread consideration.[7]

A2.5   BLANCHARD AND LEIGH'S TEST AND MACROECONOMIC THEORY

Further than debating the robustness of the empirical results of Blanchard and Leigh's test, attempts have been made to put into question its theoretical significance as well. For instance, the European Central Bank claimed that in fact the test does not add much novelty to the standard mainstream view on fiscal multipliers. The idea that contractionary policies may have depressive effects on the GDP in a time period of two years is seen by the ECB as consistent with the dominant theory: in the "short run", production may deviate from "natural" equilibrium due to movements in effective demand. As a matter of fact, Blanchard himself seems to uphold the same claim, when he suggests – in the paper co-authored by Leigh and in many other works – that fiscal multipliers exist in the "short period" only. This is the very reason why, even in his seventh edition of his macroeconomics textbook, he claims that the contractionary effect of austerity fiscal policies is only temporary, while in the "long run" these same policies would contribute to economic recovery.[8]

   The above-mentioned attempts to reduce fiscal multipliers to mere "short run" phenomena contrast with the empirical evidence highlighting the persistence of fiscal shocks well beyond the two-year period suggested by Blanchard and Leigh. Fatás and Summers,[9] for example, explore the GDP response to fiscal policy over a longer horizon in order to evaluate the persistence of such a policy shock. The exercise consists in replicating Blanchard and Leigh's test for the two-year period 2010–2011 and then extending the time span up to 2014 and 2019 by introducing a slight variation in the regression. Fatás and Summers argue indeed that the identification technique used by Blanchard and Leigh does not require matching the timing in the regression variables and so this allows them to use different time horizons to calculate the forecast errors, keeping fixed the time span 2010–2011 on the right-hand side of the regression. In this way, they find

---

   [7]   European Commission (2016), "Towards a positive euro area fiscal stance. Supporting public investments that increase economic growth", *EPSC Strategic Notes*, 20, Luxembourg: European Political Strategy Centre.
   [8]   O. Blanchard (2017), *Macroeconomics* (7th edn), Boston, USA: Pearson.
   [9]   A. Fatás and L.H. Summers (2017), "The permanent effects of fiscal consolidations", NBER Working Paper 22374.

that the correlation between change in fiscal policy and forecast errors is strong and the estimated coefficient increases over time, entailing the existence of sizeable fiscal multipliers both in the "short" and in the "long" run.

At a closer look, the distinction between the "short run" and the "long run" proposed by the mainstream has always been rather vague and mutable. The reader of the present volume does know that, according to the prevalent model, the "short run" is the time length of the process of adjustment that would bring the economic system back to "natural" equilibrium, which is indeed called "long run" equilibrium as well. On the actual duration of this process, mainstream economists have often held changing views: in effect, in recent years many of them have argued for increasing the length of the period. It will suffice to say that Blanchard himself has changed his mind on the matter: whilst in the first edition of his macroeconomics textbook he claimed the "short run" to last just a year and the "long run" to last just a decade,[10] in the next editions he adopted looser definition: "a few years" for the "short run" and "a few decades or more" for the "long run".[11]

These few notes raise some further hints for reflection with respect to the comparison between the two macroeconomic approaches described in the present volume. The reader will remember from the previous chapters that both in the AS–AD model and in the IS–LM–PC model the "natural" equilibrium is matched by a hypothetic situation in which the production level would be completely independent from effective demand, and hence from fiscal policy also. Blanchard and Leigh's test – and Fatás and Summers's test even more so – contribute to show that this equilibrium is in fact extremely difficult to reach: empirical analysis shows some degree of persistency of the effects of fiscal shocks on GDP.

One more time, the interpretation of empirical evidence in the light of traditional macroeconomics does not seem an easy task to perform. On the contrary, the very same evidence looks more consistent with an interpretation grounded on the alternative macroeconomic model, according to which effective demand – and the policies affecting it – can have persistent effects on the performance of production and unemployment. It is obvious that these few hints are just didactic traces, not a complete empirical assessment of the alternative macroeconomic paradigms. For further insights, we advise the interested student to have a look at the further reading recommended at the end of the present volume.[12]

[10] O. Blanchard (1997), *Macroeconomics*, Boston, USA: Pearson.
[11] O. Blanchard (2017), *Macroeconomics* (8th edn), Boston, USA: Pearson.
[12] The data and all the instructions needed in order to replicate Blanchard and Leigh's test step-by-step are available at: http://www.emilianobrancaccio.it/didattica/.

Appendix 3   On the pandemic trade-off between health and production

Emiliano Brancaccio and Raffaele Giammetti

A3.1   IS THERE A TRADE-OFF BETWEEN HEALTH AND PRODUCTION?

Among the many disputes raised by the Covid-19 pandemic, perhaps the most relevant one concerns whether a "trade-off" between health protection and the safeguard of production and occupation exists or not. The problem arises from the fact that almost all countries have adopted various measures of physical distancing between people to avoid the acceleration of infections and the consequent exhaustion of intensive care hospital beds. The most severe measure is the imposition of a "lockdown", that is a generalized block to the movement of people. These measures seem capable of slowing down the contagion but also have the undesirable effect of curbing demand, slowing down production and thus triggering an economic crisis. Therefore, there seems to be a clear pandemic trade-off between saving lives and keeping up the trend of production and employment. However, some argue that such a dilemma may not exist, or at least may be more complex than as it is addressed in the prevailing debate.

A3.2   MORE VICTIMS FROM THE ECONOMIC CRISIS THAN FROM THE VIRUS?

Some oppose lockdowns and deny the existence of a pandemic trade-off, arguing that the economic crisis may cause even more deaths than those caused by Covid-19. If this were the case, no choice would be left: any measure implying a reduction in economic activity should be avoided. This thesis, however, does not seem to find confirmation in the data. The literature on the impact of economic recessions on mortality generally shows that economic crises are not related to an increase in deaths; to the contrary, often they are matched by a decrease. The reason is that in periods of economic growth workers have less time to devote to healthful activities or routine medical visits; health problems associated with cardiovascular disease increase; stress related to urban traffic and to more intense work grows, especially in the case of longer working hours during short and intense economic expansions; moreover, accidents at the workplace and work-related illnesses increase, safety inspections can decrease in relation to the activity and environmental pollution can be more severe. The intensification of working activity is therefore related to an increase in deaths, primarily due to accidents at work and occupational diseases but more generally due to cardiovascular diseases, pneumonia, neoplasms, liver diseases, etc. The greater the size of the economic boom, the stronger these correlations are, and they apply to all causes of death. The only exception is suicides, which tend to increase during recessions, but the magnitude of the phenomenon is too limited to reverse the general trend. The only question that remains open concerns the possibility that a particularly violent and lasting economic crisis could fuel geopolitical tensions and eventually trigger war conflicts, and thereby increase the death rate. But this would be a possible indirect effect which is not examined by research on the subject.

Therefore, in general, the literature shows that the death rate tends to increase during economic expansions and decrease in periods of higher unemployment. The correlation between production trends and mortality rates can be more or less significant depending on other factors, but in any case it is inverse. The idea that the economic crisis may bring more deaths than Covid-19 does not seem to find empirical support.

A3.3 IS LOCKDOWN GOOD FOR ECONOMIC RECOVERY? THE IMF THESIS

A different objection to the pandemic trade-off is advanced by the International Monetary Fund, which in its October 2020 *World Economic Outlook* argued that even if the lockdown is clearly related to recession in the short term, in a longer time span it could help economic recovery. A lockdown that is able to effectively contrast the spreading of the virus could restore citizens' confidence in the reduction of the risk of contagion and thus induce them to enjoy more the possibility to go out and travel, thus favouring the revival of demand and production. In this sense, the *Outlook* states that "the short-term economic costs of lockdowns could be compensated by stronger medium-term growth, possibly leading to positive overall

Table A3.1   *Days of lockdown started in the first quarter of 2020*
and expected cumulative growth of real GDP 2020–2021
(IMF-WEO forecast October 2020). Countries are
ordered by days of lockdown

	Days of the first lockdown	Cumulative GDP growth 2020–2021
Sweden	0	–1.2
Denmark	17	–1
Finland	20	–0.4
Austria	28	–2.1
Poland	29	1
China	33	10.1
Turkey	35	0
Slovak Rep.	40	–0.2
Greece	42	–5.4
Lithuania	42	2.3
Switzerland	42	–1.7
Germany	43	–1.8
Belgium	47	–2.9
Brazil	47	–3
New Zealand	49	–1.7
United Kingdom	50	–3.9
France	55	–3.8
Netherlands	55	–1.4
Spain	56	–5.6
Argentina	66	–6.9
Italy	70	–5.4

effects on the economy".[1] Thus, even the IMF does not see a trade-off between health protection and safeguarding the economy.

The IMF does not provide evidence to support this thesis, saying that they would come from future research. However, it is interesting to note that the economic growth forecasts contained in IMF's own *Outlook* do not seem to support the idea that a lockdown could favour future recovery. Table A3.1 shows the duration of lockdown measures started in the first quarter of 2020, and the cumulative growth of real GDP that the IMF expected for the two-year period 2020–2021 (the countries are selected on the basis of the data available in the *Outlook*).

[1]   International Monetary Fund, "A long and difficult ascent", *World Economic Outlook*, October 2020, p. 66.

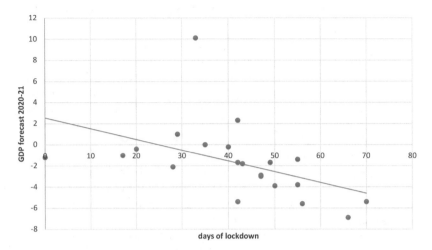

Figure A3.1   Negative correlation between lockdown duration and growth forecasts (IMF-WEO October 2020 data)

Based on the method already described in Appendix 1, students can derive the regression line drawn in figure A3.1 from these data. Placing the growth forecast on the y axis and the days of lockdown on the x axis, they can verify that the equation describing the line corresponds to $y = -0.1022 \times +2.5484$, with a p-value of 0.03 and an $R2 = 0.2243$.

The negative inclination of the line indicates that the longer the lockdown the less cumulative growth in GDP. Therefore, according to IMF's own data, the lockdown duration seems to be related to decline in production and economic crisis, albeit with a very low significance, also in the medium-term, that is beyond the year of occurrence of the lockdown.

Obviously, the degree of significance is too modest and this exercise is also too rudimentary to provide any concrete indication on the strength of the thesis put forward by the International Monetary Fund. The regression just described is relevant only for didactic purposes. It shows nonetheless that IMF's conjecture about the economic benefits of the lockdown is not proven. More in-depth studies are needed to assess the empirical evidence of the hypothesis.[2]

---

[2]   On other possible economic impacts of the lockdown, see: R. Giammetti, L. Papi, D. Teobaldelli and D. Ticchi (2020), "The Italian value chain in the pandemic: the input–output impact of Covid-19 lockdown", *Journal of Industrial and Business Economics 47*, 483–97.

A3.4   OVERCOMING THE PANDEMIC TRADE-OFF

Waiting for evidence showing that the opposite is true, it seems inevitable to accept the idea that a pandemic trade-off between health and production actually exists: lockdown and other measures of physical distancing reduce infections and victims of the virus but on the other hand depress the economy and create unemployment, both in the short and medium-long term. On closer inspection, however, the tragic dilemma of a political choice between the increase in the death toll and the increase in the unemployed is not inevitable. Under certain conditions, there are ways to loosen the constraint of the pandemic trade-off in order to overcome it. That is, it is possible to reduce both the victims of the virus and the victims of unemployment. In what follows we will examine the problem in terms of a political choice under what we can define as an "economic-scientific constraint". As the constraint changes, we shall see, the terms of the choice change.

Let us analyze the problem with an algebraic example. We denote with v the percentage of potential victims of Covid-19 in relation to the population and with u the unemployment rate, or the expected percentage of unemployed population in relation to the workforce. Then we introduce the "economic-scientific constraint" to which the political choice must be subject. Suppose for instance that this constraint is described by the following equation: $u = 20$. This constraint indicates all the possible combinations between victims of the virus and unemployment rate that can be obtained by adopting a more or less stringent lockdown, given the current state of economic policy and scientific knowledge. For example, assuming that an extremely rigid lockdown keeps the victims of the virus at one per cent of the population, that is $v = 1$, from the "economic-scientific constraint" it follows that the corresponding unemployment rate will be equal to $u = 20/v = 20/1 = 20$, or 20 per cent. If, on the other hand, milder social distancing measures were adopted that give rise to a percentage of victims equal to $v = 2$, then the constraint indicates that the unemployment rate will be $u = 20/2 = 10$, and so on.

Let us now indicate with M the level of "malaise" in the community caused by the victims of the virus and by unemployment. We assume that this malaise can be represented by the following "social malaise" function: $M = u + 8v$. In the present case, victims of the virus are supposed to cause eight times more social malaise than unemployment. Obviously, if the coefficients that multiply v and u are modified, it is possible to configure differently the relative "weight" that the community attributes to the two different social evils.

The goal of government authorities is to minimize the M level of social malaise, while being constrained by the existing "economic-scientific constraint". The problem can be represented in terms of a minimization under constraint:

$$\min \quad M = u + 8v \tag{A3.1}$$

$$sub \quad uv = 20 \tag{A3.2}$$

To find the solution, first of all we set the constraint in terms of victims, $v = 20/u$. Then we substitute the constraint in the function to be minimized. We will have: $M = u + 8(20/u)$ that is, $M = u + 160u^{-1}$. At this point we impose the first order condition for identifying the minimum of the function, that is, we calculate the derivative of M with respect to u and set it equal to zero: $dM/du = 1 - 160u^{-2} = 0$, hence $u^{-2} = 160^{-1}$. Raising both terms to minus one we get $u^2 = 160$, and therefore $u = \sqrt{160}$, that is $u = 12.64$. By substituting this result in the constraint equation, we get $v = 20/12.64 = 1.58$. Therefore, to minimize social malaise, in this case the authorities will adopt a lockdown such as to determine an unemployment rate of 12.64 per cent and a share of potential victims of the virus of 1.58 per cent. Given the economic-scientific constraint, this is the combination of death toll and unemployment that keeps social malaise as low as possible. The authorities will aim for this solution, calibrating the degree of rigidity of the lockdown for this purpose. The following graph describes the example, with the decreasing line indicating the lowest possible social malaise function, tangent to the economic-scientific constraint represented by the convex curve.

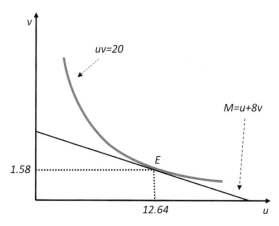

Figure A3.2   *The pandemic trade-off as a constrained minimization problem*

Obviously, if the social malaise function changes, the solution pursued by the authorities will change accordingly. One of the possibilities is that public authorities realize that the community attributes an even greater "weight" to the victims of the virus than unemployment rate, and therefore the social malaise function becomes, for example: $M = u + 10v$. Reformulating the constrained minimization problem and the related graph, the social malaise line becomes flatter, so that the optimal point of tangency moves down to the right along the constraint curve. That is, the authorities will adopt a more stringent lockdown, accepting a higher unemployment rate in order to reduce the percentage of victims. Students are invited to draw the new graph and calculate the solution.

Even in this example, until now, the pandemic trade-off has been unavoidable. Depending on the "weight" assigned to the "social evils" of casualties and unemployment, the malaise function changes and so does government's policy. In any case the choice must lie on the same curve as the economic-scientific constraint: if the lockdown is to be tightened to reduce the number of victims, an increase in unemployment must be accepted, and if the lockdown is to be eased to mitigate the economic crisis it will be necessary to accept a growth in the death toll. But is there a way to reduce both the victims of the virus and the unemployed? The answer is positive. It is a matter of adopting such measures that make it possible to lower the curve of the economic-scientific constraint, thus making it less stringent. This operation can be accomplished in many different ways, and acting either on the unemployment side, with the implementation of expansive economic policies, or on the side of the victims of the virus, through scientific research, or even on both sides, via a combination of policies and research. Students are invited to investigate these options based on the analysis carried out in the chapters on the economic consequences of the pandemic and on the comparison between planning and market in scientific research. These policies will be able to affect the economic-scientific constraint in the desired sense. In our example, the constraint could become $uv = 5$, which corresponds to a downward translation of the curve and to an optimal solution located at the bottom left, closer to the origin of the axes. Reformulating the constrained minimization problem in algebraic terms, students can verify that in this case the solution corresponds to $u = 6.3$ and $v = 0.79$. That is, thanks to better economic and research policies, it becomes possible to reduce both the unemployment rate and the victims of the virus. By following this path, the pandemic trade-off can be overcome.

Crisis and revolution in economic theory and policy: a debate[1]

Pietro Raitano: Good evening everyone. I thank the public for turning out, the Giangiacomo Feltrinelli Foundation for organizing this event, and the speakers, who we shall have the pleasure of hearing elaborate on important issues which, at the present historical moment, we all need to understand and confront.

I work at a monthly magazine, *Altreconomia*, which has for two decades subscribed to the view that the economic framework which has shaped this age of "globalization" is not only incapable of solving any of the most important problems that afflict society on a global scale – such as inequality or environmental challenges – but is in some respects responsible for these problems, and therefore that the academic thinking which accompanies this framework needs to be reconsidered.

Ten years have elapsed since the eruption of the economic and financial crisis of 2008, and today we are seeing signs that the spectre of another crisis may be on the horizon. In this sense, the debate from distant – I would even say, antithetical – positions, like those confronting each other tonight, can really help us understand how policy might cope this time and how it can be more effective than in the past.

I therefore welcome our speakers, Emiliano Brancaccio and Olivier Blanchard. I give the floor to Mr. Brancaccio, Professor of Economic Policy at the University of Sannio and proponent of the "The Economists' Warning" against European austerity policies that was published in the *Financial Times* in 2013.[2] He has also authored a macroeconomics

---

[1] This chapter contains the transcript of a debate, entitled "Pensare un'alternativa" (Thinking of an Alternative), which took place at the Giangiacomo Feltrinelli Foundation in Milan, Italy, on 19 December 2018, and was moderated by the journalist Pietro Raitano. We thank Gary Mongiovi for helpful comments, the Giangiacomo Feltrinelli Foundation for the permission to publish the transcript, and the University of Sannio for contributing funds for the translation. An English version has already been published as E. Brancaccio and O. Blanchard (2019), "Crisis and Revolution in Economic Theory and Policy: A Debate", *Review of Political Economy 31(2)*, 271–287.
[2] The document, published as an open letter in the *Financial Times* on 23 September 2013, was signed by over 100 economists; it may be found here: www.theeconomistswarning. com.

handbook with the eloquent title: *Anti-Blanchard Macroeconomics*; this book offers different tools from those which are found in Professor Blanchard's widely used textbook, *Macroeconomics*, from which many of us were taught.

Emiliano Brancaccio: Thank you very much for having me. Please allow me some preliminary citations on "Anti" books. Julius Caesar's *Anticato* was the literary representation of an epochal transition, one that in a little over a decade would bring about the end of the Republic and the beginning of the Roman Empire. The *Anticato* itself appears to have inspired Friedrich Engels, author of *Anti-Dühring*. In turn, Engels's book marked a crucial phase in the clash between two opposing philosophies of science: idealism and materialism.

And in a sense, I have drawn inspiration from these great examples in my own small way. *Anti-Blanchard* is a modest experiment, one that is confined to the narrow sphere of the critique of macroeconomics. Although its title takes aim at one particular person, the book in fact tries to bring to light a dispute of a much broader – dare I say collective – character. It concerns a dispute, now submerged and almost forgotten, between the prevailing approach to economic theory and policy and an alternative economic paradigm. *Anti-Blanchard* is, after all, the reason we asked the Feltrinelli Foundation to organize this debate. We thank the Foundation for having accepted our proposal. And of course we also thank Olivier Blanchard for accepting this invitation.

Now, why *Anti-Blanchard?* Why not "Anti-Lucas", "Anti-Prescott", or "Anti-Sargent"? First, the relevance of Olivier Blanchard's institutional experience transcends his individual persona. In my opinion, this is truer for him than for any other living economist. Professor Blanchard was appointed Chief Economist of the International Monetary Fund on 1 September 2008. This was just two weeks before Lehman Brothers filed for Chapter Eleven bankruptcy, triggering the global crisis. By an extraordinary confluence of circumstances, Blanchard's time at the IMF corresponded exactly with the tempestuous period of the Great Recession, the first eurozone crisis, and the start of the world's new protectionist tendencies, well before the advent of Trump in the White House. Needless to say, Blanchard's management of the Fund's research has not gone unnoticed. Under his leadership, we have witnessed a significant change in analysis and, to some degree, also in the policy proposals of the International Monetary Fund. I have in mind the Fund's "mea culpa" regarding the underestimation of fiscal multipliers; the expansion of deficit-financed public investment an instrument of economic growth; the consideration of controls on the movement of capital; the recognition of an inverse link between inequality and economic development; and so on.

Yet beyond Olivier's institutional role, a deeper reason led me to write *Anti-Blanchard* and then to publish an international edition with the help of Andrea Califano. This pertains to Blanchard's theoretical approach and to the structure of his analytical models. The prevailing paradigm of economic theory and policy – what we usually call the "mainstream", of which Olivier Blanchard is one of the world's leading exponents – ultimately refers to the neoclassical intertemporal general equilibrium tradition. A fundamental characteristic of this approach is the presumption that the spontaneous forces of the market, the forces of demand and supply, will generate the levels of the interest rate, the rate of profit, and the real wage required to bring the economy into a "natural equilibrium", that is, an equilibrium which corresponds to efficient levels of production and employment of labour and other scarce resources under given institutional constraints. Therefore, according to the prevailing approach, the free play of market forces, at least in principle, will bring about the unique distribution of income between wages, profits, and interest which, given the endowments of scarce resources and other relevant constraints, guarantees efficient levels of production and employment. Production and distribution are then linked to one another by a double thread according to an inexorable law of efficiency. This means, among other things, that in the mainstream's view, efforts to raise wages beyond the level determined by market equilibrium will necessarily lead to a drop in employment and production. In other words, social conflict can only do damage.

Now, it is possible to prove that on several occasions, in his textbook and in some of his important academic publications, Blanchard has deviated a bit from neoclassical orthodoxy, or at least has provided the basis for deviating from it. For example, in his textbook whose European edition was written with Alessia Amighini and Francesco Giavazzi, Blanchard assumes that the distribution of income between wages and profits is a substantially exogenous variable, that is, a variable external to the core of his analysis.[3] In other instances, for example, in his famous hysteresis models, Blanchard has gone even further, hypothesizing that income distribution is not only external to the analysis but does not even have any unique connection to the trend of production and employment. More precisely, in these models, under specified conditions the real wage can be considered a given variable, while levels of production and employment are determined by the

---

[3]   O. Blanchard (2016), *Macroeconomics* (7th edn), New York: Pearson; and O. Blanchard, A. Amighini and F. Giavazzi (2017), *Macroeconomics. A European Perspective* (3rd edn), Harlow: Pearson.

relationship between the money wage and the quantity of money.[4] The presence of Franco Modigliani, and a strong scent of MIT, can be strongly felt in this theoretical apparatus.

Now, I could give many more examples of this kind, and I could go into detail about the particular hypotheses that lead to such results. However, in all such instances, my basic thesis is as follows. When Blanchard's models assume that the distribution of income between wages and profits is a variable external to the analysis, and when his models furthermore assume that distribution is not uniquely connected to a specific level of production and employment, we arrive at a significant theoretical implication: Blanchard's models can accommodate alternative theoretical approaches; that is, they are open to interpretations grounded in the various "heretical" traditions of John von Neumann, Wassily Leontief, Piero Sraffa, Nicholas Kaldor, Luigi Pasinetti, Pierangelo Garegnani, Joan Robinson, Hyman Minsky, Paolo Sylos Labini, Augusto Graziani, and many others. This tradition of alternative schemes can admit several possible relations between production and distribution, none of which has anything to do with the neoclassical concept of optimal use of scarce resources. There are no longer any wage rates, profit rates or interest rates that as such guarantee maximum production and employment, given the existing constraints. In these alternative models, the intimate neoclassical link between production and distribution of income fades. The relation between these variables becomes more complicated, loses its aura of technical neutrality, and falls within the scope of social and political conflict.

In general, it is useful to keep in mind that what has just been described is an overall theoretical line of demarcation that applies to all existing approaches. Regarding the link between production and distribution of income, all more or less explicitly formulated theories, whether old or new, must logically be situated on one side or the other of that "Althusserian" line separating the neoclassical mainstream from the alternative view that has just been described. It is not always made explicit on which side of the demarcation line a particular theory ought to be placed. This is the case, for example, with agent-based modelling, one of the unconventional approaches enjoying some success today. In other words, no new theory can escape the need to take a position on whether to explain relative prices and distribution in conventional neoclassical terms, or to reject that framework and therefore commit to an explicit alternative.

---

[4]   O. Blanchard and L. Summers (1986), "Hysteresis and the European Unemployment Problem", in Stanley Fischer (ed.), *NBER Macroeconomics Annual*, vol. 1, Cambridge, MA: MIT Press.

Coming back to our specific case, that same line of demarcation high-lights a surprising fact. Those of Blanchard's models that are open to alternative theories can be taken across that theoretical line: they can in fact become open to conflict over the distribution of the social product. Drawing upon an old yet not obsolete language, one might go so far as to say that from time to time, more or less consciously, Blanchard opens his models to Marx's concept of class struggle.

Olivier will of course disagree with my interpretation. He may argue that these theoretical gaps, these small logical cracks that allow for such bold interpretations of his models, are merely the result of provisional simplifi-cations that can then be quietly removed at more advanced stages of analy-sis and replaced with others that are more aligned with the mainstream tradition. I believe that the truth is different. The truth is that economic models are a bit like children. At some point, they take on a personality of their own that in many ways is independent of their parents' aspirations.

It seems as though this is precisely the case with Blanchard. Unlike the models of Robert Lucas, Thomas Sargent, or Edward Prescott, yet analogous to many examples from the MIT tradition to which he belongs, Blanchard's models can be inverted and transformed. They can become alternative models even in order to solve some internal contradictions.[5] By adopting similar techniques, the great theorist and polemicist Frank Hahn[6] had once attempted to transform Sraffa's model into a "special case" of neoclassical general equilibrium theory; in doing so, however, he committed serious theoretical errors. These included, among others, the paradoxical claim of determining "the past as a function of the future".[7] Here we could instead say that Blanchard can become somewhat "Marxist" through a reversal which, in this case, passes the logical test. After all, if it had not been for this possibility to theoretically invert Olivier's models, *Anti-Blanchard* would never have been born and we would not be here today to discuss the matter.

We might add that this theoretical reversal is precisely what creates the possibility of relaunching a comparison and a competition, in a Lakatosian sense, between the different existing paradigms. The comparison that we

---

[5]   E. Brancaccio and F. Saraceno (2017), "Evolutions and Contradictions in Mainstream Macroeconomics: The Case of Olivier Blanchard", *Review of Political Economy* 29(3), 345–359.

[6]   F. Hahn (1982), "The Neo-Ricardians", *Cambridge Journal of Economics* 6(4), 353–374. For a survey, see Ch. 14 of H. Kurz and N. Salvadori (1995), *Theory of Production: A Long-Period Analysis*. Cambridge: Cambridge University Press.

[7]   E. Brancaccio (2010), "On the Impossibility of Reducing the Surplus Approach to a Neoclassical Special Case. A Criticism of Hahn in a Solowian Context", *Review of Political Economy* 22(3), 405–418.

propose between Blanchard's models and the heretical interpretations of them facilitates the task of choosing between them on scientific grounds, that is, on the basis of historical relevance, logical consistency, and empirical evidence.

In fact, the mainstream approach often appears to be in difficulty, even upon empirical grounds. Here, the alternative view is in a much stronger position to meet the standard of proof based on the data. A typical example is the analysis of the relationship between the so-called "flexibility" of the labour market on one hand, and the dynamics of real wages and employment on the other. As Olivier had observed some time ago,[8] and as several IMF, OECD, and World Bank reports have recently recognized, the prevailing thesis that greater labour flexibility reduces unemployment does not appear to be supported by the empirical evidence. According to the data, the alternative thesis instead appears more robust: the only tangible effect of flexibility is to reduce the bargaining power of workers and hence the wage share.[9] In other words, most of the impact of policies aimed at increasing labour market flexibility falls not on productive efficiency but on distributive conflict.

What, then, are the general economic policy implications of all this? I believe they are significant. In a recent article written with Larry Summers, Olivier Blanchard evoked the possibility that an 'evolution', perhaps even a 'revolution', of economic policy is at hand.[10] A key point of the "revolution" evoked by Blanchard and Summers concerns the possibility to support and stabilize employment levels through public investment spending. In general, this upholds the policy of public budget expansion in more systematic and incisive ways than in the past. According to Blanchard and Summers, "revolution" therefore means, among other things, a renewed role for state budget policies in supporting economic development and employment. Such a stance within the mainstream is an important development.

However, it should be pointed out that the "revolution" of economic policy proposed by Blanchard and Summers rests upon the assumption that in the future the interest rate will lie consistently below the rate of economic growth. An interest rate lower than the growth rate of the economy matters for various reasons. It helps reduce inequalities, reduces the burden of debt, and promotes public intervention in the economy. For only if

[8]　　O. Blanchard (2006), "European Unemployment: The Evolution of Facts and Ideas", *Economic Policy 21 (January)*, 5–59.

[9]　　For a survey and empirical evidence, see E. Brancaccio, N. Garbellini and R. Giammetti (2018), "Structural Labour Market Reforms, GDP Growth and the Functional Distribution of Income", *Structural Change and Economic Dynamics 44 (March)*, 34–45.

[10]　　O. Blanchard and L. Summers (2017), "Rethinking Stabilization Policy: Evolution or Revolution?", NBER Working Paper No. 24179.

interest rates are lower than growth rates can debt be sustainable in the face of primary government deficits, and more generally in the face of rising public spending. Curiously, in previous editions of his textbook, Blanchard argued that an interest rate lower than the growth rate was an "exotic" case, unlikely and in the end not very relevant. Today, however, Blanchard and Summers acknowledge that an interest rate lying consistently below the growth rate is a real possibility.

Blanchard and Summers, however, seem to justify this new scenario as a sort of spontaneous market phenomenon. They sometimes interpret it by updating Alvin Hansen's old concept of "secular stagnation".[11] For the most part, that is, an interest rate below the growth rate would be the result of a spontaneous increase in savings compared to investment and a consequent reduction in the "natural" rate of interest rate, which would presumably balance them. Let us think about it: this is the mainstream idea that there are "natural" levels of the distribution variables that correspond to the equilibrium level of production. It is again the typical neoclassical idea of an efficient link between production and distribution of income.

However, we know that alternative theoretical models teach that this efficient link does not exist and thus that the neoclassical concept of a "natural" rate of interest is illegitimate as well. The implication is that in the alternative models an interest rate persistently below the rate of growth can never be just a spontaneous market event, not even in situations of "secular stagnation". Thus, an interest rate that is lower than economic growth can only be the result of a deliberate political act.

More specifically, precise economic policy decisions are needed to keep interest rates below growth. In the first place, a monetary policy unbound by an anti-inflationary Taylor rule is necessary. The data indicate that such rules, which have been widely adopted in recent decades, are totally inadequate to stabilize the business cycle and inflation. On the contrary, they run the risk of causing relatively high interest rates. They are potentially destructive to the solvency of the economic system and can ultimately accelerate what Marx had identified as the tendency for the centralization of capital in fewer and fewer hands.[12] Furthermore, keeping the interest rate below the growth rate requires a policy of capital controls, so that the interest rate can be reduced without risking foreign capital flight. But above all,

[11] A. Hansen (1939), "Economic Progress and Declining Population Growth", *American Economic Review 29(1)*, 1–15.

[12] E. Brancaccio and G. Fontana (2016), "'Solvency Rule' and Capital Centralisation in a Monetary Union", *Cambridge Journal of Economics 40(4)*, 1055–1075 and E. Brancaccio, R. Giammetti, M. Lopreite and M. Puliga (2018), "Centralization of Capital and Financial Crisis: A Global Network Analysis of Corporate Control", *Structural Change and Economic Dynamics 45(June)*, 94–104.

keeping the interest rate below the growth rate requires a policy to counter-
act wage and price deflation, that is, a policy that prevents wages and prices
from falling. Wage and price deflation must be avoided as it increases real
interest rates and the ratio between debt service and incomes and therefore
risks making the burden of debt unsustainable.

The deflation of wages and prices is a delicate point. Blanchard has
expressed various positions on this matter, which he has assessed on a case-by-
case basis. With regard to the eurozone crisis in particular, when Blanchard
considered the cases of Greece and the Southern European countries he
repeatedly supported a policy of wage deflation with the hope of seeing competitiveness improve to levels that would stimulate exports, reduce imports,
and thus reabsorb the heavy trade deficits accumulated by these countries.[13]

Here I must say that I strongly disagree. Above all, before discussing how
to remedy these trade imbalances, I think that we should first ask ourselves
why they emerged. We should especially study in depth why the financial
market has long fueled imbalances within the eurozone later to discover,
all of a sudden, that these imbalances were unsustainable. For many years,
large financing flows had allowed many countries to import more than
they exported; then, suddenly, those flows dried up. Such a crazy merry-
go-round had undermined the stability of the euro far more than any public
finance imbalance. Let me remind you that along with Francesco Giavazzi,
Blanchard was for a long time substantially optimistic about the possibility
that the market was operating correctly, meaning that the external imbalances of the Southern European countries could be offset relatively quickly
through increases in productivity and production.[14] Afterwards, it became
clear that those imbalances were unsustainable, and they too changed their
minds. This is a positive change of perspective. Yet, we still face an unresolved problem. A financial market that fosters imbalances which eventually turn out to be entirely unsustainable is intrinsically inefficient and can
be a source of serious tensions in international relations. This problem taps
into a key issue of contemporary capitalism that, for all practical purposes,
has yet to be confronted. It is a completely unresolved threat that could
reappear at any moment.

Secondly, moving from the causes to the remedies, my opinion, which
differs from Blanchard's, is that wage deflation is never a valid solution.

---

[13]   O. Blanchard (2012), "The Logic and Fairness of Greece's Program", *IMF Direct*, 19
March 2012; and O. Blanchard and L. Summers (2017), "Rethinking Stabilization Policy:
Evolution or Revolution?", NBER Working Paper No. 24179.

[14]   O. Blanchard and F. Giavazzi (2002), "Current Account Deficits in the Euro Area:
The End of the Feldstein Horioka Puzzle?", *Brookings Papers on Economic Activity 33(2)*,
147–210.

Even when faced with significant foreign imbalances, the policy of wage and price deflation should be avoided and other paths should be sought. I wish to be clear on this point. If we think that the eurozone needs to rely on deflation to try to remedy its internal imbalances and survive, then not only do I suspect that it will not survive, but I believe that it is not even appropriate to hope for its survival.

Why do I insist so strongly on this point? Because history teaches us that a solution based on wage deflation is dangerous and can have violent repercussions on the economic structure, as well as on social and political institutions. Some have argued that deflation was one of the factors that led to the rise of Nazism. Now, history does not repeat itself, but remembering it may be useful in this age of frightening collective repressed memory. In the end, the memory of deflation as the engine of Hitler's rise was one of the reasons behind "The Economists' Warning" that Dani Rodrik, myself, and many others published in the *Financial Times* a few years ago, and which we still consider timely. Therefore, I say: deflation must be avoided, always and in every situation. Indeed, keeping deflation out of the economist's toolbox was a basic teaching of the most significant economic policy "revolution" that has ever taken place under capitalism: the "revolution" that bears the name of Keynes.

Let me end, therefore, with a few words on Keynes. In more or less obvious terms, Keynes is the inspiration behind Blanchard and Summers when they evoke the possibility of a revolution in economic policy. In this context, the question that has somewhat bothered me, which I would like to share with you all, is this: is a "revolution" of economic policy that in one way or another refers to Keynes feasible today? Blanchard and Summers believe it would be good for this revolution to take place, but they add that they are not at all certain it will happen. I fear their doubt is well founded. We know Keynes as a progressive intellectual, a Bloomsbury man, a civil liberties advocate, and an enemy of rentiers. Yet all of these characteristics come from the fact that Keynes was the product of an extraordinary time marked by a deep systemic conflict between capitalism and socialism. Keynes's intellect was clearly forged by the antagonism between those two great systems of social life. His ideas were modelled on that historical collision, and his success depended on the fact that he tried, in a certain sense, to embody a possible dialectical synthesis of that conflict. Not all biographers highlight this aspect, which in my opinion is decisive and raises important questions for the present day.

For, as you see, we have become used to dismissing the actual socialist experiment as a disaster. Obviously, this judgement is based on several reasons. We know it was a colossal experiment that most definitely accelerated the transition of many countries from a stage of development that was little more than medieval to a stage of modern industrialization. However, we also know that soviet socialism was a political laboratory laden with errors and stained with horrors. At the same time, even a total removal of socialist planning from political discourse can give rise to unintended consequences. The problem, though, is that when the Lacanian threat of the socialist 'Great Other' is no longer present, we cannot help but ask ourselves whether the political conditions for a Keynesian synthesis can be created in such a frightening dialectical void.

Well, I fear not. I fear that the Keynesian synthesis of the twentieth century was ultimately a direct result of the socialist threat. I fear that without the prodding of that socialist challenge it would be extremely difficult today for another Keynesian synthesis to emerge. I contend that this as an open problem for anyone trying to evoke Keynes today. I therefore think it is an open problem for many of us, even for Olivier Blanchard.

Raitano: I thank Professor Brancaccio and I give the floor to Professor Blanchard, who now works at the Peterson Institute for International Economics. As previously mentioned, he served as Chief Economist of the International Monetary Fund from 2008 to 2015, where he had to face the appalling crisis we have been discussing.

Olivier Blanchard: Good evening. First of all, I thank you for inviting me to this discussion with Emiliano Brancaccio. Emiliano raised important matters concerning the role of economic theory, the issue of distribution, and the functioning of the eurozone, among other things. However, I will leave these points for the debate and the interactive part of this evening.

I would like to start from the question of whether there are alternatives to capitalism. My answer is "No", in the following sense. For me, it is obvious that the only non-chaotic way to organize economic interactions in a world populated by seven billion people is the use of markets. I think this leaves no room for discussion. At the same time though, we do know that markets perform unsatisfactorily in various instances, such as infrastructure, health or education. This is why the solution can only be a combination of markets and the state. We have learned that some dreams of the past turned out to be a nightmare. Eliminating markets and having the state take over translated into catastrophe. The opposite path was attempted in other countries where markets were allowed to rule; but there too the results, though different in form, were equally bad. It is clear, therefore, that the only solution involves a combination. Yet the question is: how do we determine the right mix? I do not think the answer can ever be the same in all cases. Rather, I think it depends upon how the world is evolving. Markets do a good job in some cases. In others, they produce unacceptable excesses, such as growing inequalities. I think this is the way the debate should be conducted.

That said, I am going to move on to what I know best, which is macro-economics, macroeconomic policies, and what we have learned from the last decade. I will speak in the first person singular rather than the first person plural. I will do so in order to indicate what has changed my mind over the past ten years about how macroeconomics and the economy work and about the policies that it would be beneficial to implement.

Now, what happened in the last ten years? There are two very different events. First of all, the Great Financial Crisis of 2008–2009 occurred and left visible scars in a large number of countries. This event has shaped the world in a terrible way, and we are just starting to slowly recover. Second, there has been the gradual rise of populism. This is the result of many factors, among which inequality plays a key role. From the perspective of the challenges we presently face, these are the elements that dominate the scene. We can take five lessons from this.

The first is obvious: the financial system matters in the economy. I say this because before the 2008–2009 crisis, macroeconomists had largely ignored the financial system. They saw it simply as a means for transferring funds to the people or companies that needed them. Hence, many of the macro-economic models did not analyze the financial sector. This became a problem when the crisis exploded. Recognizing that the financial system is relevant is therefore an obvious conclusion, but it has more insidious consequences than one might think for how we understand the economy. Macroeconomists look at macro variables and their interactions, hoping that looking at these macro variables is enough to make sense of what is happening. In general, economists do not have the time, ability, or opportunity to look into every single micro variable. The issue is that financial sector problems may not be visible on a macro level. Outwardly, the sector may seem to be in good shape while, in fact, various problems lie in the interaction between the various players. Does this mean that macroeconomists must look at every details of the financial system in order to say something about the macro economy? I think the answer may be yes, and this is a tough challenge.

The second lesson is that in order to keep the financial system under control and avoid risks, we must use many policy tools. This makes the situation quite complex. We like to view macroeconomic policy as a small set of simple tools. In reality, a large number of tools are needed. If used well and in the right combination, such tools allow a greater range of action than applying a single instrument to this or that problem. But this makes thinking about policy much more difficult.

The third lesson deals with a problem that always occurs when a regula-tion is implemented. Whether it is a financial market or any other market, there will always be someone on the other side trying to circumvent or use the regulation in a way that best suits his own purpose. We see it in labour markets. When reforms are introduced, firms and workers adapt to them over time. It usually takes a decade, more or less, to really see the full effect. In the case of finance, there are professionals whose job is to try to find a way around whatever rules the regulators have imposed. It is a game of cat and mouse, played infinitely more quickly than in other markets. This makes financial regulation extremely difficult.

The fourth lesson is the following. Before the crisis, especially in advanced countries, most macroeconomists believed that the economy fluctuated around a trend and that policy tools could be used to keep the economy close to the trend. I have always been sceptical about this view. I have worked on hysteresis and bubbles, both of which suggest a different interpretation of fluctuations and their relations to trend. In my opinion, the crisis has made it clear that the idea that economies are stable – that, when they are hit by a shock, they return to equilibrium on their own – is simply wrong. There are countless examples of how small shocks have had large effects. We know that if someone makes a run on a bank and others see him and do the same, the bank, which until then was solvent, will become insolvent and will be forced to close. Thus, a very small event can lead to a larger one. This phenomenon is not confined to banks; it can affect the financial system and the economy. Thus, the conventional idea that small shocks have small effects on the economy is incorrect. An extreme form of this is multiple equilibria. If everyone is optimistic, then things go well. If everyone is pessimistic, then things go wrong. I think I have become much more sceptical about the ability of the economy to self-regulate, and this has an obvious implication. If I was already quite supportive of using macroeconomic policies ten years ago, today I feel the need to implement an aggressive macroeconomic policy at the earliest warnings that something is going wrong.

The past decade has led to tremendous change in the field of monetary policy and minimal change in the field of fiscal policy. This presents a problem. Given the so-called "zero lower bound" of the interest rate, central banks understood they lacked the tools needed to face the crisis. They therefore created new tools, such as what we have come to call "quantitative easing". But do we have monetary policy tools today that can allow us to prevent or at least limit the effects of the next recession? A new recession will come. We do not know when, but it will come. Today the US interest rate is around two to three per cent. Typically, in the past during a recession the central bank had reduced the rate five percentage points or more in order to avoid a deeper recession. All it can do now is decrease it by three percentage points, and I do not think this would be enough. This is a serious issue.

Central banks have an important tool, the policy interest rate, which they move up and down. However, the effects of monetary policy on distribution among various groups of people were typically thought to be small. The central banks have enjoyed a regime of independence, because the significant consequences of what they were doing in terms of inequality had not been well understood. Central banks have an even wider mandate today. They can buy all kinds of assets, but this has direct consequences on distribution. For example, when the central banks decide to slow down the real estate market by increasing the down payment needed to buy a property, not only are the brakes applied to the housing market but young people will now find it much more difficult to buy a home. This is clearly a "non-neutral" policy. We have to ask ourselves whether full independence should be granted to the central bank as it is today.

Regarding fiscal policy, governments were seriously shaken when the financial crisis showed its most brutal face at the end of 2008. We at the IMF told them that they should proceed with a fiscal expansion because private demand was collapsing and something had to be done. The governments were so afraid that they did it. There was a very important fiscal expansion in 2009 that most likely led to positive outcomes. The problem is that, as soon as the greatest danger had been avoided, most countries returned to their previous fiscal policy. This was an austerity policy aimed at deficit reduction and limiting the increase of debt. This policy is what has been implemented since then. This was a lost opportunity in two respects.

The first is that of the "automatic stabilizer". Essentially, tax revenues automatically decline during a recession, hence the fiscal deficit increases. This mechanism helps push demand up. But tax codes are not designed with macro stabilization in mind. Basically, if a country has more progressive taxation, then the automatic stabilizer will be stronger. Thus, the stabilization is stronger in some countries, weaker in others. Most countries accept the idea that automatic stabilizers work, but so far no country has tried to design better automatic stabilizers, that is, something that automatically triggers the right fiscal expansion in case of recession. This is a lost opportunity.

The second aspect involves the notion of debt as a sin. As you know, in German, the word for 'debt' (Schuld) is synonymous with 'guilt'. In a context where the interest rate is high and the growth rate is relatively low, debt becomes expensive because it accumulates quickly and must eventually be repaid. We are in a context today, however, in which the interest rate is lower than the growth rate. In countries like the United States, France, and Germany, the interest rate is less than the growth rate, and this allows for issuing debt without having to raise taxes later. Let g represent the rate of growth of GDP; over time, a unit of debt grows at the same rate as the interest rate r. Thus, if g is higher than r, and the primary deficit (the deficit not including interest payments) is equal to zero, then the debt/GDP ratio decreases. Therefore, in situations of very low interest rates, the tax cost of debt is much lower.

Nevertheless, we continue to view debt ratios above 60 per cent as dangerous, and we have rules which require nations to reduce such debt relatively quickly. I think these rules are inappropriate with regard to the current situation. A word of warning, however, given where this talk is taking place: One should not apply these conclusions to Italy. In the case of Italy, r is greater than g because investors are unsure about being repaid. If the government could convince them that they would be fully repaid, the interest rate would be much lower. However, such a promise is credible only if investors believe that the government can be trusted. At this stage, they do not.

Let us move on to the fifth lesson on the rise of populism. A lot of people are studying why populism has grown stronger. I think one main reason is inequality, as well as economic insecurity. Immigration is also a factor in many countries. The income share of the top one per cent has also exacerbated the crisis. The payment of obscene salaries to the bankers who were at the origin of the financial crisis has had a very powerful resonance. Though they play different roles in different countries, all of these elements are in fact present.

I focus on inequality because I believe it is the most important factor. We have been aware of the problem for a long time, but there was the idea that high growth rates would eventually make everyone better off. Not everyone would benefit to the same degree, but the presumption was that everyone would gain something. This used to be true but it is no longer true today, for two reasons. First, long-term growth of income is lower than it used to be. Second, the nature of technological progress and globalization also plays a role in growing inequality. What happens when the two elements are combined? The people at the bottom of the social scale record low increases in real income. They may even record decreases, as we see in the United States. This is clearly unacceptable. This trend is becoming increasingly widespread. There is no need for me to talk about what has happened in my country, France, over the past few weeks, about the government you have in this country, or about Trump in the US. The point is that many people are suffering. My question is: what can we do? I think that this is the most difficult question, and it brings us back to what I was saying at the beginning.

We have standard tools to combat inequalities. The first tool is education. Better education prepares you for jobs that exist and will exist rather than for jobs that do not exist. I know little about the level of professional training in Italy, but I do know something about the level of professional training in France, which is not good. A huge effort must be made, but it may not be enough.

Other issues: to what extent is it possible to increase the minimum wage without affecting the employment of the less-skilled workers? To what degree should we use the negative income tax as compared with higher minimum wages to raise the incomes of very-low-wage workers? These questions bring us to an issue that could touch on the future of capitalism. And it does worry me. I ask myself: if we implemented these measures and if our governments understood the necessity of implementing them, would this be enough? In recent weeks, events in France have shown that many people want much more than the state can realistically do. Here we come to the discussion of the necessary changes I mentioned earlier. We must look at much stronger measures than those that I have just cited.

We have to look at a minimum tax for corporations in various countries, an international agreement under which substantially all countries agree upon having a minimum rate. Countries that do not comply must be penalized in some way. When you ask people in France, they say: "we want more public services" and also "we want less taxes". To the response that the money isn't available, they retort: "tax the rich". But as things stand today, this would lead nowhere. Were taxes to be raised by one country alone, companies would move elsewhere. As a result, I think that in tackling inequality, an international taxation agreement on companies is needed to create a wider tax base. This would be a substantial change when compared to what we have today.

The same applies to international trade. This often benefits consumers, but it creates serious damage to workers who lose their jobs. Even if we hope to compensate for this damage, it is typically not enough. When you open the market to international trade, it probably makes sense to do so progressively, rather than all at once in hopes that everything works out. This gives more time for workers to gain new training and find new jobs.

Corporate governance is another area for action. This is the last one that I will mention. Firms maximize shareholder value, and they do this in the most optimal way. However, this is often at the expense of workers and consumers. The idea of changing corporate governance by introducing worker representation is one that comes and goes, but it makes sense.

I think we can make changes in this direction, which I hope is enough to avoid future catastrophes.

Raitano: There are many insights from these two weighty presentations. I will mention just a few: the topic of inefficiencies in international finance; the subject of state investments; and finally the issue of unequal distribution of wealth. This latter has become more acute with the crisis, so much so that seventy million people have as much wealth as the rest of the world's population. Additionally, Professor Blanchard words give an idea of how profound is the change of thinking shaping our era. Let Professor Brancaccio take the floor in response.

Brancaccio: I will limit myself to a few observations on one of the key themes examined by Olivier Blanchard, so that the public has the possibility of stepping in. Olivier seems to take a stand on a fundamental point, indicating that there is no alternative to capitalism. His proposal focuses on finding the right mix between state intervention and spontaneous market mechanisms, yet within a substantially capitalistic framework. Olivier touches upon a thesis that is characteristic of schools of thought that exclude options outside the perimeter of the capitalist market. In fact, he states that in such a complex world populated by billions of individuals, only the market can, in the final analysis, regulate, discipline, and guide processes and decisions. This is a strong thesis that, as we know, is contingent on important historical and theoretical evidence.

There is, however, a critical observation that can be applied to this thesis. As Blanchard himself acknowledged, the level of instability in the spontaneous market mechanisms has turned out to be much greater than anyone could have imagined a few years ago. The instability of free market forces has been felt beyond the boundaries of the economy itself, meaning it is generating important repercussions on the social and political structures themselves. This is a point of great significance, for it suggests that the system is more unstable and potentially more destructive than previously expected.

Blanchard cited the social and political upheavals experienced by France and other countries. He has drawn attention to the ongoing protests, stressing that the protesters' claims lie beyond the reach of the concrete possibilities of economic policy, given the existing systemic constraints. For instance, Olivier points out that if a single country increases taxation on corporate profits, then capital will flee to other countries. In order to solve this problem he evokes the possibility of an international agreement on corporate taxation. Alternatively, I would suggest, controls could also be imposed on international capital movements; Blanchard, too, has alluded to capital controls, albeit for other reasons. But it appears to me that these types of measures are not on the political agenda of any major actor. Hence, corporate taxation is constrained by the risk that capital and companies might move elsewhere.

In this scenario of social claims on the one hand and institutional constraints on the other, there is a real danger that in order to hold things together, to accept economic instability while suppressing social and political instability, an attempt will be made to reduce people's rights – not only social rights, which have already been greatly reduced, but also civil and political rights.

In other words, if it is maintained that there is no alternative to the current capitalist market system, there is the risk that, in order to defend the system from its own instability, it may become necessary to sacrifice something else. This trend is already under way, and it may intensify as the Marxian tendency towards capital centralization continues. The very fact that the former Chief Economist of the International Monetary Fund concluded his speech here by evoking the danger of "future catastrophes" and claiming that the difficult task before us is to find a way to avoid them, seems to me an authoritative testimony of the crises and contradictions of our time.

Blanchard: Let me return to the topic of the absence of alternatives. I was making a "normative", not a descriptive statement. In reality, I indeed see some politicians offer what looks like alternatives. For example, populist governments offer simple policy solutions as alternatives. However, these solutions will not work. What worries me is that when it becomes evident that these are not real alternatives, these governments will be tempted to go further. I too, like Emiliano, think that maybe they will reduce the level of democracy in order to remain in power, despite poor economic results. Or, they will try the US device of "wagging the dog", which means seeking out an enemy and waging war on them in order to distract the public.

In his presentation, Emiliano raised several other interesting points. I do not agree with all of them. The first concerns distribution. I believe that this is absolutely central to both short-term and long-term issues. I have always seen the level of unemployment as reflecting in part a distributive struggle between workers and companies. Workers want wages to match what they need to spend and firms want to set prices based on the wages they have to pay. Everyone wants more. How can this conflict be resolved? My thesis is that, unfortunately, it is partly resolved through unemployment, which increases to the point where workers' wage demands match what companies are willing to pay.

Another dimension of distribution that is significant in the long run is the transmission of wealth. Thomas Piketty[15] insists upon this point. Fundamentally, much inequality comes from wealth transmission. This is why I see the inheritance tax as a means of reducing inequality.

As for the eurozone current account deficit, I had indeed thought that several Southern countries, not Italy but Spain, Portugal, and

---

[15]   T. Piketty (2014), *Capital in the Twenty-First Century*. Cambridge, MA: Harvard University Press.

Greece, needed substantial investments. Therefore, running current account deficits looked like a good idea. In the end, this turned out to be not such a good idea. They did not invest much and ended with a very high foreign debt that had to be repaid. They have now reduced their current account deficits substantially, but largely because imports are low. This is largely why their current accounts look better than a few years ago.

But how can they return to health on the external front? They must increase competitiveness. This is a necessary condition. They can do so in two ways. One is to increase productivity, but it is easier said than done. The other is to have wages that grow more slowly than their competitors' wages. Essentially, if your competitor has an inflation rate of two per cent, then your inflation rate needs to be zero per cent. For example, if we consider Germany as a competitor, and considering the German economy is marked by very low inflation, then we should have deflation in order to improve our competitiveness. However, I agree 100 per cent with Emiliano that deflation is not a positive solution. I think that the solution lies not on a national level but on a European one. Germany should accept more than two per cent inflation, so that others can substantially improve their competitiveness without deflation.

Raitano: Let us gather some questions from the public.

First question: Both of you agree on the relevance of poor income distribution, which is consistent with Professor Blanchard's perspective and poses problems for economic growth. Is it possible that rethinking the rules of the international monetary system could contribute to repositioning this problem in a more optimistic perspective?

Second question: I would like to ask Professor Blanchard: what do you think about heterodox Post-Keynesian models?

Third question: Professor Brancaccio, at the end of your speech, you referred to the post-war context, when the socialist bloc and the capitalist system were in antithesis. Today, what interests could constitute the social bloc that will stabilize capitalism or enable it to reform itself?

Fourth question: This is for Professor Brancaccio, who initially mentioned the risk of the suppression of democracy. I would like to ask whether democracy has not already been vanquished through substantial market dominance over national parliaments, and whether, when social issues are disregarded, we are going to see the return of fascism as Karl Polanyi predicted?

Fifth question: In 2014, the Nobel Prize-winning economist Jean Tirole stated that alternative economic theories, those that correspond to critical thinking traditions, are anti-scientific. In his view, such theories cannot have space in the academy because they would promulgate a relativism of knowledge that is the antechamber of obscurantism.[16] I would like to know Professor Blanchard's opinion on this matter and whether he believes that the study of alternative theories – alongside the traditional ones, to be sure – should instead be encouraged.

Brancaccio: The last question about Tirole compels us to reflect on the fact that some prominent members of today's academic community seem quite unwilling to create the minimum conditions necessary for making a fruitful Lakatosian competition possible among alternative paradigms. This poses a major obstacle to the future progress of economic science, and I would like to hear Olivier's opinion on it. I would also have some theoretical remarks on his reflections about distribution, but we can also explore these themes elsewhere. Here I wish to take inspiration from the questions from the public and conclude by addressing the political and economic policy issues that have been raised.

Regarding the risks to democracy, the economist Dani Rodrik has advanced an interesting thesis on the conflict that might emerge between the total freedom of the circulation of capital and goods and the sustainability of democratic processes within each country.[17] The freedom of movement of capital, for example, can tie the hands of the authorities legitimized by the democratic process. This makes it impossible to lower interest rates or tax profits due to the threat of foreign capital flight. Rodrik argues that the optimal solution to this problem would be to bring the democratic process to a higher level, essentially moving it beyond the boundaries of individual states. This can be done by establishing a supranational democratic government that resolves conflicts in a coordinated way and shields political choices from the blackmail of capital movement. Rodrik clearly acknowledges that although the ideal solution involves supranational coordination of decision-making, it is often impossible to put it into practice. We should therefore look for alternatives. Even in the case of the European Economic and Monetary Union, Blanchard has implicitly suggested a coordinated supranational solution. He reminded us that the obstinacy with which Germany keeps domestic inflation at relatively low levels is a serious obstacle to coordinated resolutions. Through its anti-inflationary policy, Germany has helped fuel a dangerous tendency towards deflation in many other European countries. The fact that the strongest country in the euro area has, in relative terms, put downward pressure on wages and prices

---

[16] Tirole made the remark in 2014, a letter to the French Secretary of Higher Education and Research. The letter may be found here: http://assoeconomiepolitique.org/wp-content/uploads/TIROLE_Letter.pdf, accessed 7 January 2022.

[17] D. Rodrik (2011), *The Globalization Paradox. Democracy and the Future of the World Economy*. New York: W. W. Norton.

has triggered destructive processes of deflationary competition across a large part of Europe. Blanchard has suggested that Germany will eventually accept wage and price inflation higher than the current one in order to block this dangerous general deflationary trend. This is precisely the sort of coordinated solution Rodrik considers 'ideal', in which the strongest country would act in line with the overall interest of the European Union to avoid deflation.

Unfortunately, such coordinated solutions seldom find favourable political conditions. On the difficulty of carrying out such coordination in Europe, allow me to offer a small personal account of a very informative experience I once had. It was 2012, when the European socialist parties had strong expectations of political success in France, Germany, and Italy. During François Hollande's candidacy for the presidency of the French republic, the Foundation for European Progressive Studies, which is very close to the European Socialist Party, held a conference to elaborate a common socialist manifesto for progressive economic policy reform for the European Union. The conference took place in Paris at the National Assembly. The former French and Italian Prime Ministers Laurent Fabius and Massimo D'Alema invited me to participate in this conference. I was asked to present a proposal that I had made a few months earlier. The proposal was called "A European wage standard", and it had already been included in the Italian Democratic Party's political programs. Simply put, it involved adopting sanctions against European countries which, despite being in a systematic trade surplus with their trading partners, insisted on pushing for a competition policy based on a fall in wages and prices. Essentially, the "wage standard" was nothing more than a supranational coordination mechanism for wage bargaining to prevent Germany, the strongest country in the EU, from dragging all other countries into deflation.[18]

At that time, the proposal received approval from representatives of various countries: French, Spanish, Portuguese, and Greek, among others. At a certain point, however, from this general harmony arose the voice of two German participants, one representing labour unions, the other a representative of social democracy. They basically said: "While we appreciate Professor Brancaccio's suggestion, the problem is that he has failed to understand how the EU works. The EU was built not on the basis of solidarity and coordination, but on the basis of competition, and it is destined to remain so." One of them added that he also disagreed with the more modest French proposal to establish a European minimum wage. In

---

[18]   E. Brancaccio (2012), "Current Account Imbalances, the Eurozone Crisis and a Proposal for a 'European Standard Wage'", *International Journal of Political Economy 41(1)*, 47–65.

the end, no common manifesto emerged from that conference. For me, that
was a small life lesson. At that moment, I realized that if even the more or
less worthy heirs of the labour movement tradition exalted the virtues of
European wage competition, then finding supranational solutions to face
the crisis of the EU would be very unlikely.

From this brief anecdote, I also draw inspiration to say a last word to
those who asked me what the "social bloc" can achieve today in fighting
for an economic policy "revolution". My opinion is that all the movements
of social and civil progress we have witnessed in the capitalist era have
almost always been associated with propulsive thrusts which, in more or
less direct terms, came from an organized working class – what we have
called the international labour movement, both in its reformist and revo-
lutionary forms. To me, the idea that we can bring about changes in the
direction of social and civil progress without the subversive drive of labour
organizations, seems to be sharply denied by the facts. The problem is that,
nowadays, only the representatives of the capital seem able to organize
politically. Large-scale capital strongly rooted at the supranational level
finds political representation in what we could call the traditional, uncriti-
cal "globalist" forces. At the same time, smaller-scale capital rooted above
all at the national level, often in trouble and with solvency problems, today
finds a potential source of political representation in what might be called
"reactionary populism". Yet, labour, for its part, remains silent. In other
words, we are at the mercy of a ferocious struggle within the capitalist class
that has general repercussions on society as a whole. Meanwhile, labour is
totally silenced on the political level. I believe this political silence of labour,
today, represents the main threat to modern civilization.

Blanchard: I was asked how much international organizations can do
to tackle inequality. The Organisation for Economic Co-operation and
Development or the World Trade Organization are clearly relevant in this
context. However, they cannot solve the problem by themselves. What they
can do is a number of things, like working on corporate taxation. This is
something that needs to be done internationally.

Regarding Post-Keynesians: I must admit that I have not read all they
have written. However, in general, the importance of the concept of distribution seems to be quite an important topic for them, but less important
for us. Hence, I think they have useful points to communicate on this front.
I am in favour of drawing inspiration from their work.

As for Tirole's statements, I do not think anyone can have a monopoly
on knowledge. If other people have interesting things to say, then someone
who was once an outsider can eventually become an insider, as in the
case of Hyman Minsky. People who promote points of view that differ from
the mainstream can provide something useful. Sometimes they are right. At

the same time, however, I still believe that the direction in which the mainstream is looking is the right one. I do not think there are alternative realities, but rather that there is only one reality that needs to be understood. When people ask me what I do, I like to say I am an engineer. The way I see it, I am a social engineer. The machine that I am trying to understand is complex, and I am open to suggestions. But in the end, this is the machine and we need to understand it.

I want to make one last observation and end with that – we economists have been too "imperialistic". We have looked down on sociologists, psychologists, and political scientists. I think things are changing from this point of view. I think there has been a lot of progress in this regard, and I hope we will create a more integrated research field.

Further reading

This volume is devoted to a comparison between the prevalent approach to macroeconomics, so called "mainstream", and an alternative approach developed starting from the contributes of the "critical" schools of thought. A complete review of the academic debate over these two paradigms is well beyond the scope of this short section. Nonetheless, we will offer to the reader some suggestions for further reading.

The very definition of "mainstream" comes from a hint originally raised by Paul Samuelson, who labelled, with this expression, a proposal for a synthesis between the old neoclassical theory and the critiques put forward by John Maynard Keynes during the crisis of the 1930s. This synthesis consists of reducing the Keynesian issue of effective demand shortage to a mere problem of the "short run", while claiming that a free market capitalist economy in the long run would spontaneously get back to a "natural" equilibrium of perfect competition, characterized by full employment. Mainstream contemporary models essentially reproduce the conclusions of such a synthesis, though allowing for the possibility for the "natural" equilibrium to be characterized by market imperfections and information asymmetries such that persistent involuntary unemployment is generated. For a better definition of "mainstream" macroeconomic theory, one can look at Chapter 24 of O. Blanchard (2017), *Macroeconomics* (8th edn), Boston, USA: Pearson; O. Blanchard (2008), "The state of macro", NBER Working Paper 14259; J.B. Taylor (2000), "Teaching macroeconomics at the principles level", *American Economic Review 90(2)*, 90–94. On the theoretical foundations of the mainstream macroeconomic model, see O. Blanchard and S. Fischer (1989), *Lectures on Macroeconomics*, Cambridge, USA: MIT Press. On the validity of mainstream models after the "great recession", see P. Romer (2016), "The trouble with macroeconomics", *The American Economist*. On this subject, see also the changes in Blanchard's thought analyzed by E. Brancaccio and F. Saraceno (2017), "Evolutions and contradictions in mainstream macroeconomics: The case of Olivier Blanchard", *Review of Political Economy 29(3)*, 345–359.

As for the "critical" economic thought, we refer here, as a first approximation, to a group of contemporary scholars belonging to different

Anti-Blanchard macroeconomics

streams of research, which are present, broadly speaking, in the original works of Karl Marx, Michal Kalecki, Piero Sraffa, Wassily Leontief, Herbert Simon, Hyman Minsky, and in an interpretation of Keynes that is alternative to the mainstream one. Even if epistemological and analytical differences can be found between the scholars mentioned, they share a common refusal of the paradigm that is dominant nowadays, which is based on methodological individualism linked to the reduction of economic behaviour to a matter of utility maximization subject to the bond of the scarcity of productive factors. These authors can be identified as holding an alternative view on capitalism as a monetary economy of reproduction, characterized by the division between antagonistic groups and social classes with competing material interests, and by the inexistence of an equilibrium to be defined as "natural" in the sense typical of the dominant paradigm. In our view, this alternative view on capitalism can also provide a theoretical basis for the development of recent economic research branches, including evolutionary economics and behavioural economics. On the distinctive features of the critical theory approaches: A. Graziani (2003), *The Monetary Theory of Production*, Cambridge, UK: Cambridge University Press; L. Pasinetti (2007), *Keynes and the Cambridge Keynesians*, Cambridge, UK: Cambridge University Press; A. Roncaglia (2009), *Piero Sraffa*, Basingstoke, UK: Palgrave Macmillan; H.P. Minsky (1975), *John Maynard Keynes*, New York, USA: Columbia University Press. In the vast range of critical schools of thought, Marxist studies clearly stand out, due to their important tradition and their complexity of analysis: on the matter, see J. Eatwell, M. Milgate and P. Newman (1990), *Marxian Economics*, Basingstoke, UK: Palgrave Macmillan. If one is to look for a possible epistemological collocation for the contemporary critique to economic policy and theory, L. Althusser (1997), *Reading Capital*, London, UK: Verso may give some hints.

With respect to macroeconomics teaching, examples of "alternative" basic or advanced textbooks are: M. Lavoie (2014), *Post-Keynesian Economics: New Foundations*, Cheltenham, UK and Northampton, USA: Edward Elgar Publishing; H. Kurz and N. Salvadori (1995), *Theory of Production: A Long-Period Analysis*, Cambridge, UK: Cambridge University Press; S. Bowles (2004), *Microeconomics. Behavior, Institutions, and Evolution*, Princeton, USA: Princeton University Press. With regard to international macroeconomics textbooks, a pluralistic theoretical approach is chosen by G. Gandolfo (2016), *International Finance and Open-Economy Macroeconomics*, Berlin, Germany: Springer. On some recent developments in didactics and on the comeback of the comparative approach to macroeconomics teaching, see the collection of essays edited by G. Fontana and M. Setterfield (eds) (2010),

Macroeconomic Theory and Macroeconomic Pedagogy, Basingstoke, UK: Palgrave Macmillan.

The sections belonging to Chapter 5 of this volume draw from Emiliano Brancaccio's latest years' investigations, joined by Andrea Califano. On the different interpretations of the economic crisis, see the essays included in the collection of works edited by Emiliano Brancaccio and Giuseppe Fontana: E. Brancaccio and G. Fontana (eds) (2011), *The Global Economic Crisis. New Perspectives on the Critique of Economic Theory and Policy*, London, UK: Routledge. With respect to alternative monetary policies, refer to E. Brancaccio and G. Fontana, "Solvency rule versus Taylor rule. An alternative interpretation of monetary policy during the economic crisis", *Cambridge Journal of Economics 37(1)*, 17–33. An investigation aimed at empirically testing the theoretical insights of the latter paper has begun with the work E. Brancaccio, G. Fontana, M. Lopreite and R. Realfonzo (2015), "Monetary policy rules and directions of causality: A test for the Euro Area", *Journal of Post Keynesian Economics 38(4)*, 509–531 and brought forward in E. Brancaccio, A. Califano, M. Lopreite and A. Moneta (2018), "Nonperforming loans and competing rules of monetary policy: A statistical identification approach", *Structural Change and Economic Dynamics 53*, 127–136. On the matter of wage competition within a monetary union, a proposal for a "European wage standard" aimed at coordinating the bargaining process is presented in E. Brancaccio (2012), "Current account imbalances, the eurozone crisis and a proposal for a European wage standard", *International Journal of Political Economy 41(1)*, 47–65. The sustainability of a monetary union and the implications of a deflationary policy within it are dealt with in E. Brancaccio and G. Fontana (2015), "Solvency rule and capital centralisation in a monetary union", *Cambridge Journal of Economics 40(4)*, 1055–1075. On the comparison between alternative theories, see E. Brancaccio and D. Suppa (2019), "A comparative approach to macroeconomics: The case of the 'Anti-Blanchard'", in A. Moneta, T. Gabellini and S. Gasperin (eds), *Economic Crisis and Economic Thought: Alternative Theoretical Perspectives on the Economic Crisis*, London, UK: Routledge. E. Brancaccio (2010), "On the impossibility of reducing the surplus approach to a neoclassical special case", *Review of Political Economy 22(3)*, 405–418 proposes a further analysis of the differences between the alternative approach and the dominant economic theory. Finally, the developments of Olivier Blanchard's economic thought are examined in-depth in E. Brancaccio and F. Saraceno (2017), "Evolutions and contradictions in mainstream macroeconomics", cited above.

The first Italian edition of the present volume has raised some interesting debates. *Anti-Blanchard* has been the object of discussion in seminars organized by the Università Bocconi di Milano and the Scuola Superiore Sant'Anna di Pisa, among other institutions. Further thoughts on the didactic approach adopted in this section are gathered in A. Amighini, E. Brancaccio, F. Giavazzi and M. Messori (2012), "A new textbook approach to macroeconomics: A debate", *Rivista Italiana di Politica Economica 7*, 101–129.

Index

agent-based modelling (ABM) 202
Alesina, A. 185
Alessandrini, P. xiv
Althusser, L. 222
Althusserian 202
Altreconomia 199
Amar, R. 67
AMECO database 95, 131
American Economic Review 184, 185, 189, 205, 221
The American Economist 221
Amighini, A. 2, 201, 224
animal spirits 153, 156, 157
anti-trust 16–19, 36, 38, 59, 81, 84, 164
Ardagna, S. 185
Arestis, P. 116
Asia 125
austerity 31, 32, 184, 185, 190, 199, 211

banking system 58, 92
Bank of England 67
bank run 71, 92
bankruptcy 69, 128, 130, 200
behavioural economics 222
Bellofiore, R. xiv
Beraldo, S. xiv
Berger, R.L. 175
Berlin Wall 166
Biagioli, M. xiv
Blanchard, O. (only quoted works) viii, xi, 1, 43, 103, 116, 132, 134, 139, 184, 185, 189–91, 199, 201, 202, 204, 206, 221
Boeri, T. 138
Boitani, A. xiv
Bolshevik Revolution 166
Bowles, S. 222
Brancaccio, E. 4, 5, 101, 106, 108, 127, 132, 140, 143, 158, 199, 200, 203–5, 208, 214, 216–18, 221, 223, 224

Brookings Papers on Economic Activity 43, 206
Brown, J.R. 185

Califano, A. 5, 108, 127, 131, 143, 201, 223
Cambridge Journal of Economics 101, 106, 116, 132, 203, 205
Capital Controversy 116
capital flight 100, 124–7, 205, 217
capitalism 1, 3, 4, 100, 152, 206–8, 213, 214, 216
capitalist economy 28, 41, 148, 165
capitalist mode of production 64, 166
Casella, G. 175
Castelnuovo, E. xiv
Cellini, R. xiv
centralization of capitals 108
Cesaratto, S. xiv
Ciccone, R. xiv
class struggle 149, 203
climate change 158–61
Colombatto, E. xiv
competitiveness 121–3, 129, 132, 206, 216
correlation 172–9, 182, 183, 186, 189, 191, 193, 195
Costabile, L. xiv
covariance 174, 175
Covid-19 4, 5, 161, 165, 169, 171, 192, 193, 195, 196
credit crunch 91
credit default swap (CDS) 189
crowding out 31, 32
Cuzzola, A. xiv

D'Acunto, S. xiv
D'Alema, M. 218
De Cristofaro, F. 5, 127, 143
deflationary trap 79, 80
Dekking, F.M. 175

Delli Gatti, D. xiv
Democratic Party (Italy) 218
deregulation 84, 94
Dosi, G. xiv
Draghi, M. 132
dynamic stochastic general equilibrium
(DSGE) models ix, x

Eatwell, J. 222
Economic Policy 3–6, 78, 79, 81, 90,
185, 204, 205, 207, 217–19
Ederer, S. 101
elasticity 62, 63, 83
employment protection legislation
(EPL) 138, 172, 179–83
Engels, F. 200
euro area 101, 108, 129, 132, 190, 206,
217
Europe 116, 125, 131, 218
European Central Bank 32, 124–6, 129,
132, 185, 189, 190
European Commission 95, 126, 185,
189, 190
European Economic and Monetary
Union (EMU) 108, 128, 217
*European Journal of Economics and
Economic Policies: Intervention* 133
European Socialist Party 218
European Union 218
European wage standard 132, 218
Eurostat 128, 129
eurozone 128–33, 200, 206–8, 215,
218
evolutionary economics 222
exchange rate 122–5, 130, 132–7

Fabius, L. 218
Fama, E. 152
Fatas, A. 190, 191
Favero, C. xiv
Federal Reserve 55, 103
Ferraguto, G. xiv
Finance & Development viii
Financial Times 132, 199, 207
fiscal multiplier 186
Fischer, S. 185, 202, 221
Fitoussi, J.P. 101
Fontana, G. 101, 106, 108, 132, 205,
222, 223
Forges Davanzati, G. xiv

*Foundation for European Progressive
Studies* 218
France 130, 131, 139, 181, 187, 194,
211–14, 218
Fusco, A.M. xiv

Gabellini, T. 223
Gallegati, M. xiv
game theory 135, 167–9
Gandolfo, G. 222
Garbellini, N. 133, 140, 204, xiv
Garegnani, P. 202
Gasperin, S. 131, 223
Germany 128, 130–32, 139, 181, 185,
187, 194, 211, 216–18
Giammetti, R. 5, 140, 204, 205, xiv
Giangiacomo Feltrinelli Foundation
199
Giavazzi, F. 2, 201, 206, 224, xiv
Global crisis (2007) 5, 63, 200
globalization 123, 128, 199, 212, 217
Graziani, A. 202, 222
Great Britain 91
Great crisis (1929) 28, 42, 93
Great depression 58, 79
Great recession 2, 4, 128, 167, 184, 200
Greece 128, 129, 131, 132, 139, 181,
187, 194, 206, 216
Green, W.H. 175
Greenspan, A. 55, 105

Hahn, F. 203
Hansen, A. 205
Hein, H. 101
Hicks, J.R. 2
Hitler, A. 207
Hollande, F. 218
hysteresis of unemployment 116–21

IMF Direct 132, 206
IMF World Economic Outlook 185
immigration 60, 127, 140, 142, 143, 212
inequality 107, 199, 200, 209, 211–13,
215, 219
insolvency 69, 71, 94, 108, 110
international capital mobility 123
International Journal of Political
Economy 132, 158, 218
International Labour Organization
(ILO) 101

International Monetary Fund (IMF) 1–2, 101, 184–5, 187–9, 193–5, 200, 204, 206, 208, 215
international monetary system 216
invisible hand theorem 167, 171
Ireland 128, 129, 131, 139, 181, 187
Italy 128–31, 138, 139, 181, 187, 194, 199, 212, 215, 218

Journal of Industrial and Business Economics 195
Journal of Post Keynesian Economics 108, 223
Julius Caesar 200

Kaldor, N. 202
Kalecki, M. 222
Keynes, J.M. 42, 58, 61, 100, 148, 207, 221, 222
Keynesian 108, 115, 116, 149, 151, 156–8, 160, 163, 184, 185, 208
Keynesianism xi
Kraaikamp, C. 175
Kurz, H. 203, 222, xiv

labour flexibility 137–40, 172–5, 177, 179, 181, 183
Lacanian 208
laissez-faire 168
Lakatosian 203, 217
Latin America 125
Lavoie, M. 222
Lehman Brothers 200
Leigh, D. 5, 184–91
Leontief, W. 166, 202, 222
liberal 127, 136, 171
liberalism 168
liberalist 41, 166
liberalization 59, 94
liquidity trap 43, 49, 50, 60
Livermore, J.L. 135
Lopreite, M. 108, 205, 223
Lopuhaa, H.P. 175
Lovell, M. 43
Lucas, R. 203
Lunghini, G. xiv

Maastricht 116
Marconi, D. xiv

Marx, K. 45, 54, 59, 100, 108, 157, 203, 205, 222
Marxian 151, 156, 161, 164, 215
Marxism xi
Marxist 203
Masciandaro, D. xiv
McLeay, M. 67
Meester, L.E. 175
Messori, M. 224
Milan 199
Milgate, M. 222
Minsky, H.P. 202, 219, 222
Modigliani, F. 202
Moneta, A. 108, 223, xiv
monetary base 91–3
monetary economy of reproduction 222
monetary multiplier 91–3
monetary union 108, 122, 123, 128, 132, 205, 217
Mongiovi, G. 199, xiv
monopolistic competition 61, 63
monopoly 38, 219
Moreno-Brid, J.C. xiv
Musella, M. xiv

Nash, J. 168
Nash equilibrium 168, 169
Nazism 207
Neo-liberal 127
New Keynesian 1
Newman, P. 222
New York Stock Exchange 153
Niechoj, T. xiv
Nobel Prize 152, 158, 166, 168, 216
nonperforming loans 71, 108
Nordhaus, W. 158, 160, 161

OECD Employment Outlook 172, 182, 183
Onaran, O. 101
open economy 121, 123
ordinary least squares (OLS) 186, 188
Organisation for Economic Co-operation and Development (OECD) 5, 138–40, 172, 179–83, 185, 219
Ortona, G. xiv
output gap 74, 75
Oxford Review of Economic Policy viii

Pagano, M. 185
Pagano, U. xiv
Palma, G. 116
Papi, L. 195
Paris 172, 183, 218
Pasinetti, L. 116, 202, 222
perfect competition 62
Perotti, R. 185
Phillips, W. 2, 6, 72–4
Phillips curve 2, 6, 72–4
Pigou effect 60–63
Piketty, T. 215
Pini, P. xiv
Polanyi, K. 216
populism 209, 212, 219
populist 215
Portugal 128, 129, 131, 139, 181, 187, 215
Post-Keynesian 116, 216
Prescott, E. 203
present value model (PVM) 152–5
production function 14, 15, 73, 87, 141, 144, 145, 150, 151, 154, 159
protectionism 123
PSL Quarterly Review 158
public debt 108–12, 114–16, 125, 128
public deficit 108, 109, 112, 115, 116, 128
public planning 65, 166, 168, 171
p-value 178, 188, 189, 195

quantitative easing 210

Raitano, P. 199
Reaganomics 166
Realfonzo, R. 108, 223, xiv
Review of Political Economy 199, 203
Rivista Italiana di Politica Economica 224
Robinson, J. 202
Rodrik, D. 207, 217, 218
Roman Empire 200
Romer, P.M. 221
Roncaglia, A. 222
Ryland, T. 67

Salvadori, N. 203, 222
Samuelson, P.A. 221
Saraceno, F. 203, 221, 223, xiv
Sargent, T. 203

Sawyer, M. 116
scarcity models 149
Scazzieri, R. xiv
Schindler, M. 184
Sciences Po Document de travail 101
secular stagnation 205
Setterfield, M. 222
Shapiro, M. 43
Shiller, R. 152, 153
Simon, H. 222
Skidelsky, R. xiv
Smith, A. 167, 168
Soci, A. xiv
socialism 166, 207, 208
socialist 166, 207, 208, 216, 218
Solow, R.M. 144
solvency rule 106, 107, 132, 205
Soros, G. 135
Soviet Union 166
Spain 128, 129, 131, 139, 181, 187, 194, 215
Spaventa, L. xiv
speculation 102, 136, 154, 157, 158
Spilimbergo, A. 184
Sraffa, P. 148, 151, 202, 222
Sraffian 151, 156, 157, 161, 164
standard deviation 177, 178
Stiglitz, J.E. 101
Stirati, A. xiv
Stock, J.H. 175
Stockhammer, E. 101
stock market 102, 152–4, 156–8
structural change 108, 131, 140, 204, 205
Structural Change and Economic Dynamics 108, 131, 140, 204, 205
Summers, L.H. 116, 118–20, 190, 202, 204–7
sum of squares 177, 178
Suppa, D. 5, 223
Swedish Economic Policy Review 185
Sylos Labini, P. 202
Symansky, S. 184

Taylor, J.B. 67, 103–7, 205, 221, 223
Taylor rule 67, 103, 104, 106, 107, 205
technological unemployment 36, 39, 60, 89
Teobaldelli, D. 195

Thailand 134
Tiberi, M. xiv
Ticchi, D. 195
Tirole, J. 216, 217
Tobin, J. 125–7
Tobin tax 123, 125–7
Tortorella Esposito, G. xiv
trade balance 129, 137
treasury bond 8, 71, 108, 128, 130
Trump, D. 200, 212

under-consumption xiii
United States of America (USA) 1,
    103, 105, 134, 138, 175, 181, 184–5,
    190–91

van Ours, J. 138
Vita, C. xiv
Vogel, L. 101
von Neumann, J. 202

wage competition 121–3, 219
Watson, M.W. 175
Weale, M. xiii
Wicksell, K. 77
World Bank 204
World Trade Organization 219

zero lower bound 72, 79, 80, 210
Zezza, G. xiv
Zingales, L. xiv

'When Emiliano asked me to endorse Anti-Blanchard Macroeconomics, I was a bit taken aback. You can guess why. But I agree with him that we should always question our assumptions, confront them with the facts, and be open to change if the facts dictate it. Questions such as whether we can expect the economy to return to health by itself, whether recessions have permanent adverse effects, whether the interest rate channel of monetary policy works, are essential ones. For the time being, I stand by the conclusions of my textbook, but I am happy and indeed eager to see them challenged.'

Olivier J. Blanchard

'Beyond its provocative title, Anti-Blanchard Macroeconomics raises constructive critiques of our approach to macroeconomics teaching'

Alessia Amighini and Francesco Giavazzi,
co-authors of the European edition of Blanchard's Macroeconomics

'Even if designed for students, this book also offers food for thought to researchers interested in reopening a debate on the foundations of contemporary macroeconomics'

Mauro Gallegati

'It is an excellent way to understand both analytical strengths and weaknesses of the mainstream approach'

Tortsen Niechoj

'Anti-Blanchard Macroeconomics increases variety in macroeconomic theory: it shows what is wrong with the dominant theory and draws attention to its alternatives'

Heinz D. Kurz

'The fact that one of the cardinals of pre-crash macroeconomic orthodoxy is willing to commend this heterodox text, is evidence of the mess in which orthodox macroeconomics finds itself after the collapse of 2007–09'

Robert Skidelsky